I wish to thank John and Karen (Dworetzky) for all their help and patience and Besi, Orval, Ouida, Jennifer, and Tyler for all their love.

        Stephen S. Cooper

Appreciation is extended to John and Karen for their help and confidence. My portion of this endeavor is dedicated to Dee for his example and high standards of excellence, Bertha for always being there when I needed her, Dona for her concern and friendship, Don and Flossie for being themselves and giving so much, David for his special spirit of persistence, Carol for her glowing enthusiasm, Kenny for his playful innocence, and Terry whose faith, love, and selfless devotion made my part of this project possible.

        Richard D. Rees

895

Study Guide to Accompany

PSYCHOLOGY

John P. Dworetzky

Department of Psychology
Glendale College, Arizona

Prepared by
Stephen S. Cooper
Glendale College, Arizona

Richard D. Rees
Glendale College, Arizona

West Publishing Company
St. Paul   New York   Los Angeles   San Francisco

ISBN 0-314-63170-4

3rd Reprint—1983

CONTENTS

HOW TO USE THIS STUDY GUIDE

Have you ever tried to study a chapter in a textbook, but found it difficult to concentrate? Was it hard to focus on the really important material? Did your mind wander? If your answer is yes, you're not alone. It is easy to spend a lot of time studying without gaining much from your efforts.

This study guide was written to help you study the subject matter of psychology in an economical time-saving manner while simultaneously maximizing your learning and understanding of the material. It was designed to focus your attention, and to stress the essential ideas of each corresponding chapter of your textbook.

The study guide chapters contain the following learning tools:

Behavioral Objectives
Key Terms and Concepts
Names to Remember
Guided Review
Self Test I
Self Test II
Essay Questions

The following suggested strategy is based on the assumption that you will be devoting approximately 5 to 6 hours of study to each chapter. You should not do it all at once. Break it into 6 days for an hour a day, 3 days for 2 hours each, or some other convenient schedule. Of course, some students will require more than 5 or 6 hours to master a chapter, and some can do it in less. Adjust the following time frame to meet your individual requirements, but do follow the suggested sequence. It should produce good results for you.

A TEN-STEP TIME-EFFECTIVE PROGRAM
FOR SUCCESS IN INTRODUCTORY PSYCHOLOGY

1.   (5 minutes or less) Look over the *Behavioral Objectives* in this study

guide for the chapter you are reading. They indicate your goals, the things you should be able to do when you finish the chapter.

2. (5 minutes or less) Scan the *Key Terms and Concepts* and the *Names to Remember*. You won't remember them all now, but look them over and get yourself in the frame of mind to watch for them as you proceed.

3. (15 minutes or less) Go through the *Guided Review* verbally and visually only. Do no writing at this point. You will often need to check the answers at the end of the chapter. You have now previewed the chapter thoroughly and are ready to dig in.

4. Read the chapter in the textbook. Go section by section and pause frequently to think about what you are reading. Reflect on the names, terms, and questions that you previewed in steps 1, 2, and 3. Take one or two five-minute rest periods to space out your efforts. Do not allow your mind to wander.

5. (30 minutes or less) Come back to the study guide and identify each key term, concept, and name in the *Key Terms and Concepts* and *Names to Remember* sections. Check the textbook as needed. It is not necessary to write the definitions, just look over them.

6. (60 to 90 minutes) With your textbook open in front of you, write out the answers in the *Guided Review* section. The items closely follow the flow of discussion in the text, so use the text to find them if you get stuck. Then check your answers against those printed in the answer section at the end of the study guide chapter. Clarify, by talking to yourself, the items that give you trouble.

7. (10 minutes or less) Take *Self Test I*; check the answers that are given at the end of the chapter, and interpret as follows (if your professor tests on lecture material that is not in the textbook, be sure to study your lecture notes as well. The self-tests only reflect your knowledge of textbook material):

Number Correct	Your Grade	Interpretation
14-15	A	You should do very well on the exam over this material
12-13	B	You should do pretty well on the exam
10-11	C	You'll probably pass the exam
7-9	D	Go back and repeat steps 4, 5, and 6 (You're going to need some extra time)
0-6	F	Repeat steps 4, 5, and 6

8. (10 minutes or less) After taking *Self Test I* and reviewing those areas where you had difficulty, then, as a final check on your knowledge, take *Self Test II*. Interpret your score as before. At this point you should be doing quite well. (Note – if you do not pass *Self Test II*, you might want to consider a tutor or other help. You'll probably do poorly on the class exam. It may help to go back and write the definitions of the *Key Terms and Concepts* and definitions of the *Names to Remember*.)

9. (30 minutes or less) As a final effort to consolidate your understanding of the chapter, review the *Behavioral Objectives* section of this study guide and verbally (not in writing) determine the answers you would give. Check with the text if necessary.

10. (Optional) (60 minutes or less) Write the answers to the essay questions and verify them by checking the textbook. If your professor uses essays, this section of the study guide will help you to practice for them. If you would like to consider additional questions of this type, each of the *Behavioral Objectives* can be turned into (or simply interpreted as) an essay question.

LET'S BEGIN

If you are a good student and have your own study techniques, it may be unnecessary to adopt this approach. However, even good students may benefit from the suggested time management framework.

For all students, following this study guide strategy could save you some precious time, increase your learning and appreciation of the material, and help you perform well on exams. It's certainly worth a try.

We wish you success and enjoyment. Your textbook is carefully prepared to supply you the necessary information. This study guide is here and ready to help you zero in on the important ideas, and your professor is ready to guide and inspire you. With all of this, how can you fail? Are you ready? We hope you are. The ground work is laid, the materials are beckoning you, it is now your move. May you work hard, learn much, and enjoy your experience. Welcome to psychology.

Richard D. Rees   Stephen S. Cooper

CHAPTER 1

History, Systems, and Research Methods

BEHAVIORAL OBJECTIVES

After completing this chapter, the student should be able to:

1. Define psychology and give examples of different kinds of behavior that psychologists study.
2. Explain the educational requirements for becoming a psychologist and recognize the employment settings in which psychologists do their work.
3. Identify several areas of specialization in psychology and point out the key features of each specialty.
4. Outline the history of psychology identifying the key individuals and the schools of psychology they developed.
5. Contrast structuralism with the schools that rebelled against it.
6. Illuminate the controversy about who really developed the first experimental laboratory in psychology.
7. Demonstrate awareness of the major criticisms of psychoanalysis.
8. Identify the major components of a simple psychological experiment.
9. List and explain the six major bipolar dimensions of research.
10. Explain what an independent variable is, and what a control group is.
11. State the best and most common technique used in an experiment to overcome observer and subject bias.
12. Identify the features of an A-B-A single subject experimental design.
13. List and describe five nonexperimental research methods.
14. Distinguish between explanation, prediction, and control as common goals of psychology.
15. Describe factors in experiments that may represent a breach of ethics.

KEY TERMS AND CONCEPTS

psychology
clinical psychologist

American Psychological Association
experimental psychologist

physiological psychologist
comparative psychologist
developmental psychologist
social psychologist
industrial or organizational
   psychologist
educational psychologist
counseling psychologist
structuralism
introspection
functionalism
stream of consciousness
natural selection
behaviorism
S-R psychology
"black box" psychology
Gestalt psychology
phi phenomenon
psychoanalysis
unconscious mind
free association
humanistic psychology
third force in psychology
self-actualization
cognitive psychology
scientific method
experiment
catharsis
social learning theory

sample
interobserver reliability
control
random selection
variable
independent variable
dependent variable
observer bias
subject bias
Hawthorne effect
double-blind controlled experiment
replication
expansion
single-subject experiment
A-B-A single-subject experimental
   design
cause-effect relationship
correlation
naturalistic observation
case study
survey
sampling error
deduction
antecedent conditions
prediction
theory
explanation
reductionism
ethics

NAMES TO REMEMBER

Aristotle
Hippocrates
Wilhelm Wundt
Edward B. Titchener
William James
Charles Darwin
G. Stanley Hall
John Dewey
John B. Watson
Max Wertheimer
Wolfgang Kohler

Kurt Koffka
Sigmund Freud
Abraham Maslow
Carl Rogers
Jean Piaget
Albert Bandura
Phineas Gage
J. M. Harlow
Philip Zimbardo
Clark Hull

GUIDED REVIEW

1. Psychology is the study of the _behavior_ of organisms.

2. Although a psychologist with a doctoral degree is called doctor, he or she is not a _physician_.

3. The largest percentage of psychologists is employed by _colleges_ and _universities_ than by any other category of employer.

4. More psychologists specialize in _clinical_ and _counseling_ psychology than in the other areas of specialization.

5. _Experimental_ psychologists rely on scientific methods and experiments and often conduct their work in a laboratory.

6. _Physiological_ psychologists study biological factors in behavior, _Comparative_ psychologists focus on similarities and differences among species, and _social_ psychologists examine the effects of people on each other.

7. _Clinical_ and _Counseling_ psychologists help people resolve serious abnormal behaviors and other personal problems, _Developmental_ psychologists study changing behavior patterns over the lifespan, _Organizational_ psychologists are involved with business and working conditions, and _Educational_ psychologists study the teaching-learning process.

8. The two parent disciplines giving birth to psychology were _philosophy_ and _physiology_.

9. Aristotle thought that thinking occurred in the _heart_, and that the brain's function was to help _cool_ the blood.

10. Psychology was founded in the year _1879_, in a laboratory in _Leipzig_, Germany.

11. Many consider _Wilhelm_ _Wundt_ to be the father of psychology. He is associated with the system of psychology known as _experimental_.

12. In his laboratory, this father of psychology was interested in studying the _structure_ of the mind by using a self-observation technique known as _introspection_.

13. In 1892, structuralism was brought to the United States by Edward B. _Titchener_. He set up his laboratory at _Cornell_ University.

14. The major critical flaw of structuralism, which resulted in its being abandoned, was the method of _introspection_. Different researchers using this method in different laboratories were not getting the same _results_.

15. The structural movement was valuable to psychology for three reasons:
    (a) it provided a strong _scientific_ and _research_
    impetus, (b) it gave the _introspection_ method a thorough
    test, and (c) it served as a foundation against which
    new systems of psychology could _rebel_.

16. The first completely American psychology was _functionalism_, and
    was founded by _William_ _James_.

17. He coined his famous term " _stream_ _of_
    consciousness " to suggest that consciousness was constantly
    changing and flowing and was not fixed like a structured blueprint.

18. James was greatly influenced by _Charles_ _Darwin_,
    whose concept of _natural_ _selection_ suggested
    that animal characteristics which served a valuable function would endure
    from generation to generation. James believed that human _consciousness_
    must have a _function_, namely to steer a nervous system
    grown too complex to regulate itself.

19. The major distinction between functionalism and structuralism is that
    functionalism focuses upon _why_ a thought or behavior
    occurs as opposed to _what_ a thought or behavior is.

20. Functionalism influenced the beginning of _developmental_ psy-
    chology through the work of G. Stanley Hall, who founded the
    American _Psychological_ _Assc._.

21. Another functional psychologist, _John_ _Dewey_,
    was interested in problem solving and improving teaching and stimulated
    the birth of _educational_ psychology.

22. The areas of animal psychology and industrial psychology also have roots
    in the early psychological school of _functionalism_.

23. An argument developed in 1979 (psychology's 100th birthday) concerning
    who developed the first _psychology_ _lab_.
    Was it _Wundt_, or was it _James_ ? Don't
    forget that _Wundt_ is typically credited with that honor,
    and the 100th birthday celebrated the opening of his lab in Leipzig,
    Germany, in _1879_.

24. An influential and controversial school of American psychology, contend-
    ing that only objectively observable behavior can legitimately be the
    subject matter of psychology was _behaviorism_, and was devel-
    oped by _John_ _Watson_.

25. Watson rejected the study of conscious thought and mental activity
    because they were _unobservable_.

26. S-R psychology and "black box" psychology are synonyms for the school of _behaviorism_ .

27. Behavioristic efforts have developed behavioral _technology_ , focused on making psychology more of a _science_ , and have shown that our responses are determined by the pleasant or unpleasant _consequences_ of our actions.

28. Behaviorists have been criticized because they ignore important but _unobservable_ aspects of behavior such as _emotion_ , thought, and _unconscious_ processes.

29. The motion picture projector, which is based on the false perception of motion called the _phi_ _phenomenon_ , was basic to the development of _Gestalt_ psychology. This was another school of psychology developed in opposition to _structuralism_ .

30. "The whole experience is more than the _sum_ of its parts" is the major tenet of _Gestalt_ psychology and was defended by _Wertheimer_ , _Köhler_ , and _Koffka_ .

31. The school or system of psychology which has its roots in neurology and medicine and which postulates an unconscious mind is called _Psychoanalysis_ and was developed by a Viennese physician named _Sigmund_ _Freud_ .

32. The goal of psychoanalysis is to treat and understand _abnormal_ _behavior_ .

33. Freud argued that the mind was like an _iceberg_ because much of it is hidden beneath the surface. This concept was the last of three great blows to _human_ _pride_ .

34. Freud thought that the function of the unconscious was to keep unacceptable thoughts or desires _repressed_ or _hidden_ from the _conscious_ mind.

35. A Freudian technique wherein the patient says whatever comes to mind regardless of how foolish it seems is called _free_ _association_ .

36. Psychoanalysis has been _criticized_ because many argue that as a psychology it is un _unscientific_ . Others point out that psychoanalysis relies on techniques that have never been _validated_ .

37. The third force in psychology is _humanistic_ psychology. Its leading proponents are _Abraham_ _Maslow_ and _Carl_ _Rogers_.

38. The concepts of free will, creativity, being conscious, and striving toward self-actualization are basic to _humanistic_ psychology.

39. _Cognitive_ psychology, which focuses on thinking and conscious processes, was influenced by the early work of the Swiss psychologist _Jean_ _Piaget_.

40. All scientific research relies on systematic and objective methods of _observing_, _recording_ and _describing_ events.

41. There are six basic dimensions of psychological _research_.

42. Descriptive research tells _what_ has occurred, and explanatory research trys to explain _why_ it occurs.

43. Researchers who do not interact with the variables under study are conducting _naturalistic_ research, while others _manipulating_ variables in experiments.

44. If research focuses on past events it is _Historical_ research; if not it is _ahistorical_.

45. Investigating a theory results in _theoretical_ research, and simply investigating phenomena is called _serendipitous_ research.

46. Knowledge is advanced by _basic_ research, and technology is advanced by _applied_ research.

47. Studying one person yields _single_ _subject_ research, and studying averages of many people produces _groups_ research.

48. A most powerful research tool is the scientific _experiment_. To use this tool, an issue must be chosen for investigation which is _testable_.

49. Freud believed viewing violence can act as a _catharsis_, reducing the viewer's desire to be _violent_.

50. On the other hand, Albert Bandura (who developed a _social_ _learning_ theory) believes that viewing violence will _increase_ the viewer's inclination to imitate the _violence_.

51. To test whether viewing television violence increases children's violent acts, you must first select a _sample_ of children of many ages and backgrounds. It is important that you not _generalize_ beyond your _sample_, that is, go beyond your _data_.

52. If you are studying aggression and violence, you must first _define_ your terms. Does a tree falling in the forest make a noise? The answer depends on how you _define_ _noise_.

53. Since different observers of children's behavior may disagree on what constitutes a violent act, two or more observers can compare observations to yield what is known as _interobserver_ _reliability_.

54. In your experiment on television violence and children's violence, the group of children who watch the violent cartoons is called the _experiment_ group, and the group who do not see violent cartoons is called the _control_ group.

55. The _control_ group serves as a comparison for the experimental group. In fact, it is the use of _control_ that defines an experiment.

56. The best way to get the second (control) group of children in your study is to _randomly_ divide the original group of children in half.

57. The control and experimental groups must be treated _exactly_ the _same_, except for the one _variable_ you wish to measure. Anything that happens to the experimental group is _controlled_ for if it also happens to the control group.

58. The variable that is manipulated in an experiment is called the _independent_ variable, and the variable that may be influenced by the manipulations (usually some measure of behavior) is called the _dependent_ variable.

59. Four groups of 25 teachers saw the same videotape of the same normal fourth-grade boy. They saw him as normal, learning-disabled, emotionally disturbed, or mentally retarded because they saw what they _expected_ to see. This example illustrates the problem of _observer_ _bias_.

60. An electric company's employees increased their work output both when the lights got brighter or dimmer because they knew they were subjects and did what they thought was expected. This illustrates the problem of _subject_ _bias_ and has come to be called the _Hawthorne_ effect.

61. Two problems that may arise in an experiment are observer and subject ___bias___.

62. Bias in your experiment can be avoided by insuring that the observers do not know whether the subjects being observed are from the ___experimental___ or ___control___ group. Also, the subjects themselves are unaware of which ___group___ they are in. Such an arrangement is called a ___double___-___blind___ controlled experiment.

63. The conclusion of your "violence" experiment shows that (as found in similar experiments) viewing cartoon violence ___increase___ the probability of immediate post-viewing ___aggression___ in grade-school children.

64. The theory that best fits your observations is that of ___Albert Bandura___, not the theory of ___Sigmund Freud___.

65. An old research rule states that "If it hasn't happened twice, it ___hasn't___ ___happened___." Thus an important procedure for any study is ___replication___, which means to ___repeat___ the study to see if the results ___agree___.

66. In addition to replication it is also often desirable to ___expand___ upon the research that you have conducted.

67. ___single___-subject experiments use time as the control.

68. By giving a drug to a subject, then withdrawing it, and then giving it again, the effects of the drug on a recall task can be investigated. This illustrates an ___A-B-A___ single-subject experimental design.

69. A ___correlation___ is defined as the relationship between two variables.

70. Although correlational studies allow predictions to be made, they do not provide information about ___cause___ and ___effect___ relationships. To examine cause and ___effect___, it is necessary to create an ___experiment___ by manipulating the ___variables___ involved.

71. Sometimes things go together (and are well correlated) by ___accident___.

72. Whenever something is discovered that is quite unexpected, it is a good idea to ___replicate___ the study a few times.

73. To observe children's aggression by simply viewing them behind one-way glass without interacting with or manipulating the variables illustrates the research technique known as _naturalistic_ _observation_ .

74. Such _naturalistic_ _observation_ can be conducted in an _informal_ or in a _structured_ way.

75. In collecting naturalistic observation data, the observer should remain as _unobstructive_ as possible so as not to change the behavior of those being observed.

76. To analyze in depth the life history of a single subject is to do a _case_ _study_ .

77. Dr. J. M. Harlow reported the _case_ _study_ of Phineas Gage who had a steel rod forced through his face and out the top of his skull by an explosion.

78. Although case studies may provide valuable data, they cannot lead to solid conclusions without further _scientific_ _research_ .

79. Conducting an interview or administering a questionnaire are examples of _survey_ techniques.

80. One problem with surveys is that people often report what they wish were _true_ .

81. Married couples tended to _overestimate_ when asked about the frequency of their sexual relations.

82. Surveys are often susceptible to sampling _error_ as when names selected from the _telephone_ book were used to predict _Landon_ the winner over Roosevelt in the 1936 election. The pollsters didn't realize that only _rich_ people had phones in those days.

83. Psychological _tests_ measure aptitudes and abilities, and are often used for clinical or _personality_ assessment.

84. Some tests are given in _groups_ , and others are administered to _individuals_ singly.

85. The efforts of scientific psychology are aimed at a common three-faceted goal, namely _explanation_ , _prediction_ , and _control_ .

86. To explain or predict, psychologists make _deductions_ based on their research findings.

87. To make a prediction or derive an explanation one must consider and observe the _antecedent_ conditions. If you determine what will happen before an event occurs you are making a _prediction_, if you show <u>why</u> something is happening or has happened then you are giving an _explanation_.

88. The ultimate answer to why water boils (or to any other question) will always be, " _beats_ _me_ !" Seeking after ultimate answers by going to smaller and smaller (more molecular) antecedent conditions is an example of _reductionism_. Ultimate answers from the point of view of scientific psychology are probably _unobtainable_.

89. Psychologists hope to discover _rules_ they can apply when certain _antecedent_ conditions are present. By applying the rules they hope to _predict_ behavior or _explain_ behavior that has already occurred.

90. The power to predict the future permits the researcher or other interested parties to try to _avoid_ it or to try to _change_ it, or in other words to use the research goal of _control_.

91. Guidelines or morals outlined by a professional group are called _ethics_. To face ethical issues the _American_ _Psych_ _Assoc._ has published guidelines for psychological research.

92. One study that may have been a breach of ethics involved observing men in a restroom and confirmed that it took the subjects _longer_ to start urinating if someone were nearby.

93. Psychologist Philip Zimbardo conducted a mock _prison_ study at Stanford University. Students acted out the roles of _prisoners_ or _guards_ and many suffered severe psychological reactions. This study may have been a breach of _ethics_.

94. Clark Hull attended a _seance_ to try and make contact with his dead _sister_. After the medium called up the spirit and spoke to Hull in his sister's voice, Hull informed the medium that he _never_ _had_ a sister. Thus we see that Clark Hull loved _scientific_ _experiments_.

SELF TEST I

1. The study of the behavior of organisms is the definition of
   a. sociology
   b. behavioral science
   c. psychology
   d. all of these

2. Psychology was born of two parents, _____ and
   _____.
   a. philosophy, physics   c. philosophy, chemistry
   b. chemistry, physiology   d. philosophy, physiology

3. _____ were interested in why a thought or behavior
   occurred, and _____ were interested in what a thought
   or behavior was.
   a. functionalists, structuralists
   b. structuralists, functionalists
   c. functionalists, functionalists
   d. structuralists, structuralists

4. The perception of apparent movement that occurs when pictures are shown
   in rapid succession (as with a motion picture projector) is called
   a. stroboscopic motion   c. the phi phenomenon
   b. the neon effect   d. the horopter phenomenon

5. Psychoanalysis is most closely associated with the work of
   a. Wolfgang Kohler   c. Charles Darwin
   b. Sigmund Freud   d. Carl Rogers

6. Which of the following is not a concept associated with humanistic
   psychology?
   a. free will   c. creativity
   b. fulfilling one's potential   d. environmental rewards

7. If you are not interested in investigating a particular theory, but merely
   want to study some interesting phenomenon such as rude drivers, you
   are conducting _____ research.
   a. historical   c. serendipitous
   b. naturalistic   d. single subject

8. To answer whether a falling tree makes a noise when no creature is
   there to hear it depends totally on
   a. how you set up your instruments
   b. the force of gravity
   c. how you define "noise"
   d. all of the above

9. The variable in an experiment that is manipulated is called the _____
   variable.
   a. dependent   c. control
   b. independent   d. extraneous

10. As you observe a group of rats labeled "bright" and a group labeled
    "dull" run a maze, you find that the bright ones do better in the maze
    than the dull ones. What is the most likely explanation for such a
    finding when the rats were labeled "bright" or "dull" by the flip of a
    coin?

    a. you see what you expect to see
    b. the "bright" rats really did do better
    c. observer bias
    d. both a and c

11. Two valuable procedures to consider employing after completing an experiment are
    a. application and publication
    b. incubation and illumination
    c. replication and expansion
    d. statistical analysis and computer application

12. If you study the incidence of aggression among gorillas in their natural habitat and you wisely decide to refrain from interacting with your variables you are conducting a/an _____ study
    a. experimental
    b. correlational
    c. naturalistic observation
    d. case

13. Psychologists
    a. use psychological tests to measure aptitudes and abilities
    b. administer psychological tests to large groups of individuals at a time
    c. administer psychological tests to one individual one-on-one
    d. all of the above

14. If you have discovered rules which permit you to know the future, and you can try to avoid it or change it, you are
    a. seeking the unobtainable
    b. conducting an experiment
    c. reductionistic in your approach
    d. exerting control

15. Your English term paper is on visual illusions of motion; which early school of psychology should you consult for information about the perception of apparent motion?
    a. structuralism   c. Gestalt psychology
    b. functionalism   d. behaviorism

SELF TEST II

1. A _____ psychologist relies on scientific methods and often conducts research in a laboratory.
    a. comparative   c. organizational
    b. social   d. experimental

2. The person considered by many to be the father of psychology was
   a. Sigmund Freud
   b. Max Wertheimer
   c. John Watson
   d. Wilhelm Wundt

3. Wundt's experimental laboratory was established in/at _____ in _____ .
   a. Heidelberg, Germany, 1879
   b. Harvard University, 1876
   c. Leipzig, Germany, 1879
   d. Cornell University, 1865

4. Which of the following were Gestalt psychologists?
   a. Max Wertheimer
   b. Wolfgang Kohler
   c. Kurt Koffka
   d. all of the above

5. Freud used special techniques to probe the unconscious mind. Which of the following is not one of them:
   a. free association
   b. dream analysis and interpretation
   c. analysis of slips of the tongue
   d. helping patients to achieve self-actualization

6. Modern psychology today
   a. consists of a loose amalgam of splinter groups all going in different directions
   b. consists of many specialties in the field, all united by a common philosophy, namely, the scientific method
   c. is based on the original principles of the early psychological schools
   d. both a and c

7. To conduct a scientific experiment, you first need
   a. willing subjects
   b. a testable issue
   c. a valid theory
   d. a control group

8. When selecting subjects for assignment to the different groups in an experiment, it is important that they be _____ so as to insure similarity between the groups
   a. carefully assigned
   b. randomly selected
   c. from common backgrounds
   d. of the same sex

9. Anything that happens to the experimental group in an experiment is _____ if it also happens to the control group.
   a. a contaminating factor
   b. unimportant
   c. a dependent variable
   d. controlled for

10. When the observer in an experiment does not know which subjects are assigned to the experimental group or the control group, and when the subjects themselves do not know which group they are in, we have what is called a
    a. subject-interobserver reliability design
    b. random experimental-control phenomenon
    c. multi-controlled experimental procedure
    d. double-blind controlled experiment

11. If two variables are correlated it means that
    a. there is a cause-and-effect relationship between them
    b. there is a relationship between them
    c. the relationship between them occurred by coincidence
    d. they are similar to each other in most respects

12. Surveys
    a. include using interviews and questionnaires
    b. are difficult to conduct properly and to interpret
    c. are susceptible to sampling errors
    d. all of the above

13. To make a deduction <u>before</u> an event occurs is to make a/an
    _____, and to make a deduction <u>after</u> the event has
    occurred is to make a/an _____.
    a. analysis, explanation   c. prediction, explanation
    b. explanation, prediction   d. prediction, analysis

14. In Zimbardo's mock prison study, Zimbardo himself
    a. became very involved in his role as prison warden
    b. suffered an acute psychological reaction and broke down because of the sadistic guards
    c. used his role as "guard" to try to persuade the sadistic "guards" to treat their "prisoners" more humanely
    d. none of the above

15. Yesterday you taught your dog to sit up and beg by reinforcing it with food. Although you didn't know it at the time, you were applying the principles of _____.
    a. behaviorism   c. functionalism
    b. structuralism   d. Gestalt psychology

ESSAY QUESTIONS

1. Explain why the American Psychological Association has so many divisions. List five major areas of specialization in psychology and describe the kinds of things that are done by the psychologists in each of these specialties.

2. Compare and contrast structuralism with functionalism, behaviorism, and Gestalt psychology. Mention key personalities and points of disagreement.

3. Explain the origins, contributions, and criticisms of psychoanalysis.

4. Design an experiment to investigate whether Coca-cola influences scores on a psychology test. Include in your design an experimental group, a control group, a dependent and independent variable, a way to overcome bias, and then carefully explain the procedures you would use.

5. Discuss the problem of ethics in psychological research.

ANSWER SECTION

Guided Review
1. behavior
2. physician
3. colleges, universities
4. clinical, counseling
5. experimental
6. physiological, comparative, social
7. clinical, counseling, developmental, industrial, educational
8. philosophy, physiology
9. heart, cool
10. 1879, Leipzig
11. Wilhelm Wundt, structuralism
12. structure, introspection
13. Titchener, Cornell
14. introspection, results
15. scientific, research, introspective, test, rebel
16. functionalism, William James
17. stream of consciousness
18. Charles Darwin, natural selection, consciousness, function
19. why, what
20. developmental, American Psychological Association
21. John Dewey, educational
22. functionalism
23. experimental laboratory, Wundt, James, Wundt, 1879
24. behaviorism, John Watson
25. unobservable
26. behaviorism
27. technology, science, consequences
28. unobservable, emotion, unconscious
29. phi phenomenon, Gestalt, structuralism
30. sum, Gestalt, Wertheimer, Kohler, Koffka
31. psychoanalysis, Sigmund Freud
32. abnormal behavior

33. *iceberg, human pride*
34. *repressed, hidden, conscious*
35. *free association*
36. *criticized, scientific, validated*
37. *humanistic, Abraham Maslow, Carl Rogers*
38. *humanistic*
39. *cognitive, Jean Piaget*
40. *observing, recording, describing*
41. *research*
42. *what, why*
43. *naturalistic, manipulate*
44. *historical, ahistorical*
45. *theoretical, serendipitous or atheoretical*
46. *basic, applied*
47. *single subject, group*
48. *experiment, testable*
49. *release or catharsis, violent*
50. *social learning, increase, violence*
51. *sample, generalize, sample, data*
52. *define, define noise*
53. *interobserver reliability*
54. *experimental, control*
55. *control, control*
56. *randomly*
57. *exactly, same, variable, controlled*
58. *independent, dependent*
59. *expected, observer bias*
60. *subject bias, Hawthorne*
61. *bias*
62. *experimental, control, group, double-blind*
63. *increases, aggression*
64. *Albert Bandura, Sigmund Freud*
65. *hasn't happened, replication, repeat or duplicate, agree*
66. *expand*
67. *single*
68. *A-B-A*
69. *correlation*
70. *cause, effect, effect, experiment, variables*
71. *accident or coincidence*
72. *replicate*
73. *naturalistic observation*
74. *naturalistic observations, informal, structured*
75. *unobtrusive*
76. *case study*
77. *case study*
78. *scientific evidence*
79. *survey*
80. *true*
81. *overestimate*

82. *error, telephone, Landon, rich*
83. *tests, personality*
84. *groups, individuals*
85. *explanation, prediction, control*
86. *deductions*
87. *antecedent, prediction, explanation*
88. *beats me, reductionism, unobtainable*
89. *rules, antecedent, predict, explain*
90. *avoid, change, control*
91. *ethics, American Psychological Association*
92. *longer*
93. *prison, prisoners, guards, ethics*
94. *seance, sister, never had, scientific experiments*

Self Test I		*Self Test II*	
1.	*c*	*1.*	*d*
2.	*d*	*2.*	*d*
3.	*a*	*3.*	*c*
4.	*c*	*4.*	*d*
5.	*b*	*5.*	*d*
6.	*d*	*6.*	*b*
7.	*c*	*7.*	*b*
8.	*c*	*8.*	*b*
9.	*b*	*9.*	*d*
10.	*d*	*10.*	*d*
11.	*c*	*11.*	*b*
12.	*c*	*12.*	*d*
13.	*d*	*13.*	*c*
14.	*d*	*14.*	*a*
15.	*c*	*15.*	*a*

CHAPTER 2

The Biological Bases of Behavior

BEHAVIORAL OBJECTIVES

After completing this chapter, the student should be able to:

1. Describe the classic study of "pleasure centers" done by James Olds.
2. List the major divisions and subdivisions of the nervous system and briefly describe their functions.
3. Label the parts of a neuron and describe their functions.
4. Compare and contrast the sympathetic and parasympathetic nervous systems.
5. Explain the role of neurotransmitters and describe the synapse.
6. Label the major regions or lobes of the brain and describe the functions located in these areas.
7. Explain why the amount of brain area differs for various regions of the motor cortex and sensory cortex.
8. Describe the new PET scan procedure and explain how it may influence future psychiatry.
9. Describe the functions of the left and right hemispheres of the brain.
10. List the two main kinds of neurotransmitters, the monoamines and amino acids, and describe what neuropeptides are.
11. Summarize the different functions of the neuropeptides.
12. Describe the research attempting to explain acupuncture and placebo effects.
13. Distinguish between the endocrine and exocrine systems.
14. Describe what a nature-nurture dilemma is.
15. Explain eugenics. Define positive and negative eugenics.

KEY TERMS AND CONCEPTS

electrical brain stimulation (ESB)
pleasure center
central nervous system (CNS)
peripheral nervous system (PNS)

brain
spinal cord
somatic nervous system
afferent nerves

efferent nerves
reflex arc
autonomic nervous system
sympathetic nervous system
neuron
nerves
electrochemical messages
soma
axon
dendrites
nucleus
neural membrane
sodium-potassium pumps
impulse initiating zone
spike
nerve impulse
action potential
neurotransmitters
resting potential
graded potential
silent cells
synapse
end buttons or synaptic knobs
vesicles
presynaptic surface
postsynaptic surface
excitatory synapse
inhibitory synapse
negative potential
Golgi stain
brain mapping
sulci
gyri
myelin sheath
gray matter
cerebral cortex
neocortex
hindbrain
medulla
pons
cerebellum
reticular activating system
superior and inferior colliculi
forebrain
diencephalon
telencephalon
thalamus
olfactory bulb
hypothalamus

pituitary gland
hormones
corpus callosum
limbic system
hippocampus
amygdala
frontal lobes
parietal lobes
occipital lobes
temporal lobes
central sulcus
motor area
somatosensory areas
visual cortex
association areas
PET scan
positrons
schizophrenia
short term memory
long term memory
prosoagnosia
Broca's area
aphasia
split-brain
epilepsy
brain dominance
lateralized
norepinephrine
monoamines
amino acids
dopamine hypothesis
Parkinson's disease
L-dopa
serotonin
glycine
gamma-aminobutyric acid (GABA)
hallucinogenic drugs
neuropeptides
periaqueductal gray matter
enkephalin
beta endorphin
acupuncture
microelectrode
naloxone
placebo
placebo reactors
dynorphin
exocrine glands
endocrine glands

pituitary gland
adrenal glands
gonads
executive hormones
thyrotropin releasing hormone
    (TRH)
adrenaline (epinephrine)
noradrenaline (norepinephrine)
steroids
endocrinologists
chromosomes
genes
karyotype
autosomes
sex chromsomes

gametes
meiosis
ovum
sperm
evolution
natural selection
canalization
sensitive period
selective breeding
nature-nurture question
eugenics
negative and positive eugenics
gene pool
Marfan's syndrome

NAMES TO REMEMBER

James Olds
R. E. Myers
R. W. Sperry
M. S. Gazzaniga
Avram Goldstein

Bruce Pomeranz
Gregor Mendel
Sir Francis Galton
Charles Darwin

GUIDED REVIEW

1. In James Olds' classic rat study he used <u>*electrical*</u> <u>*brain*</u> <u>*stimulation*</u> to seemingly discover the existence of <u>*pleasure*</u> <u>*centers*</u> in the brain.

2. The <u>*nerves*</u> transmit messages throughout the body, thus permitting you to breathe or to remember your telephone number.

3. The two major divisions of the nervous system are the <u>*central*</u> nervous system and the <u>*peripheral*</u> nervous system. These are commonly abbreviated as the <u>*CNS*</u> and <u>*PNS*</u> respectively.

4. The CNS consists of the <u>*brain*</u> and <u>*spinal cord*</u>.

5. The <u>*peripheral*</u> <u>*nervous*</u> <u>*system*</u> is divided into the somatic nervous system and the <u>*autonomic*</u> <u>*nervous*</u> <u>*system*</u>. The PNS carries messages to and from the <u>*central*</u> <u>*nervous*</u> <u>*system*</u>.

6. The __somatic__ nervous system carries messages inward toward the CNS from the sense organs or outward away from the CNS to __skeletal__ __muscles__ .

7. __afferent__ nerves carry neural messages inward to the CNS, while __efferent__ nerves carry messages away from the CNS. These two types of nerves make up the __reflex__ __arc__ , which is one of the simplest arrangements in the nervous system.

8. The seemingly automatic division of the PNS is the __autonomic__ __nervous__ __system__ , which is divided into two parts, the __sympathetic__ and __parasympathetic__ subdivisions.

9. The "fight or flight" system that expends energy and prepares the body for fighting or running away is known as the __sympathetic__ __nervous__ __system__ .

10. While the sympathetic nervous system excites the body and expends energy the __parasympathetic__ nervous system slows the body and conserves energy.

11. When the sympathetic nervous system is especially active the heart beat __increases__ , __adrenaline__ is secreted, the pupils __dilate__ , and the mouth becomes dry. Following this the __parasympathetic__ nervous system calms the body down and salivation and digestion functions resume. Yet the effects of the adrenaline secretions may leave the person a little shaky for __20__ to __30__ minutes.

12. The basic unit of the nervous system is the nerve cell, which is called a __neuron__ .

13. __nerves__ are made up of thousands of neurons. Most neurons are located in the __brain__ , and while no one knows exactly how many neurons there are in the brain, the common estimate is __10__ billion.

14. The typical neuron has three distinct structures: The __soma__ , or cell body, the __axon__ , which carries the nerve impulse away from the cell body, and the __dendrites__ .

15. The soma contains the __nucleus__ , which manufactures the __enzymes__ and __molecules__ essential for the cell's life.

16. In a single neuron the __dendrites__ receive messages and send them to the soma. The __axons__ , which can vary considerably in length, carries the nerve impulse away from the soma to

to eventually stimulate other _neurons_ , _muscles_ , or _glands_ .

17. Surrounding the entire neuron is a thin skin or _membrane_ which allows the cell to maintain differences inside and out. The difference is most pronounced in the higher concentrations of _potassium_ ions inside the membrane and _sodium_ ions outside the membrane (when the neuron is at rest). The relative concentrations of sodium and potassium ions are made possible by the approximately one million _sodium_ - _potassium_ _pumps_ that are found in each neuron.

18. Neurons are stimulated when chemical messengers called _neurotransmitters_ excite the receiving neuron. If enough excitatory stimulation is stored up in the _soma_ , the _impulse_ _initiating_ _zone_ is stimulated and the axon sends the impulse on.

19. At rest a neuron has a greater concentration of _potassium_ ions inside the axon and a greater concentration of _sodium_ ions outside the axon. This state is known as the _resting_ _potential_ and the neuron is capable of generating a nerve impulse down the length of its _axon_ .

20. When the impulse initiating zone is sufficiently stimulated, a _spike_ can be seen on an oscilloscope. If the spike or _nerve_ _impulse_ is created an _action_ _potential_ has been reached.

21. Neural impulses can convey a variety of messages depending on the _number_ of neurons firing or the _rate_ of each neuron's firing.

22. _Graded_ _potentials_ include all the ranges of electrical exchanges that are not strong enough to cause an _action_ _potential_ but which are greater than those found at _resting_ _potential_ .

23. Graded potentials rapidly lose their _strength_ over distances, thus they are useful for _local_ communication rather than long distance transmissions.

24. Neurons that rely heavily on graded potentials are often called _silent_ _cells_ . Many of these neurons have no _axon_ .

25. The space or junction between a neuron and another muscle, gland, or neuron is called a _synapse_ .

26. A single axon can have thousands of end buttons or _synaptic_ _knobs_ that terminate at other neurons, muscles, or glands. The synaptic knobs are filled with _vesicles_ which contain _neurotransmitter_. Neurotransmitter spills into the synapse from the surface of the _presynaptic membrane_, and receptors on the _postsynaptic membrane_ may then respond to the neurotransmitter.

27. There are two kinds of synapses: _excitatory_ and _inhibitory_. Excitatory synapses create a _positive_ ion flow and make the postsynaptic membrane more likely to be stimulated.

28. A _negative_ ion flow is created when an _inhibitory_ _synapse_ is stimulated and the receiving neurons (muscles, glands) are less likely to be activated.

29. _Brain_ _mapping_ is often done during brain surgery to identify and thereby avoid damaging vital functions of the brain.

30. The brain's surface is wrinkled and covered with fissures known as _sulci_ and convolutions which are known as _gyri_.

31. Myelin is a white fatty sheath or covering on the _axon_ of some neurons. The gray matter of the brain is made up of _unmyelinated_ neurons, while the white matter is made up of _myelinated_ neurons.

32. Seventy percent of all the neurons in the central nervous system are contained in the _cerebral cortex_, which is also known as the _neocortex_ because of its more recent evolutionary development.

33. The brain has been divided into three major regions: The _hindbrain_, the _midbrain_, and the _forebrain_.

34. The major components of the hindbrain are the _medulla_, the _pons_ and the _cerebellum_. These structures are found in lower animals as well as humans, and being evolutionarily older, are collectively known as the _reptilian_ _brain_.

35. At the base of the brain where the spinal cord widens lies the _medulla_, whose function is to control vital _life_ _support_ systems such as _heartbeat_ and _respiration_.

36. Just above the medulla and in front of the brain stem is the _pons_, which regulates motor messages from higher

brain areas down to the _cerebellum_. It controls other functions as well, including regulating _sensory_ information and respiration.

37. Behind the pons at the lower rear of the brain lies the _cerebellum_, which coordinates _muscle tone_ and fine motor movement.

38. The _reticular activating system_ is contained within the hindbrain and is made up of a relatively few neurons which monitor the general activity of the hindbrain and regulate _sleeping_ and _waking_. The focusing of _attention_ and general arousal or alertness also seem to be controlled in this reticular formation.

39. Upper portions of the reticular formation are found in the _midbrain_ along with two important structures, the _superior colliculi_ and the _inferior colliculi_.

40. The _superior colliculi_ are known to be involved in controlling and regulating _visual_ movement and processing and relaying _auditory_ information.

41. The _diencephalon_ and the _telecephalon_ make up the forebrain. The diencephalon is further subdivided into the _thalamus_ and _hypothalamus_.

42. The _thalamus_, like the reticular activating system, seems to be involved in controlling _wakefulness_ and _sleeping_. However, the thalamus seems to have a more important functirn of acting as a _relay center_ for _sensory_ messages (although not as a relay center for _olfactory_ messages).

43. An elongated structure that has generated much interest because of its large number of important functions is the _hypothalamus_. It has a role to play in the regulation of sleep and wakefulness, control of body temperature, _hunger_ and _thirst_ as well as _blood pressure_ and body metabolism.

44. The _pituitary_ gland receives neural messages and some executive _hormones_ from the hypothalamus. The pituitary gland is known as the _master gland_, since its secretions can control glands throughout the body.

45. A band of fibers that are located in the _telencephalon_ are known as the _corpus collosum_. In severe forms of

epilepsy   this band of fibers is cut.

46. Two major components of the _limbic_   _system_
are the hippocampus and the _amygdala_   . The hippocampus has
been shown to have an important role to play in _memory_   ,
while the amygdala has been associated with _emotion_   .

47. Throughout evolution the _cerebral_   _cortex_
has grown and become the most prominent aspect of the brain. The
cortex has been mapped into four major lobes: the
frontal   lobes, the _parietal_   lobes, the occipital lobes and the _temporal_   lobes.

48. A person who suffered a stroke and was paralyzed on the left side of
the body had damage to the _right_   side of the brain.

49. The _motor_   _area_   of the brain is located in
the back of the frontal lobes and just in front of the _central_
sulcus. The sensory area, or _somatosensory_   area, lies just
behind the central sulcus in the _parietal_   lobes.

50. Behind the parietal lobes and above the cerebellum are the
occipital   lobes which make up the _visual_
cortex.

51. Auditory messages arrive at the lobes located behind your temples.
These are known as the _temporal_   lobes.

52. A new breakthrough in brain research has been the _PET_
(abbreviation) scan. When subjects listened to music the
temporal   _lobes_   clearly light up on the
scan. Also, mental patients diagnosed as _schizophrenic_
have had scans showing dark regions in the _frontal_
lobes   as compared with normal individuals' scans.

53. Charles Whitman had a malignant brain tumor pressing on, and quite
possibly influencing, the _amygdala_   , which is part of the
limbic   _system_   and has been shown in
cat studies to be associated with _emotion (rage)_ .

54. Milner first implicated the _hippocampus_   as important to memory,
when a patient of his had the hippocampus cut, resulting in the inability
to place new memories into _long_   - _term_
storage.

55. Much of our early information about the brain came from studying
damaged   brains. For example, individuals who have had
the lower portions of their occipital lobes damaged experience a disorder
known as _prosoagnosia_ . This disorder results in the individual
being unable to _recognize_   faces.

56. The _left_ hemisphere of the brain has been found to be associated with language. Damage to _Broca's_ area may result in speech disorders such as _aphasia_. Speech generation is generally impaired when Broca's area is damaged, yet the muscular function is not seemingly the reason since damaged patients can still _sing_.

57. The brain is said to be flexible or _plastic_, since other areas often seem to take up the functions of the damaged areas. For example, young children who have had their _left_ hemisphere language areas destroyed seem to have developed new centers in the _right_ hemisphere.

58. Myers and Sperry did a classic _split_- _brain_ study with cats and found that one hemisphere could learn something while the other remained ignorant. This creation of two brains takes place by cutting the _corpus_ _callosum_ and has been done on humans who suffer from _epilepsy_.

59. Split brain patients have demonstrated that each _hemisphere_ can indeed act independently. For example, if a split brain subject is shown a familiar object so that only the right hemisphere gets the input, then this person will be unable to _state_ what he has seen. However, if the _left_ hemisphere receives the input the subject can easily say what he saw.

60. The left hemisphere is specialized for _speech_ and _language_, while the right hemisphere is able to do things that require _spatial_ orientation. Emotional differences between the hemispheres are suggested, with the _right_ being more emotional.

61. Alcohol seems to affect the _right_ _hemisphere_ more, and our ability to attend to things seems to also be controlled more by the _right_ _hemisphere_.

62. Most right-handed people are _left_ brain dominant, and most left-handed people are _left_ brain dominant. About _two_-_thirds_ of the people who are left-handed write in a _hooked_ manner and it has been found that 99% of these people are _left_ _brain_ dominant.

63. Some people are highly _lateralized_ in that the hemispheres differ greatly in brain organization. _men_ tend to be more lateralized than _women_.

64. Neurotransmitters are _localized_ in specific groups of neurons

in the brain. _norepinephrine_ is a transmitter suspected to be involved in arousal, _dream_ _sleep_ _____, ____mood_____ ___regulation___, and is believed to be involved in one of the brain's ____pleasure____ _centers_.

65. The two major kinds of neurotransmitters are the _monoamines_ and the ___amino___ ___acids___. Each neurotransmitter has a characteristic _excitatory_ or __inhibitory__ effect on other neurons.

66. Neurons containing the monoamine transmitter _dopamine_ are found in greater concentrations in the _midbrain_. These neurons project to the _forebrain_ and are believed to be involved with _emotional_ responses and their regulation.

67. Most excitatory effects on neurons are believed to be caused by ___aspartic___ acid and _glutamic_ acid. The most common inhibitory transmitter in the brain is _gamma_ - _aminobutyric_ acid, while the simplest of amino acids, _glycine_, acts as an inhibitory transmitter in the spine.

68. _neuropeptides_ are molecules made from short chains of amino acids and act as chemical _messengers_. Beta-_endorphin_ has been found to be located in the _pituitary_ ___gland___ and is considered to be the body's own morphine-like substance.

69. Microelectrode studies on cats have suggested that the brain's release of __beta__ - _endorphine_ may explain how the Chinese procedure of _acupuncture_ may work in relieving pain.

70. Also supporting beta-endorphin's role in acupuncture have been human studies where _naloxone_ has been injected to block the effects of __beta__ - _endorphine_ and the acupuncture procedure than failed to block pain.

71. Research has implicated _beta_ - _endorphine_ as a possible cause of the pleasurable high runners report experiencing. Treadmill studies found higher levels of this neuropeptide in those who _exercise_ regularly than in those who are _sedentary_.

72. Research on the neuropeptides has found that excess endorphin can possibly lead to _overeating_, while met-enkephalin and _vasopressin_ have been found to enhance _memory_.

73. Avram Goldstein discovered _dynorphin_ in 1979, which means _power_ in Greek. This neuropeptide appears to be 200

times more powerful than _morphine_ .

74. _Exocrine_ glands secrete onto the body's surface and include tear and _sweat_ glands. The pituitary, the adrenal glands, and the gonads secrete _hormones_ directly into the bloodstream and are part of the _endocrine_ system.

75. _Hormones_ are messengers that are carried in the bloodstream and have a vital function in _physical_ _growth_ and _sexual_ _developement_ .

76. Some of the hormones released by glands or by the _Hypothalamus_ are called _executive_ hormones because their release may trigger the release of other _hormones_ in the endocrine system.

77. The adrenal glands secrete _adrenaline_ and _noradrenaline_ also known respectively as epinephrine and _norepinephrine_. Both of these hormones are related to actions of the _sympathetic_ nervous system to ready the body for emergency situations.

78. _adrenaline_ causes the heart to beat faster and the inhibition of digestion, while _noradrenaline_ is an executive hormone which, when acting on the adrenal cortex, causes the secretion of _steriods_ .

79. In a normal human body cell there are 23 pairs, or 46 individual _chromosomes_. On the chromosomes of each cell lie the _genes_ which contain the genetic code for the entire body. Of the chromosomes, the 23rd pair are known as the _sex_ _chromosomes_ and the remaining 22 pairs are called _autosomes_ .

80. Sperm or egg cells are called _gametes_ and only contain _23_ chromosomes (not pairs) each. The production of sex cells is accomplished by a special type of cell division known as _meiosis_ .

81. Autosomes and sex chromosomes both carry genetic codes, but only the _sex_ _chromosomes_ carry the genetic codes which determine an individual's _sex_ . The 23rd pair of chromosomes indicate a male individual if the pair is shaped _XY_ , and female if they are shaped _XX_ .

82. The _ovum_ or egg can only contain _X_ shaped sex chromosomes. Therefore boys and girls will have received one X chromosome from their _mother_ . Since sperm are either _X_ or _Y_ , the male _gametes (sperm)_ will ultimately determine the child's _sex_ .

83.   _Gregor_ _Mendel_, an Austrian monk, discovered that a number of simple _traits_ in offspring would occur at particular _ratios_ depending on the kinds of traits possessed by the _parents_ .

84.   While learning and experience are extremely important factors in determining your _behavior_ , you are also the product of billions of years of _evolution_ and _natural_ _selection_ .

85.   Clearly some basic responses in human beings are built-in or _inherited_ such as swallowing, etc. In humans more complex behaviors such as building a dog house or registering for college are _learned_ behaviors. However, _genetics_ may still be a factor by the passing on of _genetic_ predispositions.

86.   Teaching a disc pecking response is easier when using a pigeon than a pig* because of the process known as _canalization_ . A canalized behavior is _learned_ _easily_ , almost inevitably.

87.   _Sensitive_ _periods_ are special times during our development when a particular influence is most likely to have an effect because we are _biologically_ predisposed to react to that influence at that particular time.

88.   Raising "maze bright" rats is an example of _selective_ _breeding_ , which is one way psychologists have studied kinds of _inheritance_ . Since humans cannot ethically or practically be used for selective breeding studies we attempt to learn more about inheritance by examining people who are _related_ .

89.   The closer individuals are in terms of their _genetic_ relationship, the more likely they are to be similar in intelligence. But is the similarity due to _environment_ or _heredity_ ? This is a _nature_ - _nurture_ dilemma.

90.   _Eugenics_ was a term coined by Sir Francis Galton and involved a movement to create a better _human_ race.

91.   _Negative_ _eugenics_ is a process of eliminating defective genes, often by compulsory _sterilization_ . _positive_ eugenics requires select women to be fertilized by the best _sperm_ .

---

      *Never try to teach a pig to sing. It is impossible and it annoys the pig!

92. Mr. Niethold did not feel his dental pain because he had small electrodes
     implanted in the _periaqueductal, gray_
     _matter_____ of his brain which, when stimulated, increased
     the _____beta_____ =_gradasy_____ levels in his brain.
                           endorphine

SELF TEST I

1. The central nervous system consists of the _____
    and _____ _____.
    a. brain; peripheral nerves
    b. nerves; spinal cord
    c. dendrites; your body
    (d.) brain; spinal cord

2. Nerves that carry sensory messages to the CNS are called _____
    nerves.
    a. efferent   c. worker
    (b.) afferent   d. autonomic

3. When you get frightened or very angry your _____
    nervous system readies the body for fight or flight.
    a. parasympathetic   (c.) sympathetic
    b. reactive   d. none of the above

4. The _____ nervous system has two subdivisions: the
    _____ nervous system and the _____
    nervous system.
    a. autonomic; sympathetic; parasympathetic
    (b.) peripheral; autonomic; somatic
    (c.) both a and b
    d. none of the above

5. The _____ of a neuron may be very short or as long as
    three feet.
    a. nucleus   c. soma
    b. dendrites   (d.) axon

6. The structures of the neuron that receive most incoming nerve impulses
    are the
    (a.) dendrites   c. axons
    b. somas   d. nuclei

7. Many silent cell neurons do not have axons.
    (a.) true   (b.) false

8. A synapse is
    a. the same as an action potential
    (b.) the gap between neurons

    c. found only in the PNS
    d. none of the above

9.   If someone says you lack gray matter, they would technically be saying that you lack
    a. a myelin sheath
    b. nonmyelinated neurons
    c. sulci
    d. gyri

10.   The oldest portion of the brain from an evolutionary perspective, which is also known as the "reptilian brain" is the
    a. forebrain   c. cerebral cortex
    b. midbrain   d. hindbrain

11.   The rear of the frontal lobes contain the _____ areas responsible for control of our muscles.
    a. auditory   c. motor
    b. sensory   d. glandular

12.   The PET scan technology is most exciting to psychologists for
    a. diagnosis and investigation of mental illness
    b. measuring blood flow in the brain
    c. both a and b
    d. none of the above

13.   The right hemisphere or right brain
    a. controls the left side of the body
    b. generally does not have language
    c. may influence our attention span
    d. all of the above

14.   You inherit _____ chromosomes from each of your parents. On these chromosomes lie the _____.
    a. 23 pairs of; genes
    b. 23; genes
    c. 46 pairs of; genes
    d. 46; neurotransmitters

15.   Garcia and Koelling's study using rats who were drinking sweetened water under various stimulus conditions
    a. found that when nausea had followed the drinking of sweetened water the rats avoided sweetened water
    b. found that when shock preceded the drinking of sweetened water in the presence of a light and tone, that a fear or avoidance of the light and tone resulted.
    c. demonstrated canalization
    d. all of the above.

SELF TEST II

1. The nervous system that is encased in bone is the _____
   nervous system
   a. calcified   c. autonomic
   b. central   d. somatic

2. Nerves that carry messages from the CNS to the muscles of the skeleton
   are called _____ nerves.
   a. efferent   c. sensory
   b. autonomic   d. afferent

3. The emergency fight or flight system is the _____ nervous
   system, a branch of the _____ nervous system, which,
   in turn, is part of the _____ nervous system.
   a. parasympathetic; autonomic, peripheral
   b. somatic; peripheral, central
   c. peripheral; peripheral; central
   d. sympathetic; autonomic; peripheral

4. The basic unit of the nervous system is the
   a. body cell   c. neuron
   b. nerve cell   d. both b and c

5. Along the neuron's membrane lie the
   a. nuclei
   b. soma
   c. sodium-potassium pumps
   d. chlorine pores

6. When the axon of a neuron is at its resting potential
   a. it can fire if adequately stimulated
   b. the inside is about -70 millivolts relative to the outside
   c. more sodium ions are concentrated outside the membrane than inside
   d. all of the above

7. Silent cell neurons
   a. rely on graded potentials
   b. send messages great distances
   c. are found only in the peripheral nervous system
   d. generate spikes

8. The _____ are contained within the synaptic knobs.
   a. synapses
   b. postsynaptic membranes
   c. vesicles
   d. dendrites

9. The fat white matter covering some axons is called the
    a. white coat
    b. myelin sheath
    c. insulating sulci
    d. all of the above

10. The portion of the brain known as the thalamus
    a. acts as a central relay center for sensory information
    b. has no known functions
    c. is responsible for muscle tone
    d. all of the above

11. A punch to the left side of your jaw would send a sensory message to the
    _____ area on the _____ side of the brain
    in the _____ lobe
    a. somatosensory; left; parietal
    b. somatosensory; right; frontal
    c. somatosensory; right; parietal
    d. motor; left; temporal

12. The speech center known as Broca's area is located
    a. on the left side of the brain of most people
    b. on the left for left-handed people only
    c. on the right for most left-handed people
    d. either b or c

13. In a human body cell there are
    a. 23 chromosomes
    b. 46 chromosomes
    c. 23 pairs of chromosomes
    d. either b or c

14. A baby who has a 23rd pair of XX chromosomes is a
    a. male   c. mutation
    b. female   d. hermaphrodite

15. _____ is the scientific term for the selective breeding
    of human beings.
    a. cryonics   c. biogenetics
    b. eugenics   d. none of these

ESSAY QUESTIONS

1. Discuss why the autonomic nervous system is so named; then compare
    and contrast the sympathetic and parasympathetic subdivisions.

2. List and describe the functions of the major lobes of the brain.

3. Explain the role of neurotransmitters in the nervous system.

4. Describe the functions that are unique to each hemisphere and explain why split-brain surgeries have been done on humans.

5. Summarize eugenics as proposed by Sir Francis Galton.

ANSWER SECTION

Guided Review
1. *electrical brain stimulation (or ESB), pleasure centers*
2. *nerves*
3. *central, peripheral, CNS, PNS*
4. *brain, spinal cord*
5. *peripheral nervous system (or PNS), autonomic nervous system, central nervous system (or CNS)*
6. *somatic, skeletal muscles*
7. *afferent, efferent, reflex arc*
8. *autonomic nervous system, sympathetic, parasympathetic*
9. *sympathetic nervous system*
10. *parasympathetic*
11. *increases, adrenaline, dilate, parasympathetic, 20, 30*
12. *neuron*
13. *nerves, brain, 10*
14. *soma, axon, dendrites*
15. *nucleus, enzymes, molecules*
16. *dendrites, axon, neurons, muscles, glands*
17. *membrane, potassium (or K^+), sodium (or Na^+), sodium-potassium pumps*
18. *neurotransmitters, soma, impulse initiating zone*
19. *potassium, sodium, resting potential, axon*
20. *spike, nerve impulse, action potential*
21. *number, rate (or frequency)*
22. *graded potentials, action potential, resting potential*
23. *strength, local*
24. *silent cells, axons*
25. *synapse*
26. *synaptic knobs, vesicles, neurotransmitters, presynaptic membrane, postsynaptic membrane*
27. *excitatory, inhibitory, positive*
28. *negative, inhibitory synapse*
29. *brain mapping*
30. *sulci, gyri*
31. *axons, unmyelinated, myelinated*
32. *cerebral cortex, neocortex*
33. *hindbrain, midbrain, forebrain*
34. *medulla, pons, cerebellum, reptilian brain*
35. *medulla, life support, heartbeat, respiration*
36. *pons, cerebellum, sensory*

37.   *cerebellum, muscle tone*
38.   *reticular activating system, sleeping, waking, attention*
39.   *midbrain, superior colliculi, inferior colliculi*
40.   *superior colliculi, visual, auditory*
41.   *diencephalon, telencephalon, thalamus, hypothalamus*
42.   *thalamus, wakefulness, sleeping, relay center, sensory, olfactory*
43.   *hypothalamus, hunger, thirst, blood pressure*
44.   *pituitary, hormones, master gland*
45.   *telencephalon, corpus callosum, epilepsy*
46.   *limbic system, amygdala, memory, emotion*
47.   *cerebral cortex, frontal, parietal, temporal*
48.   *right*
49.   *motor area, central, somatosensory, parietal*
50.   *occipital, visual*
51.   *temporal*
52.   *PET, temporal lobes, schizophrenic, frontal lobes*
53.   *amygdala, limbic system, emotion (or rage)*
54.   *hippocampus, long-term*
55.   *damaged, prosoagnosia, recognize*
56.   *left, Broca's, aphasia, sing*
57.   *plastic, left, right*
58.   *split-brain, corpus callosum, epilepsy*
59.   *hemisphere, state (say), left*
60.   *speech, language, spatial, right*
61.   *right hemisphere, right hemisphere*
62.   *left, left, two-thirds, hooked, left brain*
63.   *lateralized, men, women*
64.   *localized, norepinephrine, dream sleep, mood regulation, pleasure centers*
65.   *monoamines, amino acids, excitatory, inhibitory*
66.   *dopamine, midbrain, forebrain, emotional*
67.   *aspartic, glutamic, gamma-aminobutyric (or GABA), glycine*
68.   *neuropeptides, messengers, endorphin, pituitary gland*
69.   *beta-endorphin, acupuncture*
70.   *naloxone, beta-endorphin*
71.   *beta-endorphin, exercise, sedentary*
72.   *overeating, vasopressin, memory*
73.   *dynorphin, power, morphine*
74.   *exocrine, sweat, hormones, endocrine*
75.   *hormones, physical growth, sexual development*
76.   *hypothalamus, executive, hormones*
77.   *adrenaline, noradrenaline, norepinephrine, sympathetic*
78.   *adrenaline, noradrenaline, steroids*
79.   *chromosomes, genes, sex chromosomes, autosomes*
80.   *gametes, 23, meiosis*
81.   *sex chromosomes, sex, XY, XX*
82.   *ovum, X, mother, X, Y, gametes (or sperm), sex*
83.   *Gregor Mendel, traits, ratios, parents*
84.   *behavior, evolution, natural selection*

85. *inherited, learned, genetics (or inheritance), genetic (or inherited)*
86. *canalization, learned easily*
87. *sensitive periods, biologically*
88. *selective breeding, inheritance, related*
89. *genetic, environment, heredity, nature-nurture*
90. *eugenics, human*
91. *negative eugenics, sterilization, positive, sperm (or men)*
92. *periaqueductal gray matter, beta-endorphin*

Self Test I		*Self Test II*	
1.	d	1.	b
2.	b	2.	a
3.	c	3.	d
4.	c	4.	d
5.	d	5.	c
6.	a	6.	d
7.	a	7.	a
8.	b	8.	c
9.	b	9.	b
10.	d	10.	a
11.	c	11.	c
12.	a	12.	a
13.	d	13.	d
14.	b	14.	b
15.	d	15.	b

CHAPTER 3

Sensation

BEHAVIORAL OBJECTIVES

After completing this chapter, the student should be able to:

1. Tell in his or her own words what a sensory threshold is, and elaborate on two kinds (absolute and just noticeable difference)
2. Compare the eye with a camera, pointing out the similarities and differences.
3. Trace a ray of light from the outside world, through the various structures of the eye, to the brain.
4. Explain in detail the functioning of rods and cones and mention their relationship to the fovea, the blind spot, and dark adaptation.
5. Contrast the Young-Helmholtz (three color) theory with the Hering Opponent Process theory and the retinex theory of color vision.
6. Distinguish the difference between an afterimage and an aftereffect and give examples of each.
7. List the various types of color blindness and give the different theoretical views that pertain to color blindness.
8. Explain edge detectors, motion detectors, and high and low frequency spatial detectors.
9. Trace a sound impulse from the outside world to the brain, noting location and function of the structures through which it passes.
10. Describe how research is permitting the deaf to hear again with inner ear implants.
11. Outline the key features of three theories of hearing.
12. Compare and contrast the senses of taste, smell, and touch, summarizing recent findings in these areas.
13. Explain the difference between the kinesthetic sense and the equilibratory sense.
14. Evaluate the possible implications of a magnetic sense.
15. Outline four kinds of extrasensory perception and what scientists are doing with, and how they feel about, such phenomena.

KEY TERMS AND CONCEPTS

vertical edge detectors
absolute threshold
difference threshold
JND
Weber's Law
retina
cornea
pupil
lens
ganglion cells
bipolar cells
rods
cones
aqueous humor
vitreous humor
iris
vitreous floaters
fovea
optic nerve
blind spot
photo receptor cells
wavelength
electromagnetic spectra
visible spectrum
acuity
depolarized
hyperpolarized
dark adaptation
light adapted
Young-Helmholtz (three color)
   theory
primary colors
subtractive mixing
additive mixing
negative afterimage
color blindness
psychological primaries
opponent process theory
anabolic
catabolic
retinex theory
edge detectors

negative aftereffect
motion detectors
superior colliculus
visual cortex
high-frequency spatial detectors
low-frequency detectors
pitch
frequency
amplitude
decibels
pinna
tympanic membrane
maleus
incus
stapes
cilia (hair cells)
auditory nerve
cochlea
middle ear
inner ear
Meniere's Disease
organ of corti
high threshold fibers
place theory
frequency theory
volley theory
salt, sweet, sour, bitter
taste buds
olfactory epithelium
lock and key principle
pheromones
estrogen
subliminal
kinesthetic sense
equilibratory sense
semicircular canals
magnetic sense
clairvoyance
telepathy
precognition
psychokinesis

NAMES TO REMEMBER

Ernst Weber
Thomas Young

Herman von Helmholtz
Ewald Hering

Edwin Land
Donald Eddington
The Great Randi

Uri Geller
Walter R. Miles

GUIDED REVIEW

1. The only way we can contact the world outside our bodies is through our ~~senses~~ .

2. The amount of energy required to create a noticeable sensation is called the _absolute_ _threshold_ , and the minimum amount of energy difference necessary before you are able to tell two stimuli apart is the _difference_ _threshold_ .

3. Ernst Weber said that the _just_ _noticeable_ _difference_ for a stimulus is a fairly constant fraction of the stimulus intensity; this relationship has come to be known as _Weber's_ _law_ .

4. Although there are many similarities between the eye and a _camera_ , the two are actually more _different_ than they are alike.

5. Light passing through the eye first passes through the transparent _cornea_ , then the _aqueous_ humor, and through the _pupil_ that dilates and contracts. The light is bent for focusing by the _lens_ , passes through the _vitreous_ humor, and focuses on the _retina_ , which contains the photoreceptors in the back of the eye.

6. Before light reaches the photoreceptor cells, called _rod_ and _cones_ , it must pass through two layers of cells which also make up the retina. The first layer contains _ganglion_ cells whose axons form the optic nerve, and the second layer contains _bipolar_ cells.

7. In some instances evidence of lateral "cross-talk" has been found where stimulated cone cells may directly affect other _cone_ or _rod_ cells that have not been _stimulated_ .

8. The most sensitive portion of the retina, which gives clarity and acuity to our vision, is the _fovea_ .

9. The fovea is the centermost part of the retina where we focus images that we look at directly. Other parts of the retina that permit us to see things "out of the corner of our eye," are referred to as the _peripheral_ retina.

10. One portion of the peripheral retina, in which there are no photorecep-
    tors (rods and cones), is called the _blind_ _spot_ because this is where the _optic_ _nerve_ passes through on its way to the _brain_.

11. The first neurons that respond to incoming light are the _photoreceptor_ cells (rods and cones) which are sensitive to only a small portion of the _electromagnetic_ _spectrum_, called the _visible_ _spectrum_.

12. Longer wavelengths of light appear _red_ and shorter wavelengths appear _blue_.

13. Rods will respond to all of the light within the visible spectrum except for _red_, and _rods_ function best under reduced illumination which helps us see in the _dark_. Also, the fovea is completely packed with _cones_ and contains no _rods_.

14. Looking at a very dim star, and then focusing it directly on the fovea, reveals a second _blind_ _spot_, since looking off to the side (thereby stimulating some rods) is the only way to make the star appear.

15. Rods and cones are called contrary neurons because they rely only on _graded_ potentials and not on _action_ potentials, and because when stimulated by light, they become _hyperpolarized_ rather than depolarized. That means the interior of the neuron becomes even more strongly _negative_ than it had been before it was stimulated.

16. Unlike other neurons, the secretion of transmitter by rods and cones _decreases_ when they are stimulated.

17. Getting fully used to the dark takes about _30_ to _40_ minutes, and is called _dark_ _adaptation_ (which is due to a slow chemical change in the _rods_).

18. Oncoming headlights disrupt dark adaptation, and glare recovery time is lengthened by the ingestion of _alcohol_.

19. Poor night vision is associated with a deficiency of vitamin _A_. The _B_ vitamins are also important for good vision.

20. Most animals such as bulls and dogs are totally _color_ _blind_, seeing only blacks, whites, and grays.

21. Some fire trucks are painted ___yellow___ - ___green___ because under dim illumination this color can still be seen when other colors appear gray.

22. The ___Young___ - ___Helmholtz___ three color theory of color vision claims we see many colors because the three primary colors of ___red___, ___green___, and ___blue___ can be mixed. Mixing pigments or paints is called ___subtractive___ mixing and will not produce all colors, but mixing lights (called ___additive___ mixing) will. The presence of all primary colors in equal strengths creates ___white___, and the absence of all color is ___black___.

23. Modern research has supported the Young-Helmholtz theory's contention that there are indeed three different kinds of ___cones___ in the eye sensitive to ___red___, ___green___, and ___blue___.

24. When you stare at yellow and fatigue the receptors, you will see the color ___blue___ when you shift your gaze to a white page. This phenomenon is called a ___negative___ ___afterimage___.

25. Ewald Hering proposed the ___opponent___ ___process___ theory of color vision by suggesting that red, green, yellow, and blue are the four psychological primaries.

26. The most common kind of color blindness is ___red___ - ___green___ color blindness, which is more common among ___males___ than ___females___.

27. Hering believed that if red-green receptors were resting no color would be sensed, but that a red stimulus would depolarize the receptor putting it in the ___anabolic___ (or building up) phase. Removing red causes the cell to shift to the ___catabolic___ (or tearing down) phase resulting in a ___green___ afterimage.

28. The ___three___ ___color___ theory explains the first stage of visual processing in the retina better, but the ___opponent___ ___process___ theory explains color vision better at higher brain levels.

29. Edwin Land proposed his ___retinex___ theory of color vision and demonstrated that the full color spectrum could be produced from ___black___, ___white___, and ___red___. It has been shown that ___rods___ can contribute to the perception of color.

30. After constantly watching a waterfall, the cliffs to the side appear to be moving upward, illustrating a negative ___aftereffect___.

31. ___aftereffects___ can transfer from one eye to the other, but ___afterimages___ cannot, suggesting that the detectors responsible for aftereffects are not located in the ___retina___ but at some higher level of the ___brain___.

32. If you are looking at fine detail you are using your high frequency ___spatial___ detectors, but looking at larger or nondetailed objects requires using your ___low___ ___frequency___ detectors. These two kinds of detectors ___compete___ for dominance with each other.

33. Although light can do so, sound cannot travel in a ___vacuum___.

34. In comparing light waves to sound waves, wavelength in vision corresponds to color, and wavelength in sound corresponds to ___pitch___. The range of human hearing is from a frequency of 20 to ___20,000___ cycles per second with the short (faster) wavelengths associated with ___higher___ pitches.

35. The amplitude or height of a sound wave determines ___loudness___, which is measured in ___decibels___.

36. In following a sound wave through the ear, it first is collected by the outer ear or ___pinna___, travels down the external auditory canal, strikes the ear drum, or ___tympanic___ ___membrane___, and then vibrates three tiny bones (the ___malleus___, ___incus___ and ___stapes___). In the ___cochlea___ of the inner ear are approximately 15,000 ___cilia___ or ___hair___ ___cells___ which trigger nerve impulses that are sent by the ___auditory___ ___nerve___ to the brain.

37. Donald Eddington worked with George, who was totally deaf due to Meniere's disease. Eddington implanted six tiny ___platinum___ ___electrodes___ in George's cochlea to stimulate the ___auditory___ ___nerve___ by generating electric shocks in response to different sound frequencies, and thus George had a partial return of his ___hearing___.

38. The cilia are located in the ___organ___ of ___corti___ which is in the cochlea of the inner ear.

39. Three theories have been developed to explain the perception of pitch: The ___place___ theory, the ___frequency___ theory, and the ___volley___ theory.

40. High pitched (and high middle range) tones from 4,000 to 20,000 cycles per second are received due to the location of stimulated cilia within the organ or corti. This defines the ___place___ theory of hearing.

41. Low pitched tones of 20 to 1,000 cycles per second stimulate cilia throughout the entire organ of corti. This demonstrates what is meant by the _frequency_ theory.

42. Sounds pitched between 1,000 and 4,000 cycles per second result from neurons firing in sequence to generate up to 4,000 cycles per second, even though a single neuron can fire only _1,000_ cycles per second. This is the essence of the _volley_ theory.

43. The major taste sensations are _salt_, _sweet_, _sour_, and _bitter_.

44. If you damage your taste buds by burning your tongue, you can rest easy because taste buds are replaced every _seven_ days.

45. In terms of decreasing preferences, newborns like _sweet_ best, followed by _salty_, then _sour_, and then _bitter_ in that order.

46. In the sense of taste dogs and humans have a sense of _sweet_ but cats do not. This sense may have evolved to protect root and berry eating animals from being _poisoned_. Cats in the wild are _carnivors_ (meat eaters) and have no need to be attracted to _sweet_ vegetation.

47. The receptors for the sense of smell are located in the _olfactory_ _epithelium_ high up within the nose, and smell is one of the very _oldest_ of the senses.

48. Molecules of a substance that have a certain shape will fit into receptors in the nose which are responsive to them. That is, smell works according to the _lock_ and _key_ principle. Molecules with a shape that will not stimulate nasal receptors have no _odor_.

49. Sexual communication occurs in some animals when sexually active substances called _pheromones_ are secreted and the odor arouses sexual interest in an opposite-sexed member of the same species.

50. In the experiment on Genevieve's perspiration odor, her coworkers' _menstrual_ cycles started near the same time each month as her's after they were "treated" to odors from Genevieve's _underarms_. This finding may be related to the female hormone _estrogen_.

51. Brooklyn College researchers found that mice painted with human male _urine_ became _aggressive_, but mice painted with human _female_ _urine_ were not affected.

52. Female students exposed to vaginal acid odors rated shy candidates _higher_, and when exposed to men's perspiration rated assertive candidates _higher_.

53. Memory for ___odor___ is apparently different than memory for sights or sounds, perhaps occurring at a level in the brain that is ___preverbal___, primitive, and noncognitive.

54. Many researchers believe that olfaction is closely tied to ___emotion___ in ways not yet understood.

55. The senses of touch include ___pressure___, light ___touch___, vibration, aching ___pain___, sharp ___pain___, ___cold___, warmth, and ___heat___.

56. Simultaneous stimulation of cold and warm receptors produce the sensation of ___hot___.

57. The two point discrimination example showed that touch receptors on the skin are more sensitive (highly concentrated) on the ___fingertips___ than on the ___back___.

58. People rated a library as more enjoyable if they were ___touched___ on the ___hand___ by the librarian as they checked out books even though the majority were unaware that the ___touching___ had even occurred.

59. We gain information about the position of our body and limbs through the sense of ___kinesthesis___.

60. The equilibratory sense (or the sense of ___balance___) has receptors in the ___semicircular___ ___canals___ in the inner ear.

61. A ___magnetic___ sense is a sense of direction in response to the magnetic field of the earth. Magnetic material, mostly ___lodestone___, has been found in the ___joints___ of birds, bees, and other animals, as well as in bacteria.

62. A high degree of magnetic material has been found in the ___heads___ and ___necks___ of homing pigeons and migratory white crowned sparrows through dissection with ___glass___ knives.

63. Since the geomagnetic field changes in the presence of underground water, the claimed successful use of ___divining___ rods by human beings may be due to the newly discovered ___magnetic___ sense.

64. The four kinds of extrasensory perception (ESP) are ___clairvoyance___ (becoming aware of current distant events), ___telepathy___ (transferring thoughts from one person to another), ___precognition___ (predicting the future), and ___psychokinesis___ (moving physical

objects with the mind).

65. Most researchers feel that no *extrasensory* *perception* has ever been demonstrated to a degree that is any better than *chance* .

66. Most scientists, in throwing their hands up in disgust when ESP is mentioned, are demonstrating a poor *attitude* , because such claimed phenomena do merit *investigation* .

67. Psychologist B. F. *Skinner* , astronomer Carl *Sagan* , and a magician, the Great *Randi* are among members of a committee that was formed to investigate unusual phenomena.

68. Uri Geller, who claimed extraordinary powers, was exposed as a fraud by the *Great* *Randi* , who duplicated every one of Geller's *tricks* .

69. The man who claimed psychokinesis by turning the pages of a telephone book without touching them was actually turning the pages by *blowing* a fine puff of *air* through his lips.

70. The researcher who put $5,000 in a box along with a person's name has offered the money to any *psychic* who can state the name. So far there have been no *takers* .

71. Instead of sitting in total darkness to remain dark adapted, British fighter pilots used *red* lights by which to read books and play cards.

SELF TEST I

1. Cats exposed only to vertical stripes during their early development lost the functioning of their non-vertical edge detectors, resulting in an inability
   a. to go up or down stairs
   b. to walk around legs of tables and chairs
   c. to negotiate the corners of a room
   d. all of the above

2. Which of the following does not belong with the others:
   a. difference threshold   c. Weber's Law
   b. absolute threshold   d. JND

3. The fact that cone cells in the retina that <u>have</u> been stimulated may directly affect other cone or rod cells that <u>have not</u> been stimulated is referred to as lateral

a. "cross talk"   c. "optic transfer"
b. "bipolar cross communi-   d. "switching"
   cation

4. The most sensitive portion of the eye upon which visual clarity and
    acuity depend is/are the
    a. optic nerve   c. rods
    b. fovea   d. bipolar cells

5. The periphery of the retina contains _____, whereas
    the fovea contains _____.
    a. only rods, only cones
    b. only cones, only rods
    c. rods and cones, rods and cones
    d. rods and cones, only cones

6. It has been said that visual neurons are contrary neurons because
    a. the rods and cones are antagonistically opposed to one another
    b. it takes them over 24 hours to dark adapt
    c. they do not behave like most neurons
    d. researchers have had such a difficult time experimentally isolating
       the exact functions of the different kinds of rods and cones

7. Under very dim illumination, which color might still be perceived, although
    other colors may appear to be shades of gray?
    a. yellow-green   c. blue
    b. red   d. green-blue

8. Which theory of color vision was developed to explain why people who
    are red-green color blind can still see yellow?
    a. retinex theory
    b. Young-Hering theory
    c. Young-Helmholtz theory
    d. Hering's opponent-process theory

9. A negative aftereffect occurs when, for instance, you stare at a
    _____ for a period of time and then _____.
    a. waterfall; look to the side and see the cliffs moving upward
    b. green, black and yellow flag; see a red, white and blue flag
    c. book or newspaper; experience receptor fatigue
    d. bright light; have the difficult dark adaptation experience of
       bleached rods

10. Hearing sounds that are pitched in the 1,000 to 4,000 cycles per second
    range is explained best by the _____ theory of hearing.
    a. place   c. volley
    b. frequency   d. decibel

11. Many animals secrete sexually active substances called _____
    which are carried down wind, creating sexual interest in another animal.

a. hormones
b. pheromones

c. estrogen
d. testosterone

12. To discriminate whether you are being touched by two points or one point, the pencil points need to be about _____ apart on your _____ .
    a. one millimeter, fingertips
    b. 2½ inches, back
    c. one half inch, lips
    d. both a and b

13. To study the _____ sense in birds it was necessary to use _____ knives for dissection.
    a. homing, stainless steel
    b. mating, sterile
    c. magnetic, glass
    d. nesting, plastic

14. Under carefully controlled conditions most researchers feel that _____ extrasensory perception has been demonstrated in a manner that is better than chance.
    a. no
    b. all

    c. some
    d. much

15. Your best friend has a $50.00 bet with a man who claims he can look at a telephone book at eye level and turn the pages by concentrating on them. Your friend is betting he can't do it. What advice would you give to your friend?
    a. tell her to forget the bet
    b. tell her to go ahead with the bet but watch the man's hands very carefully
    c. tell her to place tiny styrofoam balls around the telephone book and go ahead with the bet
    d. tell her to kneel down opposite the man and watch his eyes very carefully and go ahead with the bet

SELF TEST II

1. The only contact we have with the world outside our bodies is through our
    a. perception of radiant energy
    b. knowledge
    c. senses
    d. experience

2. In comparing the eye with a camera, we find that.
    a. there are some similarities
    b. the two are more different than they are alike

    c. the comparison provides an understanding that the eye is just like
       a camera
    d. both a and b

3.   The three layers of the retina are, first the _____
    whose axons form the optic nerve, second the _____,
    and the light sensitive third layer called _____.
    a. rods and cones, bipolar cells, ganglion cells
    b. bipolar cells, ganglion cells, rods and cones
    c. bipolar cells, rods and cones, ganglion cells
    d. ganglion cells, bipolar cells, rods and cones

4.   The portion of the retina which contains no photoreceptors, because it
    is at this point where the optic nerve passes through the retina on its
    way to the brain, is called the
    a. contrary neuron   c. fovea
    b. blind spot   d. ciliary muscle

5.   In the visible spectrum the longest wavelength appears _____
    and shortest wavelength appears _____.
    a. red, green   c. green, red
    b. blue, red   d. red, violet

6.   When entering a darkened theater, it takes about _____
    to become fully dark adapted
    a. 5 to 10 minutes
    b. 30 to 40 minutes
    c. 3 hours
    d. all of these depending on the size of the theater

7.   Modern research _____ the notion that there are three
    different kinds of cones in the eye sensitive to red, green, and blue
    light.
    a. has supported
    b. has discredited
    c. is inconclusive about
    d. none of these, modern research substantiates only the retinex theory
       which includes rods as color receptors

8.   To date, which theory completely explains all we know about color vision?
    a. Young-Helmholtz theory   c. retinex theory
    b. Hering theory   d. none of the above

9.   Wavelength in hearing corresponds to _____, while wavelength in
    vision corresponds to _____.
    a. pitch, brightness
    b. loudness, brightness
    c. loudness, color
    d. pitch, color

10. The most important factor influencing what we consider taste is the
_____ of the food we are eating.
   a. texture
   b. temperature
   c. amount
   d. smell

11. Women who smelled _____ rated _____
   candidates for a secretarial job more favorably.
   a. vaginal acids, assertive
   b. wild pig scent, shy and retiring
   c. men's perspiration, assertive
   d. none of these, the candidate ratings were not affected by the sense
      of smell

12. Which of the following does not belong with the others?
   a. ganglion cells
   b. organ of corti
   c. semicircular canals
   d. vestibular sacs

13. A magnetic sense has been identified
   a. between male and female homing pigeons forming the basis for their
      mating instinct
   b. between male and female human beings forming the basis for mutual
      attraction
   c. both a and b
   d. none of the above

14. Which of the following is/are among the 40 members of a committee formed
   especially to investigate bizarre and unusual phenomena?
   a. B. F. Skinner
   b. Carl Sagan
   c. the Great Randi
   d. all of the above

15. You just bought a new $450.00 camera and want to impress your psychology
   teacher with your knowledge of how a camera and the eye are exactly
   alike. Your professor will probably
   a. tell you that a camera and the eye are more different than they are
      alike
   b. commend you for your perceptive insight
   c. tell you to sell the camera
   d. none of the above

ESSAY QUESTIONS

1. Compare and contrast the difference threshold and the absolute threshold.
   Point out the key investigator and the law that pertains to the difference threshold.

2. Trace a ray of light from the outside world to the brain, noting the
   structures through which it passes. Point out the location and function

of each of those structures.

3. Discuss the three theories of hearing and tell which range of sound each explains best.

4. Compare and contrast the sense of smell with the sense of taste using recent discoveries to illustrate your discussion.

5. Evaluate the current status of ESP in scientific circles. Include an explanation of the different kinds of ESP and cite the results of research and demonstrations to support your answer.

ANSWER SECTION

Guided Review
1. senses
2. absolute threshold, difference threshold
3. just noticeable difference (or JND), Weber's Law
4. camera, different
5. cornea, aqueous, pupil, lens, vitreous, retina
6. rods, cones, ganglion, bipolar
7. cone, rod, stimulated
8. fovea
9. peripheral
10. blind spot, optic nerve, brain
11. photoreceptor, electromagnetic spectrum, visible spectrum
12. red, blue (or violet)
13. red, rods, dark, cones, rods
14. blind spot
15. graded, action, hyperpolarized, negative
16. decreases
17. 30, 40, dark adaptation, rods
18. alcohol
19. A, B
20. color blind
21. yellow-green
22. Young-Helmholtz, red, green, blue, subtractive, additive, white, black
23. cones, red, green, blue
24. blue, negative afterimage
25. opponent process
26. red-green, males, females
27. anabolic, catabolic, green
28. three color, opponent process
29. retinex, black, white, red, rods
30. aftereffect
31. aftereffects, afterimages, retina, brain
32. spatial, low frequency, compete
33. vacuum

34. *pitch, 20,000, higher*
35. *loudness, decibels*
36. *pinna, tympanic membrane, maleus, incus, stapes, cochlea, cilia, hair cells, auditory nerve*
37. *platinum electrodes, auditory nerve, hearing*
38. *organ, corti*
39. *place, frequency, volley*
40. *place*
41. *frequency*
42. *1,000, volley*
43. *salt, sweet, sour, bitter*
44. *seven*
45. *sweet, salty, sour, bitter*
46. *sweet, poisoned, carnivores, sweet*
47. *olfactory epithelium, oldest*
48. *lock, key, odor*
49. *pheromones*
50. *menstrual, underarms, estrogen*
51. *urine, aggressive, female urine*
52. *higher, higher*
53. *odor, preverbal*
54. *emotion*
55. *pressure, touch, pain, pain, cold, heat*
56. *hot (or heat)*
57. *fingertips, back*
58. *touched, hand, touching*
59. *kinesthesis*
60. *balance, semicircular canals*
61. *magnetic, lodestone, joints*
62. *heads, necks, glass*
63. *divining, magnetic*
64. *clairvoyance, telepathy, precognition, psychokinesis*
65. *extrasensory perception, chance*
66. *attitude, investigation*
67. *Skinner, Sagan, Randi*
68. *Great Randi, tricks*
69. *blowing, air*
70. *psychic, takers*
71. *red*

Self Test I
1. *a*
2. *b*
3. *a*
4. *b*
5. *d*
6. *c*
7. *a*

Self Test II
1. *c*
2. *d*
3. *d*
4. *b*
5. *d*
6. *b*
7. *a*

8.	d		8.	d
9.	a		9.	d
10.	c		10.	d
11.	b		11.	c
12.	d		12.	a
13.	c		13.	d
14.	a		14.	d
15.	c		15.	a

CHAPTER 4

Perception

BEHAVIORAL OBJECTIVES

After completing this chapter, the student should be able to:

1. Define perception and contrast it with sensation.
2. Summarize the basic premises of the image and cue theory of perception.
3. List and summarize the monocular depth cues.
4. Convey an understanding of how a pilot uses monocular depth cues to land a plane.
5. Explain how the movie King Kong was made and tell how the image and cue theory relates to this.
6. Explain the moon illusion.
7. Describe binocular vision, including the processes of convergence and retinal disparity.
8. List and describe the perceptual constancies.
9. Describe holographic photography and convey an understanding of the possibilities for future television.
10. Explain the research findings of the visual cliff studies and what conclusions have been drawn from them.
11. Summarize the Gestalt position on the nature-nurture explanation of perception.
12. List and briefly explain the Gestalt organizing principles.
13. Summarize the image and cue and direct perception explanations of the Muller-Lyer illusion.
14. Describe both John M. Kennedy's work on sightless vision and Carter Collins' work with tactile sensory replacement (TSR).
15. Give the results and discuss the implications of Buckhout's eyewitness testimony data.

KEY TERMS AND CONCEPTS

perception

illusion

Fraser's spiral

image and cue theory

perception
illusion
Fraser's spiral
image and cue theory
depth perception
monocular depth cues
height on a plane
linear perspective
overlap
relative size
gradient of texture
aerial perspective
relative motion
two-dimensional image
moon illusion
attention
sudden change
novelty
complexity
intensity
repetition
binocular cues
convergence
retinal disparity
3D movies
holographic photography
motion picture holograms
perceptual constancies
size constancy
shape constancy
brightness constancy
Ames Room

direct-perception
motion perception
peripheral vision
rotary-drum room
foveal vision
blindsight
innate
visual cliff
auditory perception
sound localization
Gestalt view
nearness
similarity
continuity
simplicity
nativist
illusions
upside-down T illusion
Lipps illusion
Ponzo illusion
Muller-Lyer illusion
Judd illusion
Poggendorff illusion
Zollner illusion
Titchener illusion
Delboeuf illusion
edge detectors
spatial frequency detectors
canalized perceptual mechanisms
tactile sensory replacement (TSR)
affordances
biological motion perception

NAMES TO REMEMBER

Colin Turnbull
J. J. Gibson
Michael Wertheimer

John M. Kennedy
Carter Collins
Robert Buckhout

GUIDED REVIEW

1. Anthropologist _Colin_ _Turnbull_ rode with
    a native pygmy named Kenge who grew up in a _rain_
    forest. Kenge saw buffalo on the plains as
    insects, and he was totally unable to judge
    distances.

2. _Perception_ is the interpretation of sensory material. Under-
    standing perception helps us to comprehend how people are

_Organized_____ to deal with their environment.

3. A false perception of __sensory_____ information is an
   __illusion_____.

4. __Frasers_____ spiral is an __illusion___. Because
   of the brain's __perception_____ of what it has sensed, we tend to
   perceive a spiral but we are actually sensing __circles_____.

5. __Sensation_____ occurs when the sense organs are stimulated,
   whereas __perception____ is an __active_____ interpretation of sensory material.

6. Recently new technologies such as __computer___ __controled__
   equipment, the __PET_____ scan, and modern electronic equipment for examining the __senses_____ have stimulated new
   research.

7. Both the __image___ and __cue_____ theory and
   the ___direct_____ __perception____ theory attempt to explain
   how we make __sense____ of the incredible amount of sensory
   information we receive.

8. The ability to interpret visual cues to judge distance is known as
   depth __perception___.

9. The __image___ and __cue____ theorists contend
   that the way the brain makes __three___ dimensional sense
   from a two dimensional retinal __image___ is through learning
   and experience.

10. O'Brien made the movie King Kong by manipulating the
    __cues_____ we use in our daily lives.

11. Only one eye is needed for perceiving __monocular___ depth cues.
    __hieght____ __on___ __a_____
    __plane____ is one of these cues in which objects higher on a
    plane appear __more____ distant and conversely, objects
    lower on a plane appear __closer_____.

12. A second monocular depth cue is __linear___ __perspective___
    in which parallel lines appear to __converge___ at the horizon.

13. __overlap____ is another monocular depth cue that occurs when
    one object appears to overlap another.

14. Given that two objects are known to be the same size; the one project-
    ing the smaller retinal image will be perceived as being more
    __distant____. This is the monocular depth cue of
    __relative____ __size___.

15. Closer objects have more ___detail___ while objects that are
    farther away have less ___detail___. This is the monocular
    depth cue known as ___gradient___ of ___
    ___texture___.

16. The monocular depth cue of ___aerial___ ___perspective___
    explains why on a hazy day nearby mountains seem to be
    ___more___ distant than on clear days when the mountains
    appear ___closer___.

17. It takes an actual ___three___ dimensional scene for the
    monocular depth cue of ___relative___ ___motion___
    to work.

18. Relative motion is the term describing the fact that ___close___
    objects move great distances when the head is moved side to side
    compared to ___distant___ objects, which appear to move
    very little.

19. The ___moon___ illusion can be explained by examining
    ___monocular___ ___depth___ cues. When the moon is on
    the horizon there are more ___depth___ cues, which cause us
    to ___perceive___ a larger moon.

20. How we perceive a particular image depends on how we
    ___attend___ to and ___organize___ cues within that
    image.

21. Verbeek's cartoon panels show different scenes if viewed upside down
    or rightside up because we are drawn to attend to different
    ___cues___.

22. Verbeek's narrative focused our attention on different aspects of the
    cartoon, which, in turn influenced our ___perception___ of each
    panel.

23. Attention and perception are interrelated. Television ___commercials___
    rely on a variety of devices to influence our ___attention___ and
    perception.

24. Parents may attend to the surprising absence of noise in the house.
    This ___sudden___ ___change___ attracts attention.

25. Unusual things that are ___novel___ also attract our atten-
    tion.

26. A rapid sequence of stimuli is commonly used by advertisers because
    ___complexity___ is a factor that increases attention.

27. The volume of the television is just right until a commercial comes on because ___intensity___ is another factor that increases attention.

28. A slogan is often presented several times in a commercial because ___repetition___ increases attention.

29. Whenever we look at objects closer than approximately ___25___ feet our eyes ___converge___. This is the ___binocular___ depth cue of ___convergence___.

30. ___Retinal___ ___disparity___ is a powerful binocular depth cue resulting from the slightly different view each eye gets; this cue was used in the 1950s to make ___3 - D___ movies.

31. A new photographic development that allows a three dimensional picture to be seen from any angle is ___holographic___ ___photography___. Holograms are made by scanning objects with ___laser___ ___beams___.

32. Holograms are not printed on paper; they are ___projected___ into space, and the depth cue of ___retinal___ ___disparity___ operates at any angle. This new technology may well be used in the ___television___ of the future.

33. Our world is made more stable by perceptual ___constancies___. Kenge the pygmy failed to learn ___size___ ___constancy___ because of his limited environment.

34. Looking straight ahead at a partially opened door would cause us to sense a ___trapezoidal___ shape, yet we perceive a rectangularly shaped door due to ___shape___ ___constancy___.

35. We perceive ___white___ as bright and gray as darker due to ___brightness___ ___constancy___.

36. The power of the ___perceptual___ ___constancies___ has been demonstrated in a special room known as an ___Ames___ ___room___.

37. The Ames room depends on your use of ___size___ and ___shape___ constancy. When looking at the Ames room our ___senses___ send accurate messages to our brain. However, due to our ___perception___ we see bizarre things such as people growing or shrinking.

38. The image and cue view has been opposed by the ___direct___ ___perception___ theory.

39. The direct perception theory argues that it is not so much our _experiences_ and _learning_ that influences our perception, but rather our _biological_ organization to directly perceive the world in a specific way.

40. The image and cue theorists contend that a _two_ _dimensional_ image rests on the _retina_, but because of the brain's experience with _cues_ we see the third dimension.

41. J. J. _Gibson_, a leading proponent of the direct perception theory, contended that the analogy of the _eye_ as a _camera_ had been taken too far.

42. Gibson believed that the eyes' movement is extremely important to our _perception_, since we don't see a _static_ _image_, but rather a whole series of images in motion.

43. Gunnar Johansson suggests that there are _decoding_ principles within each organism that may be located in the neural system, working in a "_blind_ _mechanical_ _way_."

44. Direct perception theory argues that built in or _prewired_ perceptual mechanisms exist. The discovery of brain cells _specifically_ _tuned_ to respond to _movement_, size, or _retinal_ _disparity_ support this theoretical position.

45. Since Gibson's work an interest in _motion_ perception has developed. Direct perceptionists argue that either the motion of objects, or the motion of your own _eyes_ are the foundations of _perception_.

46. The fovea responds to _local_ changes in the visual field. _peripheral_ _vision_ responds to _global_ changes of the visual field.

47. Movement projected onto the _fovea_ leads us to perceive motion of an _object_, while motion within the periphery causes us to perceive self _motion_.

48. The _rotary_ _drum_ room can be used to demonstrate perceived _motion_ because the _peripheral_ vision is totally involved. This peripheral-foveal distinction demonstrates that there is a physiological _organization_ which helps us to perceive motion.

49. The involvement of peripheral vision in our sense of balance may be explained by the fact that _neurons_ from the foveal regions

project back to the *occipital* lobes. However, peripheral messages tend to be projected to the *temporal lobes* near the area that receives messages from the *semicircular canals*.

50. The two visual systems, the foveal and peripheral, also seem to be related to *hand* *eye* coordination. Reaching is under the control of *peripheral vision*, while fine object manipulation is under the control of *foveal vision*.

51. The case of Mr. D.B., whose *occipital lobes* had been damaged so that he was unable to see out of the *left* side of either eye, demonstrated the phenomenon of *blindsight*.

52. The explanation of the blindsight phenomenon relies on the fact that *peripheral* vision and *foveal* vision project to different areas in the brain.

53. A device designed to test innate *cliff* avoidance has been used to test various species of animals, including humans. This apparatus is known as the *visual cliff*.

54. Baby animals studied on the visual cliff demonstrate that they possess innate *cliff avoidance*. With human babies the common avoidance of the *deep* side may be either the result of *learning* or *inheritance*.

55. Rader's study suggests that the avoidance of the deep side of the visual cliff is due to an *inherited* predisposition.

56. It takes sound waves slightly less time to reach the ear *closest* to the sound source. In such a situation, the brain is actually receiving two separate sensory *messages* but we hear only *one* sound. We also use the two sounds to *locate* the source (unless the source is equidistant from both ears).

57. Michael *Wertheimer* suggests that a newborn's *visual* and *auditory* perceptual abilities are already *integrated*.

58. Much of the early work and interest in the psychology of *perception* can be traced to the *Gestalt* psychologists.

59. The Gestalt psychologists noted that people tend to *organize perception* in certain ways. Among their organizing principles are *nearness*, *similarity*, *continuity*, and *simplicity*.

60. The Gestalt psychologists attacked the school of _structuralism_, since their approach was quite contrary to the basic Gestalt premise that the _whole_ _is_ _greater_ _than_ _the_ _sum_ _of_ _the_ parts.

61. Although no one really knows why _illusions_ occur, the major theoretical debates are between the _image_ _and_ _cue_ and the _direct_ _perception_ theorists.

62. The _Muller_ - _Lyer_ illusion has been studied in an ingenious way, demonstrating that it apparently does not occur in the _retina_ but at a _higher_ level in the brain.

63. Direct perception theorists contend that the Muller-Lyer illusion results from the _organization_ of our _biology_.

64. The image and cue theorists argue that the Muller-Lyer illusion occurs because we have _learned_ the illusion, since the illusion has the components of _floors_ and other rectangles. The _inward_ turned arrows are seen as being closer, while the _outward_ turned arrows appear further away. If the arrow further away makes the same sized image on the retina it must be _larger_ because of _size_ constancy.

65. Studies of _culturally_ different individuals such as the _Zulus_ who live in a more rounded world, have found that the Muller-Lyer illusion doesn't _occur_.

66. Illusions tend to lose their effect the more you _see_ them.

67. John M. Kennedy has concluded that the principles that underlie visual _perception_ are the same principles used in _touch_ _perceptions_. Both sight and touch are _sensation_ generated by the brain based on incoming _stimuli_. Thus _blind_ individuals may organize and understand their _perceptions_ in ways similar to sighted persons.

68. Collins and others have developed a technique called _tactile_ sensory replacement (TSR) to send messages from a person's _back_ to his or her _brain_.

69. Collins' technique of tactile sensory replacement relies on images from a television _camera_.

70. Gibson's idea of an __*affordance*__ argues that properties of any sensed object are __*perceived*__ by any one species of animal in a way that will promote its __*survival*__.

71. A new branch of research known as __*biological*__ __*motion*__ __*perception*__ is trying to find if any particular __*affordances*__ are apparent in humans.

72. Studies have shown subjects can recognize individuals in __*darkened*__ __*rooms*__ with only the aid of dots of lights in __*motion*__ that have been attached to major joints. Thus biological motion may well be a human __*affordance*__.

73. Robert Buckhourt has argued strongly that __*eyewitness*__ testimony cannot always be trusted, since the eye is not like a __*camera*__.

SELF TEST I

1. _____ refers to how we interpret messages from our senses.
   a. learning   c. perception
   b. sensation   d. eugenics

2. Understanding how we perceive our world can help us learn more about how we are organized.
   a. true   b. false

3. It takes two eyes to have depth perception accurate enough to land a plane or drive a car.
   a. true   b. false

4. Relative to our point of view objects higher on a plane are seen as
   a. closer
   b. farther away
   c. the same distance as lower objects
   d. off to one side

5. The perceived larger moon on the horizon is known as the
   a. large moon phenomenon
   b. relative moon sensation
   c. moon illusion
   d. eclipse effect

6. When viewing objects with both eyes the depth can sometimes be judged by how much the eyes cross. This depth cue is known as
   a. retinal disparity   c. relative size
   b. overlap   d. convergence

7. Which of the following are <u>true</u> of retinal disparity?
    a. it is a binocular depth cue
    b. close objects create greater retinal disparity
    c. three dimensional movies (3-D) are based on retinal disparity
    (d.) all of the above

8. Size constancy is learned and has been shown to be absent in blind
    people who have recently had their vision restored.
    (a.) true   b. false

9. Which theory of perception claims we are already perceptually organized
    due to our genetics and biology?
    a. Gestalt theory
    b. image and cue theory
    (c.) direct perception theory
    d. genetic perception theory

10. Gibson's work emphasized the concept of a static or stationary image
    on the retina as an explanation of perception.
    a. true   (b.) false

11. _____ _____ is tuned to respond to <u>local</u>
    changes in the visual field, i.e., objects moving within the visual
    field.
    a. relative size
    b. peripheral vision
    (c.) foveal vision
    d. rod vision

12. Things that are close to each other appear to be grouped together.
    This defines the Gestalt principle of
    (a.) nearness   c. similarity
    b. simplicity   d. parallel contact

13. Studies of the Muller-Lyer illusion have found
    a. it to be the result of learning only
    b. it to be the result of "prewired" organization
    c. it holds up even in curvilinear cultures
    (d.) no clear answer yet as to why the illusion occurs

14. Which of the following is <u>true</u> of Kennedy's findings with blind
    children?
    a. their pointing arms converged more as they walked toward the
        target corners.
    (b.) their tracings of the perimeter of a plate were circular directly over
        the plate and elliptical when pointing from the side.
    c. they showed a better perceptual understanding than sighted
        individuals
    d. all of the above

15. The TSR device
     a. has been unsuccessful to date
     b. allows deaf persons to hear again
     c. allows blind subjects to sense through feeling what sighted
        people can see
     d. none of the above

SELF TEST II

1. _____ occurs when sense organs are stimulated.
     a. perception
     b. sensation
     c. learning
     d. an illusion

2. Not only do we see (or sense) things, we also understand or
    _____ them.
     a. question
     b. reason
     c. perceive
     d. none of the above

3. _____ theorists believe that the only way the brain can
    make sense of a two dimensional retinal image is through learning and
    experience.
     a. direct perception
     b. image and cue
     c. both a and b
     d. neither a nor b

4. Monocular depth cues only require the use of one eye.
     a. true   b. false

5. How your attention is focused affects your perception.
     a. true   b. false

6. The fact that each eye gets a slightly different view helps us judge
    depth and distance. This cue is known as
     a. convergence
     b. binocular vision
     c. monocular vision
     d. retinal disparity

7. Which of the following is not one of the perceptual constancies?
     a. size constancy
     b. shape constancy
     c. brightness constancy
     d. disparity constancy

8. People walking across a/an _____ room will appear to grow or shrink.
    a. Gibson   c. rotary drum
    b. Ames   d. Weiskrantz

9. J. J. Gibson
    a. supported the direct perception theory
    b. said that the eye-is-like-a-camera view had been overstated
    c. argued that motion is important to perception
    d. all of the above

10. Gibson and his colleagues have argued that the motion of objects, or the motion of our own eyes, are the foundations of our three dimensional perceptions.
    a. true   b. false

11. The Gestalt psychologists viewed perception to be best explained by the image and cue theory.
    a. true   b. false

12. The _____ illusion shows two horizontal lines, one with inward and one with outward turned arrowheads.
    a. Ponzo
    b. Poggendorff
    c. Muller-Lyer
    d. Titchener

13. Studies of the Zulu tribe have clearly demonstrated that learning and experience account for the Muller-Lyer illusion.
    a. true   b. false

14. Kennedy has concluded from studying blind children that the principles that underlie visual perception are basically the same principles used in touch.
    a. true   b. false

15. J. J. Gibson has called the properties of the environment that are relative to any particular organism's perceptual arrangement
    a. affordances
    b. perceptuals
    c. prewired
    d. neural parameters

ESSAY QUESTIONS

1. Describe the experiences of the pygmy Kenge when he first left the rain forest and explain why he had them.

2. Explain the image and cue theory of perception and describe how the movie King Kong relates to this theory.

3. Describe how television might be in the future. Include a discussion of holography and its effect on perception.

4. Explain the concept of affordance and give an example of it in humans.

5. Discuss the direct perception theory and compare it with the image and cue theory.

ANSWER SECTION

Guided Review
1. *Colin Turnbull, rain forest, insects, distances*
2. *perception, organized*
3. *sensory, illusion*
4. *Fraser's, illusion, perception (or interpretation), circles*
5. *sensation, perception, active*
6. *computer controlled, PET, senses*
7. *image, cue, direct perception, sense*
8. *perception*
9. *image, cue, three, image*
10. *cues*
11. *monocular, height on a plane, more, closer*
12. *linear perspective, converge*
13. *overlap*
14. *distant, relative size*
15. *detail, detail, gradient of texture*
16. *aerial perspective, more, closer*
17. *three, relative motion*
18. *close, distant*
19. *moon, monocular depth, depth (or distance), perceive*
20. *attend, organize*
21. *cues*
22. *perception*
23. *commercials, attention*
24. *sudden change*
25. *novel*
26. *complexity*
27. *intensity*
28. *repetition*
29. *25, converge, binocular, convergence*
30. *retinal disparity, 3-D*
31. *holographic photography, laser beams*
32. *projected, retinal disparity, television*
33. *constancies, size constancy*
34. *trapezoidal, shape constancy*

35. *white, brightness constancy*
36. *perceptual constancies, Ames room*
37. *size, shape, senses, perception*
38. *direct perception*
39. *experiences, learning, biological*
40. *two dimensional, retina, cues*
41. *Gibson, eye, camera*
42. *perception, static image*
43. *decoding, blind mechanical way*
44. *prewired, specifically tuned, movement, retinal disparity*
45. *motion, eyes, perception*
46. *local, peripheral vision, global*
47. *fovea, object, motion*
48. *rotary drum, motion, peripheral, organization*
49. *neurons, occipital, temporal lobes, semicircular canals*
50. *hand eye, peripheral vision, foveal vision*
51. *occipital lobes, left, blindsight*
52. *peripheral (or ambient), foveal (or focal)*
53. *cliff, visual cliff*
54. *cliff avoidance, deep, learning, inheritance (or genetics)*
55. *inherited*
56. *closest, messages (or inputs), one, locate*
57. *Wertheimer, visual, auditory, integrated*
58. *perception, Gestalt*
59. *organize perceptions, nearness, similarity, continuity, simplicity*
60. *structuralism, whole is greater than the sum of the*
61. *illusions, image and cue, direct perception*
62. *Muller-Lyer, retina, higher*
63. *organization, biology*
64. *learned, floors, inward, outward, larger, size*
65. *culturally, Zulus, occur*
66. *see*
67. *perception, touch (or tactile) perceptions, sensations, stimuli, blind, perceptions*
68. *tactile, back (or chest), brain*
69. *camera*
70. *affordance, perceived, survival*
71. *biological motion perception, affordances*
72. *darkened rooms, motion, affordance*
73. *eyewitness, camera*

Self Test I		*Self Test II*	
1.	*c*	*1.*	*b*
2.	*a*	*2.*	*c*
3.	*b*	*3.*	*b*
4.	*b*	*4.*	*a*
5.	*c*	*5.*	*a*
6.	*d*	*6.*	*d*

7.	d
8.	a
9.	c
10.	b
11.	c
12.	a
13.	d
14.	b
15.	c

7.	d
8.	b
9.	d
10.	a
11.	b
12.	c
13.	b
14.	a
15.	a

CHAPTER 5

States of Consciousness

BEHAVIORAL OBJECTIVES

After completing this chapter the student should be able to

1. Define consciousness and mention one or two ways in which it has been studied.
2. List the stages of sleep and the brain wave patterns associated with each.
3. Compare paradoxical sleep with orthodox sleep, giving the distinguishing characteristics of each.
4. Tell what a healthy insomniac is and contrast the adaptive theory of sleep with the conserving energy theory.
5. Describe studies of sleep deprivation, stating the major conclusions.
6. Give two major causes of insomnia, mention ways to combat insomnia, and explain two other kinds of sleep disorders.
7. Elaborate on the various theories of the purpose and meaning of dreams.
8. Briefly trace the history of hypnosis noting what it is and its limitations.
9. List and explain the seven hypnotic effects.
10. Evaluate claims of hypnotic age regression.
11. Distinguish meditation from biofeedback and give the major characteristics and results of each.
12. List three classifications of psychoactive drugs and give one example of each.
13. Distinguish amphetamines from cocaine.
14. Give the common name for benzodiazepines and tell how extensively they are used.
15. Compare and contrast heroin with PCP and marijuana.

KEY TERMS AND CONCEPTS

consciousness
electroencephalograph (EEG)

daydreaming
altered states

stages of sleep
alpha waves
theta waves
delta waves
slow wave sleep
REM sleep
NREM sleep
orthodox sleep
beta waves
paradoxical sleep
REM rebound
healthy insomniacs
adaptive theory
conserving energy theory
hallucinations and delusions
microsleep
REM deprivation
endogenous depression
insomnia
circadian rhythm
jet lag
narcolepsy
sleep apnea
tracheotomies
psychoanalytic interpretation
   of dreams
activation-synthesis model
   of dreams
lucid dreaming
M.I.L.D.
mnemonic device
animal magnetism
Mesmerism
hypnosis
Stanford Suggestibility Scale

dissociation
automatic writing
self-hypnosis
highway hypnosis
actual pain vs. expected pain
disinhibition
post-hypnotic suggestions
age regression
meditation
yogi
biofeedback
migraine headaches
psychoactive drugs
stimulants
amphetamines
"uppers," "speed," or "bennies"
mainline
cocaine
narcotic
caffeine
alcohol
delirium tremens
benzodiazepines
GABA
heroin
opium, morphine, codeine
"chasing the dragon"
hallucinogens
mescaline, psilocybin, LSD
PCP
"angel dust"
marijuana
THC
placebo reaction

NAMES TO REMEMBER

John Pappenheimer
John Watson
William C. Dement
Fritz Perls

Alan Hobson
Robert W. McCarley
Anton Mesmer
Eugene Aserinsky

GUIDED REVIEW

1. The mental state in which you are aware of your external environment
   and internal events is called *consciousness* .

2. In 1913, the study of consciousness was rejected by ___John Watson___ as being too subjective to be scientific.

3. Two objective ways of measuring conscious states include the use of the ___EEG___ and the ___PET___ scan.

4. Students of Eric Klinger wrote down what they had been ___Thinking___ about, right after a randomly set ___Beep___ went off. This research demonstrated that people spend a great deal of their time ___daydreaming___.

5. About ___one___ - ___third___ of our sleeping time is spent in night dreams, and about ___one___ - ___third___ of our waking time is spent ___daydreaming___.

6. Any time the content or quality of a conscious experience undergoes a significant change, that conscious state is said to be ___altered___.

7. Sleeping, dreaming, hypnosis, and meditation are all examples of ___altered___ states of ___consciousness___.

8. ___Alpha___ waves are associated with a "drowsy but awake" state, ___theta___ waves are associated with stage 1 sleep, and ___delta___ waves are associated with the deeper stages 3 and 4 sleep.

9. Delta wave sleep is sometimes known as ___slow wave___ sleep, and such sleep ___decreases___ with age.

10. Sleep progressively grows ___less___ deep throughout the night, and ___dreams___ tend to lengthen and intensify.

11. Compared with humans, horses, cows, and elephants sleep much ___less___, and opossums and bats sleep much ___more___.

12. In 1953, graduate student ___Eugene___ ___Aserinsky___ observed that a sleeping person's eyes move rapidly back and forth beneath closed eyelids. Such rapid eye movements have been abbreviated ___REM___.

13. REM sleep has been called ___Paradoxical___ sleep and NREM sleep is sometimes called ___orthodox___ sleep.

14. Brain wave patterns for the awakened state and ___REM___ sleep are very similar.

15. Increased blood pressure and heart rate, loss of muscle tone, and semi-paralysis are all characteristic of ___REM___ sleep.

16. Semiparalysis while sleeping may occur to prevent people from
    ___acting___ out their dreams.

17. Sleep walking and sleep talking occur mostly during ___NREM___
    sleep.

18. A person who is deprived of REM sleep will experience an increase in
    REM sleep on succeeding nights. This phenomenon is referred to as
    ___REM___ ___rebound___.

19. Although the ___Soviet___ claim sleep learning is an effective
    method of study, no one anywhere else in the world has shown that
    people can learn complicated material while ___sleeping___.

20. People who make an active plan to awaken at a certain hour have less
    ___slow___ ___wave___ sleep, ___less___
    REM, and more occasional ___awaken___ during the night.
    These same things happen when laboratory subjects are told they
    will be ___shocked___ while they are sleeping.

21. The average young adult needs between ___6½___ and
    ___8½___ hours of sleep a night.

22. People who can get by just fine on only three hours sleep have been
    called ___healthy___ ___insomniacs___.

23. The ___adaptive___ theory of sleep argues that, for each species,
    a certain amount of wakeful time is necessary to survive.

24. Less calories are burned while sleeping, which is the basis for the
    ___conserving___ ___energy___ theory of sleep.

25. Long term sleep ___deprivation___ in healthy subjects has not been
    found to be physically detrimental.

26. After about 60 hours of sleep deprivation, subjects experienced
    ___hallucinations___ and ___delusions___, but heart rate,
    ___blood___ ___pressure___, respiration and
    ___temp___ did not show much change.

27. William Dement awakened his experimental group subjects during the
    night preventing ___REM___ sleep. Subjects in the control
    group were awakened only during ___NREM___ sleep. The
    ___Experimental___ group tried desperately to get REM sleep and
    became hostile, paranoid and aggressive.

28. People who stay awake for long periods often slip into a few seconds
    of sleep without knowing it. These brief sleep episodes are known as
    ___microsleeps___.

29. Rats deprived of REM sleep for extremely long periods of time did not experience serious _psychological_ problems.

30. Modern researchers have concluded that long term REM deprivation in humans _will_ _not_ cause permanent psychological harm.

31. REM deprivation has been shown to be beneficial in the treatment of _endogenous_ _depression_.

32. Approximately 50 million people in the United States have _sleep_ problems.

33. Tranquilized sleep is not the equivalent of _normal_ sleep because the amount of _REM_ is lessened and the amount of time spent in the different _stages_ is altered.

34. Difficulty in going to sleep or staying asleep is known as _insomnia_.

35. The two major reasons for insomnia are _depression_ and an irregular _circadian_ _rhythm_.

36. A person who misses a night's sleep does not need a full _eight_ _hours_ extra sleep to make up for it.

37. A person who goes to bed and gets up at different times may have a weak main _circadian_ rhythm and a number of _ghost_ _rhythms_. This kind of confusion can lead to _insomnia_.

38. To overcome circadian rhythm-related insomnia you should go to bed and arise at the _same_ _time_ every day for about _three_ weeks.

39. When you travel a lot, passing through different time zones, thus trying to change your sleep schedule, you may experience _jet_ _lag_.

40. The uncontrollable, recurring, and sudden onset of sleep during daytime waking hours is called _narcolepsy_. There is strong evidence that this is an _inherited_ disease.

41. The cessation of breathing during sleep is termed _sleep_ _apnea_.

42. The vast majority of subjects awakened during REM sleep reported that they were _dreaming_.

43. Particularly among light sleepers, occasional dreaming or dream-like experiences occur during ___NREM___ sleep.

44. Dreams coming later in the course of a night's sleep are progressively ___longer___, more ___vivid___, and more unrealistic than early dreams.

45. Dreams are disguised representations of repressed desires according to ___psychoanalytic___ theory.

46. Fritz Perls argued that dreams are expressions of what is ___missing___ in life.

47. When subjects were exposed to certain experiences and told to dream about them, most of them dreamed about ___something else___.

48. One function of dreams may be to help protect the ___self___-image.

49. Hobson and McCarley developed the ___activation-synthesis___ model of dreams.

50. In Hobson and McCarley's theory, a time-triggered mechanism in the back of the brain generates impulses stimulating both the ___oculomotor___ and ___reticular___ systems.

51. The activation-synthesis theory argues that dreaming may be nothing more than the brain's attempt to make some ___sense___ out of what may amount to ___random___ electrical activity that enters the forebrain.

52. When you are aware that you are dreaming while you are dreaming, you are having a ___lucid___ dream.

53. LaBerge uses MILD (which is the abbreviation for ___mnemonic___ induction of ___lucid___ dreams) to control ___nightmares___.

54. British psychologist Keith Hearne has developed a ___nightmare alarm___ that goes off when the number of breaths per minute reach a stressful level.

55. Austrian physician Anton ___Mesmer___ cured people by applying magnetic forces. He coined the term ___animal magnetism___.

56. The term ___hypnosis___ refers to the effects of suggestion.

57. People who are hypnotized are not ___asleep___. Further,

hypnosis is not a single _phenomenon_ , but really a word describing a number of separate _phenomena_ .

58. Many people _can_ be hypnotized and many others _cannot_ be hypnotized.

59. To see how suggestible a potential hypnosis subject is, the _Stanford_ Suggestibility _Scale_ may be employed.

60. When a hypnotized subject engages in two things simultaneously but only remembers one of them, he or she is in a state of _dissociation_ . If the person discusses something while writing something else, he or she has exemplified _automatic_ writing.

61. If, by yourself, you fix your gaze and daydream (and engage in a very deep daydream) you are probably in a state of _self_ - _hypnosis_ .

62. Hypnosis can enhance _memory_ by relieving anxiety.

63. Studies have not yet shown that _endorphin_ is related to hypnotic pain relief.

64. Pain relief through hypnosis may result from the fact that people are distinguishing _expected_ pain from _real_ pain.

65. Hypnotized subjects who forget, see things that are not there, or don't see things that are there may in fact be _lying_ according to many researchers.

66. Many people who volunteer to be a subject for a stage hypnotist behave the way they do to _please_ the hypnotist and do what is _expected_ of them.

67. The belief that someone will not do something while hypnotized that he or she wouldn't do while "awake" is not necessarily _true_ .

68. A hypnotic subject who, at a later time, responds to a predetermined stimulus has been given a _post_ - _hypnotic_ _suggestion_ .

69. When a subject goes back in time (even perhaps to an earlier life) he or she is undergoing hypnotic _age_ _regression_ .

70. There is no _evidence_ to support hypnotic age _regression_ . The subject is probably merely saying and doing what is _expected_ of him or her.

71. If you sit back, relax, and concentrate on a specific word for 15 minutes you are engaging in _meditation_ . Your _heart_ rate and _blood_ pressure will become _lower_ , and _oxygen_ consumption will decrease. Also, body temperature at the extremities will _increase_ and _muscles_ will relax.

72. In India, the _Yogis_ have learned how to considerably reduce blood pressure and heart rate.

73. If you watch a machine reveal the temperature of your fingertips, and then relax to raise that temperature, you are using a technique known as _biofeedback_ .

74. _biofeedback_ has been found useful in relieving _migraine_ headaches.

75. A _psychoactive_ drug alters conscious awareness or perception.

76. Three classifications of psychoactive drugs are _stimulants_ , _depressants_ , and _hallucinogens_ .

77. Powerful stimulants which were developed to keep soldiers awake are called _amphetamines_ , and, in street language, are called _uppers_ .

78. Sustained use of dexedrine, benzedrine or methedrine (amphetamines) results in paranoia, _anger_ , and prolonged _restlessness_ .

79. In the early 1970s, amphetamines were prescribed as _diet_ pills, but that use has been discontinued because people developed a _dependency_ on them.

80. The drug _cocaine_ (a stimulant) was used by Sigmund Freud and was an early ingredient in Coca Cola. This drug is not a _narcotic_ and is very _expensive_ .

81. Cocaine can result in sudden and unexpected _death_ among both long time users and _first_ time users.

82. Like small amounts of cocaine, _caffeine_ also produces increased energy and alertness.

83. People consuming more than .75 of a gram of caffeine daily may suffer from _withdrawl_ symptoms when the caffeine is removed. These symptoms include excess _urination_ , anxiety, and _dizziness_ .

84. Although alcohol is a _depressant_, it is sometimes thought of as a _stimulant_ because it may create greater _sexual_ arousal.

85. Blood alcohol content above _.001_ often defines legal intoxication, and a content level of _.004_ may be fatal.

86. Between _30_ and _50_ percent of all automobile deaths are related to intoxicated driving.

87. Alcoholics who hallucinate about bugs crawling on them during alcohol withdrawal are experiencing _delirium_ _tremens_.

88. The most widely prescribed drugs in the world are benzodiazepines (or _tranquilizers_). Two common brand names are Librium and _Valium_.

89. The _brain_ may produce its own natural Valium. Although very little has been isolated, it seems to _bind_ with inhibitory synapse receptors more tightly than the anti-anxiety drugs do.

90. Heroin is a derivative of _opium_ as are morphine and codeine. _Heroin_ is a powerful narcotic and its use can lead to strong physical _addiction_. It is an effective _pain_ killer, and recently smoking it has become popular (though it is usually _injected_). Smokers refer to it as "_chasing_ the _dragon_."

91. Mescaline, psilocybin, LSD, and DMT are classified as _hallucinogens_.

92. PCP (commonly called _angel_ _dust_) causes hallucinations but may represent a new class of _psychoactive_ drug.

93. The three distinct phases of a PCP reaction include (1) _violent_, psychotic behavior, (2) unpredictable and _restless_ behavior, and (3) rapid _improvement_ and _personality_ reintegration.

94. PCP may be naturally produced in the _brain_. Animal research shows that it is highly _desirable_ and may be involved in the brain's own _reward_ mechanism.

95. Marijuana is classified as an _hallucinogen_. In higher doses it may act as a _stimulant_, and at lower doses, a _depressant_.

96.   The major effect of marijuana taken in small or medium doses may be
      mostly a ___*placebo*___ reaction.

SELF TEST I

1.   Rats and rabbits injected with cerebral-spinal fluid from sleep-deprived
     goats _____ than those receiving fluid from rested,
     wide awake goats.
     a. fell asleep sooner but slept less
     b. fell asleep later but slept longer
     c. fell asleep sooner and slept longer
     d. fell asleep later and slept less

2.   Delta wave sleep is associated with
     a. light sleep
     b. dreaming
     c. "drowsy but awake" state
     d. deep sleep

3.   When a person has been deprived of REM sleep, he or she is likely
     to experience _____ the following night.
     a. more orthodox sleep   c. more slow wave sleep
     b. REM rebound   d. sleep apnea

4.   How much sleep does the average young adult need per night?
     a. 3 hours
     b. 6½ to 8½ hours
     c. 9 hours
     d. none of the above

5.   Typically the first REM sleep period begins after you have been asleep
     for about _____ minutes.
     a. 30   c. 90
     b. 60   d. 120

6.   The rat who had to try sleeping while standing up on a tiny platform
     over some water was being deprived of
     a. all sleep   c. NREM sleep
     b. REM sleep   d. slow wave sleep

7.   The best way to overcome insomnia due to confused circadian rhythms
     is to go to bed and arise at the same time every day for about
     a. 3 weeks   c. 6 months
     b. 8 weeks   d. a year

8.   Which view argues that dreams are expressions of what one is missing
     in life?
     a. the psychoanalytic view   c. the activation synthesis view
     b. Fritz Perls' view   d. none of the above

9. When you are aware that you are dreaming while you are dreaming, you are having a
   a. REM alarm
   b. lucid dream
   c. mnemonic dream
   d. vivid induction of lucid dreams (VILD for short)

10. Hypnotic susceptibility
    a. is high for subjects who are alert and curious about the hypnotic effect
    b. is measured by the Stanford Suggestibility Scale
    c. is characteristic of all people, that is, all people are capable of being hypnotized by someone else
    d. all of the above

11. A hypnotized person who is taken back to an earlier stage of his life or even back prior to birth to an earlier life has undergone
    a. post-hypnotic regression
    b. dissociation
    c. Mesmerism
    d. age regression

12. Which of the following is considered to be a psychoactive drug?
    a. caffeine
    b. nicotine
    c. both a and b
    d. none of the above

13. What blood alcohol concentration is considered legal intoxication in most states?
    a. .0003
    b. .001
    c. .004
    d. .009

14. Which powerful narcotic mimics the brain's own endorphin, leads to strong physical addiction, and is an excellent pain killer?
    a. cocaine
    b. librium
    c. heroin
    d. LSD

15. The major effect of marijuana reported by subjects taking small doses
    a. results from its large effect on higher brain functions
    b. may be mostly a placebo reaction
    c. includes hallucinations of lights and colors
    d. both a and b

SELF TEST II

1. Approximately _____ of our waking time is spent in daydreaming and _____ of our sleeping time is spent in night dreaming.
   a. one-third, one-half
   b. one-half, one-third
   c. one-third, one-third
   d. one-half, one-half

2. When people are not engaging in REM sleep, they are in
    _____ sleep.
    a. paradoxical   c. NREM
    b. light   d. both a and b

3. People who make an active plan to get up at a certain time show
    a. less slow wave sleep, less REM, and more awakenings
    b. more slow wave sleep, more REM, and fewer awakenings
    c. usually sleep past the appointed time
    d. less slow wave sleep, more REM, and more awakenings

4. The conserving energy theory of sleep suggests that
    a. animals with high metabolism sleep more
    b. animals who face more danger from their environment sleep more
    c. limited food supplies will last longer with increased sleep time
    d. all of the above

5. A sleep deprived person may catch a few seconds of sleep unintention-
    ally now and then even though he or she is standing up and trying to
    stay awake. This is
    a. narcolepsy
    b. microsleep
    c. NREM rebound
    d. none of the above, a person who sleeps while standing up is consi-
       dered to be suffering from somnambulism

6. Difficulty in going to sleep or staying asleep is the definition of
    a. sleep apnea   c. insomnia
    b. somnambulism   d. sleep deprivation

7. In severe cases of sleep apnea, _____ are sometimes
    used to treat the disorder
    a. exorcisms
    b. regular bed time wake up time patterns
    c. tracheotomies
    d. nose plugs

8. Motor neurons associated with eye muscles are called _____
    neurons.
    a. reticular   c. pontine
    b. oculomotor   d. forebrain

9. Hypnosis
    a. is a state of sleep
    b. cannot be used to influence someone to do something they would
       not do while "awake"
    c. is used to completely block both real and expected pain
    d. none of the above

10. Highway hypnosis and automatic writing are examples of the hypnotic effect known as
    a. animal magnetism   c. dissociation
    b. biofeedback   d. post-hypnotic suggestion

11. If you change the temperature of your fingertips by watching a digital temperature display on a machine you are using a technique known as
    a. biofeedback   c. Yogi-Zen feedback
    b. transcendental meditation   d. none of the above

12. Cocaine is a
    a. stimulant but not a narcotic
    b. depressant but not a narcotic
    c. stimulant and a narcotic
    d. depressant and a narcotic

13. Benzodiazepines include Librium and Valium, and are more commonly called _____ or _____.
    a. uppers, bennies
    b. mescaline, LSD
    c. tranquilizers, anti-anxiety drugs
    d. none of the above

14. The brain's own naturally occurring PCP might be involved in the brain's
    a. endorphin-like pain control
    b. reward mechanism
    c. both a and b
    d. none of the above

15. A client of yours in a mental health clinic complains of excessive daytime sleepiness, headaches upon awakening, and other symptoms of a poor night's sleep. You should probably suspect
    a. sleep apnea   c. endogenous insomnia
    b. narcolepsy   d. jet lag

ESSAY QUESTIONS

1. Name and describe the brain wave patterns associated with the various stages of sleep. Include a discussion of the characteristics of REM sleep.

2. List and discuss three different sleep disorders and mention possible causes, treatments and related research.

3. Discuss the different theories that explain what dreams are and what the purpose of dreams is.

4. List five of the seven hypnotic effects and indicate what kinds of beha-
    viors are associated with each. Mention the possible reasons for each
    of the hypnotic effects you are listing.

5. Compare and contrast stimulant, depressant, and hallucinogenic psycho-
    active drugs. Give examples in each category and include the symptoms
    and adverse effects related to each example.

ANSWER SECTION

Guided Review
1. *consciousness*
2. *John Watson*
3. *EEG, PET*
4. *thinking, beep (or tone), daydreaming*
5. *one-third, one-third, daydreaming*
6. *altered*
7. *altered, consciousness*
8. *alpha, theta, delta*
9. *slow wave, decreases*
10. *less, dreams*
11. *less, more*
12. *Eugene Aserinsky, REM*
13. *paradoxical, orthodox*
14. *REM*
15. *REM*
16. *acting*
17. *NREM*
18. *REM rebound*
19. *Soviets, sleeping*
20. *slow wave, less, awakenings, shocked*
21. *$6\frac{1}{2}$, $8\frac{1}{2}$*
22. *healthy insomniacs*
23. *adaptive*
24. *conserving energy*
25. *deprivation*
26. *hallucinations, delusions, blood pressure, temperature*
27. *REM, NREM, experimental*
28. *microsleep*
29. *psychological*
30. *will (or does) not*
31. *endogenous depression*
32. *sleep*
33. *normal, REM, stages*
34. *insomnia*
35. *depression, circadian rhythm*
36. *eight hours*
37. *circadian, ghost rhythms, insomnia*
38. *same time, three*

39. *jet lag*
40. *narcolepsy, inherited*
41. *sleep apnea*
42. *dreaming*
43. *NREM*
44. *longer, vivid*
45. *psychoanalytic*
46. *missing*
47. *something else*
48. *self*
49. *activation-synthesis*
50. *oculomotor, reticular*
51. *sense, random*
52. *lucid*
53. *mnemonic, lucid, nightmares*
54. *nightmare alarm*
55. *Mesmer, animal magnetism*
56. *hypnosis*
57. *asleep, phenomenon, phenomena*
58. *can, cannot*
59. *Stanford, Scale*
60. *dissociation, automatic*
61. *self-hypnosis*
62. *memory*
63. *endorphin*
64. *expected, actual*
65. *lying*
66. *please, expected*
67. *true*
68. *post-hypnotic suggestion*
69. *age regression*
70. *evidence, regression, expected*
71. *meditation, heart, blood, lower, oxygen, increase, muscles*
72. *Yogis*
73. *biofeedback*
74. *biofeedback, migraine*
75. *psychoactive*
76. *stimulants, depressants, hallucinogens*
77. *amphetamines, uppers (or speed or bennies)*
78. *anger, restlessness*
79. *diet, dependency*
80. *cocaine, narcotic, expensive*
81. *death, first*
82. *caffeine*
83. *withdrawal, urination, dizziness*
84. *depressant, stimulant, sexual*
85. *.001, .004*
86. *30, 50*
87. *delirium tremens*

88. *tranquilizers*, Valium
89. *brain, bind*
90. *opium, heroin, addiction, pain, injected, chasing, dragon*
91. *hallucinogens*
92. *angel dust, psychoactive*
93. *violent, restless, improvement, personality*
94. *brain, desirable, reward*
95. *hallucinogen, stimulant, depressant*
96. *placebo*

Self Test I
1. c
2. d
3. b
4. b
5. c
6. b
7. a
8. b
9. b
10. b
11. d
12. c
13. b
14. c
15. b

Self Test II
1. c
2. c
3. a
4. d
5. b
6. c
7. c
8. b
9. d
10. c
11. a
12. a
13. c
14. b
15. a

CHAPTER 6

Learning and Conditioning

BEHAVIORAL OBJECTIVES

After completing this chapter the student should be able to

1. Summarize the early ethological work of D. A. Spalding and the more recent work of Konrad Lorenz.
2. Define and give examples of sensitization and habituation.
3. List the three ways behavior theory explains learning.
4. Describe the work of Ivan Pavlov on conditioned reflexes and include explanations of unconditioned stimulus, unconditioned response, neutral stimulus, conditioned stimulus, and conditioned response.
5. Describe the Little Albert study and contrast it with H. B. English's replication efforts.
6. Convey an understanding of instrumental learning and the concept of shaping.
7. Compare and contrast positive and negative reinforcement.
8. Recognize the negative aspects of spanking as a punishment.
9. Define and give examples of primary and secondary reinforcement.
10. Distinguish between, and explain, interval and ratio schedules of reinforcement, including the distinction between partial and continuous reinforcement.
11. Explain what is meant by stimulus control.
12. Summarize the background and contributions of B. F. Skinner.
13. Describe social learning and explain the process of modeling.
14. Discuss the growth and impetus behind the cognitive psychological approach to learning.
15. Define and contrast negative and positive transfer.

KEY TERMS AND CONCEPTS

learning
unlearned behaviors

behavior patterns
ethology

innate
imprinting
critical period
fixed response patterns
releasers (sign stimuli)
stimulus
species-specific behaviors
instincts
reflexes
habituation
sensitization
unconditioned stimulus (US)
unconditioned response (UR)
conditioned stimulus (CS)
classical conditioning
stimulus generalization
countercondition
extinction (classical)
associative learning
instrumental learning
operant conditioning
law of effect
reinforcement
stimulus consequence
reinforcer
shaping
discrimination
generalization
generalization gradient
positive reinforcement

negative reinforcement
superstitious learning
punishment
extinction (instrumental)
primary reinforcers
secondary reinforcers
time out
reinforcing incompatible responses
schedules of reinforcement
continuous reinforcement
intermittent reinforcement schedule
discriminative stimulus (SD)
cues
stimulus control
operant chain
habit
Skinner box
air crib
social learning
model
performance vs. acquisition
latent learning
behavior modification
cognition
cognitive psychology
cognitive map
place learning
negative transfer of learning
positive transfer of learning

NAMES TO REMEMBER

Kenneth Clark
D. A. Spalding
Konrad Lorenz
Ivan Pavlov

B. F. Skinner
E. L. Thorndike
Albert Bandura
Edward Tolman

GUIDED REVIEW

1. The Clarks' 1947 study of black and white children found that white children labeled the _black_ doll more often as being _dirty_. Also, black children tended to see the black doll as the _bad_ one.

2. _learning_ may be defined as a relatively permanent change in behavior that results from _experience_.

3. Fatigue would not be learning, since it is only a <u>temporary</u> change resulting from experience.

4. Some behaviors are learned through experience while other behaviors are <u>inherited</u>, such as birds' <u>nest</u> building behaviors.

5. Researchers investigating inherited behaviors through the use of naturalistic observation are called <u>ethologist</u>.

6. D. A. Spalding discovered that <u>baby</u> <u>chicks</u> tend to follow the first <u>moving</u> <u>objects</u> they see. He demonstrated that the following response was not learned but seemed to be <u>innate</u>.

7. Expanding ethological studies, <u>Konrad</u> <u>Lorenz</u> referred to the following response as <u>imprinting</u>.

8. Imprinting occurs in ducks soon after hatching during a <u>critical</u> <u>period</u> which lasts about two days.

9. <u>species</u> <u>specific</u> behaviors are fixed response patterns that are triggered by releasers or <u>sign</u> <u>stimuli</u>. For example, a dangling worm to a baby robin is a sign stimuli for a <u>fixed</u> <u>response</u> <u>pattern</u>.

10. Inborn human behaviors such as blinking and swallowing tend to be classified as simple <u>reflex</u> rather than the more complex fixed response patterns known as <u>instincts</u>.

11. People do tend to be attracted to small cuddly animals and <u>babyishness</u> may well be a <u>sign</u> <u>stimuli</u> for a parental instinct.

12. Animals that can <u>learn</u> are not restricted to fixed response patterns and thus they have greater <u>flexibility</u> of behavior resulting in a greater chance of <u>survival</u>.

13. Some of the simplest species can learn. The experiment with <u>fruitfly</u> <u>larvae</u> demonstrated a learned <u>avoidance</u> of substances A and O.

14. One of the simplest human forms of learning is <u>habituation</u>.

15. The value of habituation is in the fact that we come to ignore a stimulus that has lost its <u>novelty</u> or <u>importance</u>.

16. <u>Sensitization</u> occurs when an animal or human being is exposed

to a stimulus that is accompanied by ___pain___ of some kind.

17. During habituation the amount of ___neurotransmitter___ secreted into synapses along the skeletal muscles becomes progressively ___reduced___. During sensitization ___more___ neurotransmitter is secreted than normal.

18. Behavior theory suggests three ways learning occurs: first by ___association___, second through rewards and ___punishment___, and third by observing others, known as ___social___ ___learning___.

19. Ivan Pavlov, while studying ___digestion___ wondered why dogs often began to ___salivate___ before receiving food.

20. In Pavlov's experiments he paired an unlearned or ___unconditioned___ ___stimulus___ of meat with a ___neutral___ ___stimulus___, a bell. When the bell alone became a ___conditioned___ ___stimulus___ salivation was elicited.

21. Pavlov's experiments showed how a new stimulus, the ___conditioned___ stimulus, could elicit a ___reflexive___ behavior.

22. The noise of someone preparing dinner often elicits a ___conditioned___ ___response___ of salivation because the noise has often been followed by the ___uncond.___ ___Response___ of food being in your mouth.

23. Salivating when food is in your mouth is an unlearned or ___Uncond___ ___Response___.

24. The bell in Pavlov's experiments, the noise of food being prepared, and the words "pop quiz" are all ___conditioned___ ___stimuli___ that have been acquired through ___experience___.

25. Pavlov's methods became known as ___classical___ ___conditioning___ and were first tried on humans when ___Watson___ and ___Rayner___ did the ___Little___ ___Albert___ in 1920.

26. In the Little Albert study a loud noise or ___Uncond___ ___stim___ elicited a ___uncond___ ___stim___ of crying. By pairing the loud noise with a white rat the ~~response~~ ___rat___ soon became a ___cond___ ___stim___ eliciting a conditioned response of crying.

27. Little Albert not only came to fear the white rat, but other objects such as a rabbit and a Santa Claus mask. This is known as stimulus ___generalization___.

28. One strategy to rid Albert of his fear was to _counterconditon_ him by either having the rat associated with his _favorite_ food or by stimulating his _erogenous_ zones.

29. Repeatedly presenting the rat to Little Albert without any loud noise, that is putting Albert through _extinction_, was another strategy that was considered by the researchers.

30. Attitudes may be acquired through _associative_ _learning_. For example, Nunnally and his colleagues demonstrated that _positive_ _assoc_ could be made with _nonsense_ _syllables_.

31. The kinds of discrimination the Clarks found with black and white children were probably the result of ~~associa~~ _learning_. _associative_

32. Not all behavioral responses are _elicited_ responses; many responses are emitted because they are _instrumental_ for reaching a goal.

33. Instrumental behaviors are _learned_ behaviors. For example, not intentionally putting your hand on a hot burner is _instrumental_ in avoiding pain.

34. _instrumental_ and _operant_ conditioning both refer to conditioning of behaviors by the _stimulus_ _consequences_ following a response.

35. E. L. Thorndike studied cats in _puzzle_ _boxes_ and developed the concept known as the _law_ of _effect_.

36. According to the law of effect responses followed by _pleasure_ are more likely to reoccur while responses followed by _discomfort_ are less likely to reoccur.

37. Crying may be an unlearned _reflex_, a _classically_ _cond_ response or an _instrumentally_ _learned_ response.

38. In classical conditioning _extinction_ takes place when the CS is no longer followed by the _uncond_ _stim_.

39. In instrumental learning extinction takes place when a response is no longer _reinforced_.

40. The strength of any instrumental behavior can be measured by its _resistance_ _to_ _extinction_.

41. _reinforcement_ is defined as a _stimulus_ _consequence_ that increases the strength of the emitted response that it _follows_ .

42. Classical conditioning focuses on elicited behaviors while instrumental learning focuses on _emitted_ responses.

43. Reinforcing successive _approximations_ of a desired behavior is known as _shaping_ .

44. Shaping a pigeon's behavior so that it appears to read directions on signs is done by _extinguishing_ the inappropriate response until a _discrimination_ is learned.

45. A pigeon trained to turn right when shown "right" will probably turn right if shown a sign that says "left" due to _generalization_ .

46. Reinforcement by definition _strengthens_ the responses it _follows_ . A distinction is made between _positive_ _reinforcement_ and _negative_ reinforcement.

47. Positive reinforcement occurs when an organism is reinforced for having _approached_ or obtained something.

48. Negative reinforcement occurs when an organism is reinforced for successfully _avoiding_ an _aversive_ stimulus.

49. Negative reinforcement _strengthens_ behavior; positive reinforcement _also_ _strengthen_ behavior.

50. Positive and negative reinforcement can occur _simultaneously_ .

51. _superstition_ learning occurs when a response becomes associated with a reinforcing consequence by coincidence; the response does not directly influence the presentation of the reinforcer.

52. Delivering a _punishment_ following a response will decrease the _rate_ of that response.

53. _people_ are not reinforced or punished, _behaviors_ are.

54. Cooking bacon while nude is unlikely to reoccur since this behavior would typically result in _punishing_ consequences.

55. Punishment often occurs when a response is followed by an _aversive_ stimulus. Negative reinforcement occurs following the successful _avoidance_ of an aversive stimulus.

56. Punishment can be effective. However, if the punishment is too *severe* there is often a general *suppression* of other behaviors. In addition, *hostility* and *aggression* may result.

57. During the training of *seeing eye dogs*, the use of *punishment* is avoided because the drawbacks are too great.

58. In instrumental learning the removal of a *reinforcer*, known as *extinction*, may be an alternative to punishment.

59. Even after a response has been estinguished _____ _____ may occur in which the behavior briefly reappears.

60. Adults who spank children sometimes severely hurt them because the adults become too _____. Most _____ _____ begins with an intent to spank.

61. A parent who spanks his or her child may become a fear stimulus to the child through _____ _____.

62. Spanking may cause the child to become _____ reinforced for running away from home. _____ _____ usually have only a _____ effect.

63. Research on instrumental learning has shown that many _____ techniques are successful in _____ and _____ children's behavior.

64. _____ _____ is a nonphysical form of control where _____ _____ is removed by placing the subject in a boring environment.

65. Another successful nonphysical approach to eliminating undesirable behavior is the _____ _____ _____ responses, which is based on the premise that opposite behaviors can _____ occur at the same _____.

66. Many child abusers were themselves _____ as children.

67. Some _____ are naturally satisfying, such as food, water and air; that is, they are _____ reinforcers.

68. _____ _____ or acquired reinforcers are reinforcing because they are associated with _____ reinforcers or other _____ reinforcers.

69. Various instrumental responses are easier to learn than others because of the species' _____ organization. This may explain the fact that we can remember _____ responses longer than _____ responses.

70. Generally _____ reinforcement schedules are less resistant to extinction, while _____ reinforcement schedules are much more resistant.

71. If you want to train an animal or a person to have a persistent behavior, an _____ schedule of reinforcement is best.

72. Intermittent schedules of reinforcement that are based on the passage of time prior to reinforcing an appropriate response are called _____ schedules.

73. Intermittent schedules of reinforcement that are based on the number of responses required per reinforcement are called _____ schedules.

74. Ratio and interval schedules of reinforcement can also be either _____ or _____ schedules.

75. Slot machines pay off on _____ _____ schedules of reinforcement.

76. A slight pause after receiving the reinforcer is typical of _____ _____ schedules, while a scalloped shaped schedule is typical of _____ _____ schedules.

77. Stimuli in whose presence a response is likely to be emitted are _____ stimuli. They function as _____ for responding.

78. Once discriminative stimuli control the time and place that certain behaviors occur, _____ _____ has occurred.

79. Habits are referred to as _____ chains and are composed of _____ , _____ , and _____ .

80. Probably one of the best known contemporary American psychologists and the leading proponent of _____ _____ is B. F. _____ .

81. B. F. Skinner worked for the navy during World War II and in one project successfully taught _____ to guide _____ . He also gained some notoriety for the way he

raised his _____ in an _____ crib.

82. Albert Bandura and his colleagues have studied _____
    _____ , which is learning by _____ others.

83. In one of Bandura's studies children were more _____
    after watching an aggressive _____ . From this experi-
    ment it was shown that children who observed a model being
    _____ for aggressive behavior were unlikely to
    _____ the behavior even though they had
    _____ the aggressive behavior.

84. Rats allowed to wander about an empty maze later learned the maze
    faster because of _____ _____ .

85. Early _____ _____ experiments demonstra-
    ted that behaviors of entire groups of people could be changed by
    influencing the behavior of the group's _____ .

86. Models who are nurturant, aggressive, or _____ to the
    observers are _____ likely to be _____ .

87. _____ _____ is an application of learning
    theory that arranges particular _____ between stimuli
    or particular _____ following behavior, or
    _____ of desired behaviors in order to bring about a change
    in a person's behavior.

88. Bandura had some success helping people overcome _____
    _____ by using _____ .

89. _____ and _____ learning are often
    incorporated into a comprehensive _____
    _____ program such as the _____
    _____ procedures of Azrin and Foxx.

90. John _____ would not even consider cognitive issues,
    since they were not based on directly _____ events.
    However, there is a growing understanding and appreciation of how
    our _____ and _____ influence our
    behavior.

91. You can use your cognitive understanding to orient yourself to parti-
    cular problems or situations. For example, you no doubt travel
    through your own city or town with the use of a _____
    _____ that gives you an internal understanding of where
    things are located in relation to each other.

92. In a maze study using rats, Tolman determined that rats could find

their way even if the usual path were blocked. He referred to this
as _____   _____ .

93. Many people have learned a skill such as driving a manual shift car.
     But when these people get into another car in which the shifting
     pattern is different a _____ _____
     may take place in which the previous skill interferes with the new
     one.

94. Typists who have been trained on typical keyboards have, surpris-
     ingly, been found to learn the new Maltron keyboard faster than novices
     because of _____   _____ .

SELF TEST I

1. Which of the following statements is false regarding the 1947 Clark
    study of black and white children:
    a. black children thought the black doll looked like them
    b. white children judged the white doll to be the "good boy"
    c. black children judged the black doll as the "good boy"
    d. all of the above

2. Ethologists often study complex inherited behaviors known as
    a. reflexes
    b. fixed-response patterns
    c. learned behaviors
    d. none of the above

3. Human beings have inborn reflexes. Most psychologists, however, are
    doubtful that humans have instincts.
    a. true   b. false

4. The learning experiment using fruitfly larvae demonstrated
    a. that most larvae would learn to avoid or escape from substances
        that had previously been associated with shock
    b. that larvae could not learn
    c. that all larvae failed to respond to electric shocks
    d. that electric shock was pleasant to the larvae

5. Biological evidence has shown that during sensitization
    a. neurotransmitters have been secreted at very high levels in the
        synapses adjacent to the skeletal muscles
    b. neurotransmitters have been reduced to low levels in the skeletal
        muscle synapses
    c. the neurotransmitter levels show no change around the skeletal
        synapses
    d. none of the above

6. The food in Pavlov's classical conditioning experiments was termed the
   a. conditioned stimulus (CS)
   b. unconditioned stimulus (US)
   c. conditioned response (CR)
   d. unconditioned response (UR)

7. Until Watson and Rayner's 1920 "little Albert" study no one had clearly demonstrated classical conditioning in human beings.
   a. true   b. false

8. The researcher who studied instrumental learning by placing cats in "puzzle boxes" was
   a. Tolman
   b. Thorndike
   c. Skinner
   d. Pavlov

9. Each time a rat gets closer to the lever that you want it to press you reinforce its behavior. Soon, the rat is at the bar and actually pressing it. You have conducted an instrumental procedure called
   a. stimulus generalization
   b. extinction
   c. modeling
   d. shaping

10. _____ increases or strengthens behaviors it follows, while _____ decreases or eliminates behaviors it follows.
    a. punishment, negative reinforcement
    b. reinforcement, punishment
    c. food, rewards
    d. primary reinforcement, secondary reinforcement

11. Mild spankings as a form of punishment have been shown to have only a temporary effect.
    a. true   b. false

12. Reinforcing each and every response is a requirement of _____ schedules of reinforcement.
    a. partial
    b. intermittent
    c. variable
    d. none of the above

13. An "out of order" sign posted on a pop machine is a/an _____ stimulus for your to look for another machine.
    a. generalized   c. discriminative
    b. aversive   d. intermittent

14. The researcher most often associated with the social learning approach is

a. B. F. Skinner   c. E. L. Thorndike
b. John Watson   d. Albert Bandura

15. Reinforcement affects whether a socially learned behavior will be performed.
a. true   b. false

SELF TEST II

1. D. A. Spalding noted that
    a. baby chicks never followed the first moving object they saw
    b. the following response of baby chicks was learned
    c. the following response was innate
    d. fruitfly larvae exhibited a following response

2. Dangling a worm above a baby robin is a _____
    for a fixed response pattern of behaviors.
    a. sign stimulus   c. either a or b
    b. releaser stimulus   d. neither a nor b

3. Fruitfly larvae have been shown to have learning capabilities.
    a. true   b. false

4. Due to _____, a ticking clock is soon ignored.
    a. latent learning
    b. habituation
    c. instrumental learning
    d. classical conditioning

5. In Pavlov's experiments a _____ was used as the
    _____ stimulus.
    a. bell, unconditioned
    b. bell, conditioned
    c. rat, conditioned
    d. rat, unconditioned

6. A small child is bitten by a large brown dog and as a result fears all dogs. The process being demonstrated is
    a. extinction   c. generalization
    b. discrimination   d. both a and b

7. In the 1965 Nunnally et al. study in which children played a spinner game
    a. the nonsense syllable associated with a payoff became well liked
    b. the nonsense syllable associated with a loss became associated with the friendly boy picture
    c. no associations were made
    d. none of the above

8. A mother who gives candy to quiet a disruptive child may well find the child becoming more disruptive because
   a. she has reinforced the disruptive behavior
   b. she has classically conditioned the child
   c. the child is in a critical period
   d. the child is habituated

9. A trip to the gambling tables at Las Vegas might lead to
   a. positive reinforcement
   b. negative reinforcement
   c. punishment
   d. any of the above

10. Seeing eye dogs are rarely punished during their training because
    a. other desirable behaviors may be suppressed
    b. the dog may become aggressive
    c. reinforcement works best
    d. all of the above

11. Stimuli that acquire reinforcing properties, like awards or trading stamps, are known as
    a. primary reinforcers   c. biologically inherited reinforcers
    b. secondary reinforcers   d. rewards

12. Getting paid by the piece (piecework) is a _____ schedule of reinforcement
    a. variable ratio   c. fixed ratio
    b. fixed interval   d. variable interval

13. An office worker always turns left towards the bar instead of right towards home and proceeds to have a few drinks before finally arriving home. This response sequence would be known as an _____, collectively known as a _____.
    a. operant chain, punishment
    b. operant response, instinct
    c. operant chain, habit
    d. instinct, habit

14. Bandura's description of training a student driver demonstrated
    a. the advantages of associative learning
    b. the advantages of social learning
    c. that operant conditioning can easily be used to teach one to drive
    d. that classical conditioning speeds the learning of driving

15. Models who are nurturant, aggressive, or similar to observers are less likely to be imitated by observers.
    a. true   b. false

ESSAY QUESTIONS

1. Describe the experiments done by Dr. Kenneth Clark and explain why he found the results he did.

2. Describe an everyday example of classical conditioning not covered in the text using the appropriate terms.

3. Describe how you would teach a dog to sit up using instrumental conditioning procedures.

4. Explain how modeling and instrumental learning can be used to expedite toilet training.

5. Explain the difference between, and give examples of, performance and acquisition.

ANSWER SECTION

Guided Review
1. *black, dirty (or ugly), bad*
2. *learning, experience*
3. *temporary*
4. *inherited (or innate), nest*
5. *ethologists*
6. *baby chicks, moving object, innate*
7. *Konrad Lorenz, imprinting*
8. *critical period*
9. *species specific, sign stimuli, fixed response pattern*
10. *reflexes, instincts*
11. *babyishness, sign stimuli (or releaser stimuli)*
12. *learn, flexibility, survival*
13. *fruitfly larvae, avoidance*
14. *habituation*
15. *novelty, importance*
16. *sensitization, pain*
17. *neurotransmitter, reduced, more*
18. *association, punishments, social learning*
19. *digestion, salivate*
20. *unconditioned stimulus, neutral stimulus, conditioned stimulus*
21. *conditioned, reflexive*
22. *conditioned response (or CR), unconditioned stimulus (or US)*
23. *unconditioned response (or UR)*
24. *conditioned stimuli (or CS), experience (or learning)*
25. *classical conditioning, Watson, Rayner, Little Albert*
26. *unconditioned stimulus (or US), unconditioned response (or UR), rat, conditioned stimulus (or CS)*

27. *generalization*
28. *countercondition, favorite, erogenous*
29. *extinction*
30. *associative learning, positive associations, nonsense syllables*
31. *associative learning*
32. *elicited, instrumental*
33. *learned, instrumental*
34. *instrumental, operant, stimulus consequences*
35. *puzzle boxes, law of effect*
36. *pleasure, discomfort (or pain)*
37. *reflex, classically conditioned, instrumentally learned*
38. *extinction, unconditioned stimulus (or US)*
39. *reinforced*
40. *resistance to extinction*
41. *reinforcement, stimulus consequences, follows*
42. *emitted*
43. *approximations, shaping*
44. *extinguishing, discrimination*
45. *generalization*
46. *strengthens, follows, positive reinforcement, negative*
47. *approached*
48. *avoiding (or escaping), aversive*
49. *strengthens, also strengthens*
50. *simultaneously*
51. *superstitious*
52. *punishment, rate (or frequency)*
53. *people, behaviors*
54. *punishing*
55. *aversive, avoidance (or escape)*
56. *severe, suppression, hostility, aggression*
57. *seeing eye dogs, punishment*
58. *reinforcer, extinction*
59. *spontaneous recovery*
60. *emotional (or angry), child abuse*
61. *classical conditioning*
62. *negatively, mild spankings, temporary*
63. *nonphysical, controlling, modifying*
64. *time out, positive reinforcement*
65. *reinforcement of incompatible, not, time*
66. *abused*
67. *reinforcers, primary*
68. *secondary reinforcers, primary, secondary*
69. *biological (or genetic), motor, verbal*
70. *continuous, intermittent*
71. *intermittent*
72. *interval*
73. *ratio*
74. *fixed, variable*
75. *variable ratio*

76. *fixed ratio, fixed interval*
77. *discriminative, cues*
78. *stimulus control*
79. *operant, cues, responses, reinforcements*
80. *behavioral psychology, Skinner*
81. *pigeons, missles, daughter, air*
82. *social learning, observing*
83. *aggressive, model, disciplined, perform, acquired (or learned)*
84. *latent learning*
85. *social learning, leader*
86. *similar, more, imitated*
87. *behavior modification, associations, consequences, modeling*
88. *snake phobia, models*
89. *associative, instrumental, behavior modification, toilet training*
90. *Watson, observable, thinking, cognition*
91. *cognitive map*
92. *place learning*
93. *negative transfer*
94. *positive transfer*

Self Test I		Self Test II	
1.	c	1.	c
2.	b	2.	c
3.	a	3.	a
4.	a	4.	b
5.	a	5.	b
6.	b	6.	c
7.	a	7.	a
8.	b	8.	a
9.	d	9.	d
10.	b	10.	d
11.	a	11.	b
12.	d	12.	c
13.	c	13.	c
14.	d	14.	b
15.	a	15.	b

CHAPTER 7

Memory and Information Processing

BEHAVIORAL OBJECTIVES

After completing this chapter, the student should be able to:

1. Construct a list of nonsense syllables and plot a classic curve of forgetting.
2. Sketch the memory model and label the following parts or functions: Sensory memory, short-term memory, long-term memory, and rehearsal.
3. Compare short-term memory with long-term memory, noting the capacity and duration of each.
4. Explain the effects of chunking and meaning on the retention of memories.
5. Give three examples of mnemonics and use at least one or two specific mnemonic strategies to facilitate his or her own recall.
6. Describe two experiments involving the hormone vasopressin and indicate potential uses for that hormone.
7. Briefly summarize the research into the biology of memory specifically noting the work and findings pertaining to Lashley's engram, McConnell's planaria, and Ungar's scotophobin.
8. Explain the dual-code theory of memory.
9. Discuss in detail propositional network theory giving specific examples of nodes and links.
10. Compare and contrast trace column theory with propositional network theory and indicate which theory is more likely to be correct and why.
11. Distinguish between proactive interference and retroactive interference and give examples of each.
12. Name the chemical associated with flashbulb memory and explain how that chemical enhances memory.
13. Evaluate the arguments and give evidence on both sides of the issue as to whether all long-term memories are permanent.
14. Give three explanations which account for forgetting information in long-term memory.
15. Distinguish between consolidation and elaboration.
16. Tell in his or her own words the meaning of motivated forgetting and explain what repression and retrograde amnesia have to do with it.

17. Summarize the research indicating the effects of mood, mental state, and physical location upon retrieval from long-term memory.
18. List the advantages and disadvantages of spaced practice and massed practice (cramming).

KEY TERMS AND CONCEPTS

consonant-vowel-consonant trigrams
nonsense syllables
forgetting curve
memory model
sensory memory
sensory register
encode
decay
short-term memory
rehearsal
serial position effect
displacement
chunk (chunking)
long-term memory
retrieve
mnemonics
method of loci
vasopressin
hypermnesic
engram
equipotentiality
planaria
RNA
scotophobin
dual-code theory
eidetic image
photographic memory
acoustic code
verbal codes
propositional network theory

proposition
nodes
links
trace column
parallel access
proactive interference
retroactive interference
tip of the tongue phenomenon
retrieval cue
recall test
recognition test
one-way links
flashbulb memory
ACTH
forgetting
pseudo-forgetting
consolidation
retrograde amnesia
motivated forgetting
repression
reconstruction
creative remembering
elaboration
locus-dependent memory
state-dependent learning
spacing effect
encoding variability
spaced practice
massed practice
cramming strengths
cramming weaknesses

NAMES TO REMEMBER

Hermann Ebbinghaus
George Sperling
Karl Lashley
James McConnell

Georges Ungar
Donald Hebb
Kurt Koffka
Wilder Penfield

GUIDED REVIEW

1. A consonant-vowel-consonant trigram is called a _nonsense_ syllable.

2. Hermann _Ebbinghaus_ was the pioneer memory investigator who memorized long lists of nonsense syllables to plot a curve of _forgetting_ .

3. A picture or depiction to help organize our thinking about memory is called a memory ~~memory~~ _model_.

4. The memory model is composed of three main parts: The _sensory_ register, _short_ -term memory, and _long_ - _term_ memory.

5. The sensory register (or sensory memory) lasts for only a _fraction_ of a second. You must successfully _encode_ the sensory image into short-term memory or it will _decay_ and be lost. If you don't pay _attention_ to a sensation it will rapidly be lost.

6. Generally, the short-term memory can hold about _7_ items, plus or minus _2_ .

7. The length of time you can hold information in your short-term memory is about _thirty_ _second_ . To keep it there longer than that you must use _rehearsal_ .

8. Remembering the first few and the last few items from a long list is known as the _serial_ _position_ effect. You remembered about seven of the items, whereas the lost items were _displaced_ .

9. Material must be _transferred_ from short-term memory to long-term memory or it will be rapidly _lost_ .

10. A unit or item of memory was referred to by George Miller as a _chunk_ . Short-term memory can hold about seven _chunks_ regardless of the number of things they contain.

11. _long_ - _term_ _memory_ has, for all purposes, an unlimited storage capacity.

12. When a long-term memory is called up into the short term or _working_ memory, we say you have _retrieved_ the memory.

13. Three ways in which short-term memories are stored in long-term memory are (1) important or unusual (memorable) experiences,

(2) _rehearsing_ an item many times, and (3) through the use of _mnemonics_ .

14. The number eight in a telephone number is merely a _placeholder_ ; it is abstract and meaningless.

15. It is easier to remember lists of items if they have _meaning_ .

16. Memory aids or systems which impose meaning upon abstract material to be remembered are called _mnemonics_ .

17. To remember a list of items by mentally placing them in specific locations along a familiar pathway is to use the mnemonic device known as the _method_ of _loci_ .

18. The mnemonic to remember the colors of the rainbow is the man's name, _Roy_ _G._ _Biv_ .

19. The brain peptide known as _vasopressin_ has been shown to help people improve their memories.

20. Hypothesized biochemical brain structures that contain memories were called _engrams_ by Karl Lashley. He espoused the principle of _equipotentiality_ which states that memory is distributed throughout the brain and is not contained in one place.

21. The engram is also referred to as the _memory trace_ .

22. McConnell showed that chopped up _flatworm_ fed to other _flatworm_ caused the others to receive a memory by transfering the biochemicals responsible for memories.

23. Today it is believed that _RNA_ itself is not responsible for memories. It is the small proteins made by _RNA_ that contain memories.

24. One protein, _scotophobin_ , used by Georges Ungar to cause rats to avoid the dark corner of a maze, actually contained a small _peptide_ responsible for that particular memory. Other _peptides_ have been isolated which are associated with specific memories and experiences.

25. The _dual_ - _code_ theory of memory argues that memories contain both sensory and verbal information.

26. To visualize something in your mind's eye after the object is removed from view is to have an _eidetic_ _image_ . People who can use such images well have been said to have a _photographic_ memory.

27. Much of our memory is based on a network of abstract representations which are tied to ___meanings___, rather than to sensory or ___verbal___ information. In other words, your memory stores ___meanings___, not words or ___sensations___.

28. The most popular current way of describing how meaning is represented in memory is with ___propositional___ network theory.

29. The smallest unit about which it makes sense to make the judgment true or false is called a ___proposition___.

30. In propositional network theory, each proposition is represented by a ___circles___ which is connected to the relations and arguments of the proposition by ___arrows___. Parts of the propositions are called ___nodes___ and the arrows are called ___links___.

31. Kurt Koffka thought that memory was a continuous record of experiences or a ___trace___ ___column___, which is analogous to a ~~red~~ ___videotape___. However, Koffka was ___wrong___.

32. Our memories are best thought of as being located at ___intersection___ inside a city with many different entrances or ___access___ points.

33. When previously learned material interferes with your ability to remember something that you have learned later, then you are experiencing ___proactive___ interference.

34. When newly learned material interferes with your ability to remember something that you learned long ago, then you are experiencing ___retroactive___ ___interference___.

35. When you can't remember something that you are certain you know, you are experiencing the ___tip___ of the ___tongue___ phenomenon.

36. A multiple choice test is a ___recognition___ test and is much easier than a test that requires strict ___recall___.

37. Multiple choice tests are loaded with ___retrieval___ cues.

38. In propositional network theory, links between nodes will be ___strong___ if the experienced events are shocking, surprising, or powerful. Such an effect is sometimes called ___flashbulb___ memory.

39. At times of stress the hormone ___ACTH___, which enhances memory, is secreted.

40. Some researchers believe that long-term memories are _permanent_, while other researchers believe that some long-term memories may _decay_ and be lost.

41. A long-term memory may be forgotten due to decay or because you can't find the appropriate _links_ through your network to the memory _node_ that you are trying to retrieve.

42. In Jenkins and Dallenbach's study, subjects who _slept_ for eight hours remembered a list of nonsense syllables better than those subjects who stayed _awake_ for eight hours.

43. When you are surprised that you can't remember something that you really never knew in the first place, you are experiencing _pseudo_ - _forgetting_.

44. Recent information placed into long-term memory is fragile, but after a few hours it becomes _consolidated_.

45. The consolidation of long-term memories is adversely affected by the _nicotine_ in cigarette _smoke_.

46. If a person forgets everything that happened within a span of time prior to a terrifying accident, that person has _retrograde amnesia_.

47. If you purposely forget something unpleasant you are experiencing _motivated_ forgetting or _repression_.

48. Wilder _Penfield_ elicited long-forgotten memories by electrically _stimulating_ certain places within the brain.

49. Elizabeth and Geoffrey Loftus argue that not _all_ long-term memories are _permanent_.

50. Under hypnosis, some memories can be retrieved, but a lot of _reconstructing_ and "_creative_ remembering" can occur.

51. The process of linking one proposition to another in propositional network theory which enhances your ability to remember a particular proposition, is known as _elaboration_.

52. When we learn something, elements in the _environment_ become paired with the items to be remembered.

53. Both your surroundings and your _emotional_ state may influence your ability to remember something.

54. If you learn something when you are in a bad mood, you will be better able to remember it when you are in a _bad_ _mood_ .

55. To remember something better by returning to the same emotional or physical state you were in when you learned it is called _state_ - _dependant_ learning.

56. People who learn something while intoxicated may not be able to remember it when _sober_ , but will recall it when they are _intoxicated_ again.

57. Remembering something presented to you twice with a long interval between the first and second presentation illustrates the _spacing_ effect.

58. Studying in different places, at different times, and in different moods is known as _encoding_ _variability_ , and helps enlarge the elaboration _network_ of a particular memory.

59. Studying repeatedly, but only after long delays in between study sessions, is called _spaced_ practice, and cramming is called _massed_ _practice_ .

60. Cramming has its _weaknesses_ , but it also has its _strengths_ .

61. To merely get through an exam it is better to _cram_ , but for long-term retention, _spaced_ practice is best.

SELF TEST I

1. The world's first memory experiment, which made use of nonsense syllables, was conducted by
   a. Karl Lashley
   b. Wilder Penfield
   c. Hermann Ebbinghaus
   d. Sigmund Freud

2. The process by which new memories are held in the short-term memory is called
   a. attention
   b. sensory input
   c. rehearsal
   d. retrieval

3. Without rehearsal, new information is held in short-term memory for approximately _____ second(s)
   a. $\frac{1}{4}$
   b. 15
   c. 5
   d. 30

4. Which of the following would facilitate the transfer of short-term memories into long-term memory?
   a. having an experience that is unusual or important
   b. rehearsing an item many times
   c. using mnemonic strategies
   d. all of the above

5. If you remember a list of items by mentally placing them along a familiar path you are using
   a. the method of loci
   b. a menmonic
   c. the principle of equipotentiality
   d. both a and b

6. Which of the following is associated with the work of Karl Lashley?
   a. searching for the engram
   b. propositional network theory
   c. the serial position effect
   d. both b and c

7. According to modern theories, memories may be stored as
   a. sensory images (pictures or sounds)
   b. words
   c. meanings
   d. all of the above

8. Which theory of memory is rapidly becoming accepted?
   a. eidetic consolidation theory
   b. meaningful reconstruction of sensations (MRS) theory
   c. propositional network theory
   d. trace column theory

9. The tip of the tongue phenomenon
   a. occurs when you can't find a path through your memory network to the desired information
   b. produces frustration because you feel close to the desired information
   c. is a good example of retroactive inhibition
   d. both a and b

10. In the Jenkins and Dallenbach study, subjects who slept for eight hours remembered _____, and subjects who stayed awake eight hours remembered _____ of the nonsense syllables they had memorized.
    a. 50%, 10%   c. 50%, 50%
    b. 10%, 50%   d. 10%, 10%

11. Long term memories
    a. are permanently stored and, once consolidated, are never forgotten
    b. may be permanently lost and can never be recovered regardless of the technique used

c. there are prominent researchers who agree with both a and b
d. none of the above; there is no evidence yet available to support either of the positions in a or b

12. In the study where subjects learned 40 unrelated words either on the beach or 20 feet under the sea, those who learned them under the sea could recall the words better when they were _____, and those who learned them on the beach could recall them better _____.
  a. on the beach, under the sea
  b. under the sea, on the beach
  c. on the beach, on the beach
  d. under the sea, under the sea

13. If people return to the same emotional or physical condition that they were in when they learned something, they will find it easier to remember. This phenomenon is called
  a. state-dependent learning
  b. flashbulb memory
  c. the serial position effect
  d. parallel access learning

14. If you have to begin studying long before you are to take a test, it would be best to use
  a. massed practice
  b. spaced practice
  c. cramming
  d. both a and c

15. You have a burning need to remember that Homer is unhappy (you want to cheer him up). To insure that you will remember, you add the following facts: Homer wrecked his car, he's in the hospital, his dog died, his wife left him, and he owes you $50.00. You are using
  a. elaboration
  b. consolidation
  c. short-term encoding
  d. none of the above

SELF TEST II

1. A model
  a. is similar to a theory in terms of being thought of as right or wrong
  b. helps you organize your thinking
  c. of human memory consists of the remembering ellipse and the forgetting ellipse
  d. all of the above

2. How did George Sperling get his subjects to focus their attention on a particular row of letters and numbers and thus encode that information into short-term memory?
    a. he sounded a high, middle, or low-pitched tone to indicate which row should be recalled
    b. he illuminated the particular row with brighter lights as the letters and numbers were displayed
    c. he flashed an arrow indicating the particular row to be remembered
    d. none of these, Sperling didn't want his subjects to focus on any particular row of letters and numbers

3. If you try to place 20 items in your short-term memory, which ones will be the most difficult to recall?
    a. the first few items
    b. the last few items
    c. the middle items
    d. both a and b

4. A single digit within a telephone number (like the "8" in 831-9011) is
    a. merely a placeholder
    b. abstract and has no specific meaning
    c. may just as well be a letter
    d. all of the above

5. Vasopressin and a placebo were given to men ages 50 to 65 who suffered memory loss. Those who received the _____ improved their memories, concentration, learning, and attention.
    a. vasopressin   c. both a and b
    b. placebo   d. endorphin

6. A memory theory that claims memories contain both sensory and verbal information is the
    a. parallel access theory
    b. dual-code theory
    c. proactive-retroactive theory
    d. sensori-linguistic theory

7. Propositional network theory suggests that
    a. many memories are linked together, some vividly and some poorly
    b. memory is laid out like a city with many streets and intersections
    c. memory is a continuous record of experiences much like a videotape
    d. both a and b

8. When the learning of something new interferes with old memories you are experiencing
    a. proactive interference
    b. retroactive interference
    c. bilateral inhibition
    d. both a and c

9. An essay test is
   a. a recognition test
   b. loaded with retrieval cues
   c. both a and b
   d. none of the above

10. After a memory is first placed in long-term memory, a certain amount of time is necessary for that memory to _____ or take a more permanent place in the long-term memory.
   a. consolidate   c. encode
   b. rehearse   d. elaborate

11. One way to strengthen memory is (according to propositional network theory) to link several propositions together. This process is known as
   a. consolidation   c. extension
   b. elaboration   d. retrieval cueing

12. In one study, individuals in a sad mood could remember better the events in a _____ story, and individuals in a happy mood could remember better the events in a _____ story.
   a. happy, sad   c. happy, happy
   b. sad, happy   d. sad, sad

13. The fact that a person will remember an item presented twice in a list better if the interval between the first and second presentation is a long one is referred to as
   a. the spacing effect   c. state-dependent learning
   b. the rehearsal effect   d. both a and b

14. If you're interested in long-term retention and in doing well on your next exam, it would be best to use
   a. massed practice   c. cramming
   b. spaced practice   d. all of the above

15. After driving a car with a standard transmission for many years, you find that you still stomp on the nonexistent "clutch" from time to time, even though you own a new automatic. This illustrates
   a. positive transfer   c. proactive interference
   b. retroactive interference d. both a and c

ESSAY QUESTIONS

1. Compare and contrast sensory memory, short-term memory, and long-term memory. Indicate how information is stored in each of these, how long it stays there, and how much information each can hold.

2. Discuss the concept of mnemonics. Give examples.

3.   Compare and contrast the dual-code theory of memory with the propo-
     sitional network theory. Give an example of how the propositional
     network theory works and identify the specific nodes and links in your
     example.

4.   Some researchers believe that long-term memories are permanent;
     others have concluded that some long-term memories may decay and
     be lost. Which position best agrees with your thinking on the matter?
     Defend your answer.

5.   It is absolutely essential that you remember your wedding anniversary
     date so as not to disappoint your spouse. How may you use elabora-
     tion to insure that you do remember?

ANSWER SECTION

Guided Review
 1.   nonsense
 2.   Ebbinghaus, forgetting
 3.   model
 4.   sensory, short, long-term
 5.   fraction, encode, decay, attention
 6.   seven, two
 7.   thirty seconds, rehearsal
 8.   serial position, displaced
 9.   transferred (or stored), lost
10.   chunk, chunks
11.   long-term memory
12.   working, retrieved
13.   rehearsing, mnemonics
14.   placeholder
15.   meaning
16.   mnemonics
17.   method, loci
18.   Roy G. Biv
19.   vasopressin
20.   engrams, equipotentiality
21.   memory trace
22.   flatworms (or planaria), flatworms (or planaria)
23.   RNA, RNA
24.   scotophobin, peptide, peptides
25.   dual-code
26.   eidetic image, photographic
27.   meanings, verbal, meaning, sensations
28.   propositional
29.   proposition
30.   circle, arrows, nodes, links
31.   trace column, videotape, wrong

32. *intersections, access*
33. *proactive*
34. *retroactive interference*
35. *tip, tongue*
36. *recognition, recall*
37. *retrieval*
38. *strong, flashbulb*
39. *ACTH*
40. *permanent, decay*
41. *links, node*
42. *slept, awake*
43. *pseudo-forgetting*
44. *consolidated*
45. *nicotine, smoke*
46. *retrograde amnesia*
47. *motivated, repression*
48. *Penfield, stimulating*
49. *all, permanent*
50. *reconstructing, creative*
51. *elaboration*
52. *environment*
53. *emotional*
54. *bad mood*
55. *state-dependent*
56. *sober, intoxicated*
57. *spacing*
58. *encoding variability, network*
59. *spaced, massed practice*
60. *weaknesses (or drawbacks), strengths (or advantages)*
61. *cram, spaced*

Self Test I
1. *c*
2. *c*
3. *d*
4. *d*
5. *d*
6. *a*
7. *d*
8. *c*
9. *d*
10. *a*
11. *c*
12. *b*
13. *a*
14. *b*
15. *a*

Self Test II
1. *b*
2. *a*
3. *c*
4. *d*
5. *a*
6. *b*
7. *d*
8. *b*
9. *d*
10. *a*
11. *b*
12. *b*
13. *a*
14. *d*
15. *c*

CHAPTER 8

Thought and Language

BEHAVIORAL OBJECTIVES

After completing this chapter, the student should be able to:

1. Briefly summarize Wolfgang Kohler's studies with Sultan.
2. Define thinking and discuss how the behavioral explanation of subvocal speech was discredited.
3. Distinguish between routine and creative problem solving.
4. Explain and distinguish algorithmic problem solving, heuristic problem solving, and means-end analysis problem solving.
5. Define mental set and describe how Luchins' water jug problem is used to demonstrate it.
6. Summarize Robert Pirsig's criticism of the scientific method and convey an understanding of "unstuckness."
7. Describe the Whorfian hypothesis of linguistic relativity and summarize the evidence against it.
8. Explain and distinguish phonetic expansion and phonetic contraction.
9. Explain how accents are learned and how comedians can "speak" so many languages.
10. Describe the one-word stage and the two-word stage.
11. Describe telegraphic speech and define syntax, phonology, and semantics.
12. Convey an understanding of the acquisition and order of "functional words."
13. Summarize the nativist versus the learning theorist positions of language development.
14. Describe the research concerning teaching language to primates and the controversy involved.
15. Define and contrast Wernicke's and Broca's aphasia.

KEY TERMS AND CONCEPTS

insight   thinking

subvocal speech
concept
routine problem solving
creative problem solving
initial state of problem
    solving
incubation effect
algorithms
heuristics
similarity to final goal
general problem solver (GPS)
means-end analysis
mental set
functional fixedness
language
communication
grammar
novel construction
linguistic relativity
focal colors
Whorfian hypothesis
phonemes
phonetic expansion
babbling stage
tonal languages

phonetic contraction
one-word stage
syntax
phonology
two-word stage
telegraphic speech
semantics
function words
caretaker speech
baby talk
linguist
transformational grammar theory
surface structure
deep structure
twin speech
language acquisition device
nativist versus learning theorist
Wernicke's aphasia
Wernicke's area
Broca's area
arcuate fasciculus
Broca's aphasia
angular gyrus
dyslexia

NAMES TO REMEMBER

Wolfgang Kohler
Sultan
John Watson
A. S. Luchins
Benjamin Lee Whorf
Roger Brown
Noam Chomsky
Grace and Virginia Kennedy

Beatrice and Allen Gardner
Washoe
Koko
Francine Patterson
Herbert Terrace
Paul Broca
Carl Wernicke
Peter Goldmark

GUIDED REVIEW

1. In 1917, on Tenerife Island, Wolfgang _Kohler_ worked with
    a chimpanzee named _Sultan_ in a series of experiments
    studying _insight_ .

2. According to Kohler, Sultan demonstrated _insight_ when
    he put _two_ _sticks_ together to reach
    a banana.

3. Psychologists study _thinking_ , _problem solving_ , and _language_ because these aspects are the essence of the human experience.

4. _thinking_ refers to the use of mental combinations and internal representations of _symbols_ , _objects_ , and _concepts_ .

5. John Watson believed thinking to be nothing more than _subvocal speech_ .

6. Smith et al. (1947) used _curare_ to determine that thinking is an internal _mental_ activity.

7. Seeing a brand new model of a car doesn't confuse you because the _concept_ of "car" enables you to recognize objects by the _properties_ that they share.

8. For children, rules classifying _concrete_ objects and ideas are generally more easily acquired than those rules that encompass more _abstract_ qualities.

9. How we develop _concept_ depends on how we _classify_ objects according to the way in which we perceive them as similar or different from one another.

10. _problem solving_ is defined as a sequence of cognitive operations directed toward achieving a particular goal.

11. _routine_ problem solving makes use of thoughts and concepts already possessed, while _creative_ problem solving requires the development of new thoughts or concepts.

12. When you first read the "cheap necklace" problem you are in the _initial state_ of problem solving.

13. Experiments with the "cheap necklace" problem have shown that subjects who took a _break_ did significantly better than subjects who didn't.

14. Finding the solution to a problem more rapidly upon returning to it than had you been working on it all along demonstrates the _incubation_ effect.

15. Computers "solve" problems by using _algorithms_ , while human beings usually attempt to use _heuristics_ , which aren't as _systematic_ .

16. People using heuristics often rely on _similarity_ to the

final _goal_ in order to choose their next step. This is not always efficient, however, as the maze problem demonstrated.

17. Newell and Simon have developed a computer program they call the _general_ _problem_ _solver_ (or GPS).

18. The GPS is a planning and strategy computer program that uses a _means_ - _end_ analysis heuristic. It requires you to proceed from where you are to the _goal_ through _intermediate_ steps until the goal is reached.

19. The _Luchin_ water jug problems demonstrated how _mental_ _set_ may impede problem solving. The effects of mental set can cause us to ignore the _obvious_.

20. The nine dot problem often is hard to solve because people have a _mental_ _set_ to stay within the imagined _boundaries_.

21. A form of mental set known as _functional_ _fixedness_ occurs when we cannot see a creative or novel use for familiar objects.

22. _routine_ problem solving is often facilitated by _mental_ _set_ and _functional_ _fixedness_, whereas _creative_ _problem_ _solving_ is generally not facilitated by them.

23. In his book Zen and the Art of Motorcycle Maintenance, Robert Pirsig describes the phenomenon of being _stuck_.

24. Pirsig points out that the _scientific_ method is useful for hindsight, but not helpful for developing _hypothesis_.

25. Experts have stored in their memory many different _routines_ ways of solving _problems_.

26. A dog bringing its leash to its master provides an example of _communication_ without the use of _language_.

27. A language requires the use of _signs_ or _symbols_ within a _grammar_ and enables you to create _novel_ constructions.

28. _Benjamin_ _Whorf_ argued that language can influence, modify, or limit thinking because of the words and concepts available in the language. He proposed the hypothesis of _linguistic_ _relativity_.

29. According to the Whorfian hypothesis the _Eskimos_ were aware of many variations of snow because of the _words_ available to them in their _language_ .

30. The Dani language contains _Two_ color words.

31. The Whorfian hypothesis would suggest that English speaking people would be able to distinguish the eleven _focal_ _colors_ better than the Dani! Experiments testing this found the Dani were able to distinguish many _colors_ . These results suggest that Dani and English-speaking subjects make color distinctions independent of their _language_ .

32. Newborn infants do not possess _language_ .

33. _phonemes_ are the smallest units of speech that can be discriminated. These begin to appear in human beings at the age of _6_ or _7_ months.

34. Anthropologists have determined that infants younger than _6_ _months_ may be incapable of making the sounds necessary for _language_ .

35. During an infant's babbling stage" his phonetic repertoire increases as _phonetic_ _expansion_ takes place.

36. Studies of hearing children of _deaf_ parents support the notion that _babbling_ is genetically triggered and independent of _experience_ .

37. One of the first detectible linguistic differences that infants display during language development is _tonality_ .

38. During the later stages of the babbling stage infants who have been exposed to a _tonal_ language often engage in _pitch_ modulation; thus, acquisition of _inflections_ may be one of the earliest language developments.

39. _phonetic_ _contraction_ occurs when infants narrow their use of phonemes to the ones they will later use.

40. If you can imitate a _accent_ , then you have learned the _phonemes_ of that language.

41. Typically, children speak their first _word_ by the age of ten months to a year. Children seem to acquire _concrete_ nouns and _verbs_ first. The _abstract_ words occur later and tend to start with _adjectives_ such as tall, red, or little.

42. The typical one-year-old uses words _individually_ rather than in _sentences_. This time period is known as the _one_ - _word_ stage.

43. The _syntax_ of a language refers to rules that describe how words may be put together to form sentences. _grammar_ includes both syntax and phonology. The study of how sounds or phonemes are put together to form words is known as _phonology_.

44. Children in the one-word stage, while unable to construct sentences, have demonstrated some _syntax_ through their ability to comprehend _sentences_ addressed to them.

45. When we look at children's one-word speech _vertically_ rather than _horizontally_ some evidence of early syntactic structure has been noted.

46. Recent investigations of children's responses to _sentences_ during the one-word stage and the way in which they order their _one_ - _word_ utterances suggests that children are forming hypotheses about how to put words together and make sentences.

47. Most children have acquired or mastered over _two_ _hundred_ words by the time they begin to speak sentences.

48. Generally, between the ages of 18 to 20 months, children enter the _two_ - _word_ _stage_ and begin to utter two-word statements.

49. No three-word stage seems to exist. Following the two-word stage children create many short _sentences_ and word combinations referred to as _telegraphic_ speech by Roger Brown.

50. _function_ "words" are missing in telegraphic speech. During this stage children adopt a grammar of rigid word order with the _subject_ placed before the _verb_.

51. The development of grammar is closely associated with _semantics_, which refers to the meaning in a language.

52. Between the ages of two-and-a-half and five children the _world_ over start using _function_ "words" to add meaning to their sentences.

53. The fact that children understand rules of language, and are not just repeating words, was shown in the experiment in which _wugs_ were identified.

54. Whenever adults talk with children they typically restructure their language into short, simple sentences known as _caretaker speech_, which is more complex than _baby talk_.

55. Caretaker speech allows children to learn _language_ more easily.

56. Linguists study _language_.

57. People create the _syntax_ of a sentence so that it expresses a _meaning_, and they appear to do so before speaking.

58. Transposing words or accidentally rearranging words is known as a _Spoonerism_, named after William A. _Spooner_, an English clergyman.

59. The study of Spoonerisms has demonstrated that people construct their _sentences_ before they say them.

60. Noam Chomsky, a _psycholinguist_, has developed _Transformational grammar_ theory.

61. Chomsky believes we do not retain the grammatical structure, or as he calls it, the _surface structure_, but rather we transform grammar into another form he calls _deep structures_. One surface structure can have several possible _deep structures_.

62. The Kennedy twins displayed "_twin_ speech", which is quite _rare_.

63. Chomsky takes the _nativist_ position, as opposed to the learning theorist position, regarding how we develop _language_. He hypothesizes that humans have what he calls a _language acquisition approach_ by which people are "prewired" biogenetically for _language_ acquisition.

64. In the 1950s the Hayeses attempted to teach _Vicki_, a _chimp_, to talk.

65. The Gardners taught a chimpanzee named _Washoe_ to "speak" or communicate using _American sign language_, or ASL.

66. _Francine Patterson_ studied language acquisition in a _gorilla_ named Koko who mastered _four hundred_ signs.

67. Koko appears to have developed ___syntax___ and a number of novel constructions like " ___lemon___ " o'clock.

68. Both the great apes' ability to learn ___language___ and their inability to match the complexity of human language, support an ___interactionist___ position.

69. The interactionist position is that both ___learning___ ability and ___brain___ organization are important factors in acquiring language.

70. Terrace argues that language acquisition in the great apes is just ___instrumental___ conditioning produced by inadvertent cueing.

71. In the 1860s a French physician, ___Paul___ ___Broca___, discovered that damage to the ___left___ side of the ___frontal___ lobes causes ___aphasia___, a speech disorder.

72. Damage to ___Broca's___ area causes aphasia, in which people have difficulty expressing themselves in fully formed or ___grammatical___ sentences.

73. Wernicke's area is located in the ___left___ side of the brain, mostly in the ___temporal___ lobe, and is connected to Broca's area by the ___arcuate___ ___fasciculus___.

74. People with Broca's aphasia have impaired ___articulation___, and slow labored speech.

75. People with Wernicke's aphasia have ___grammatically___ normal speech, but the ___semantic___ content is bizarre.

76. The ___angular___ ___gyrus___ transforms a visual image of a word into an ___auditory___ form.

77. If the arcuate fasciculus is destroyed or damaged, ___semantic___ content may be severely affected.

78. Damage to the angular gyrus does not affect the ___spoken___ word, only the ___written___ word. This may explain the disorder known as ___dyslexia___.

79. ___Peter___ ___Goldmark___ was a creative problem solver who invented the color television and long ___playing___ ___record___.

SELF TEST I

1. The researcher who studied Sultan's "insight" solution to the two
    stick problem was
    a. John Watson   c. Noam Chomsky
    b. Wolfgang Kohler   d. None of the above

2. The experiment described in the text that used a curare derivative
    to paralyze a subject demonstrated that
    a. problem solving could not take place under the effects of
       curare
    b. thinking was not a muscular activity
    c. mental set was in fact a real phenomenon
    d. none of the above

3. A /an _____ requires a systematic search of every possible
    avenue or approach towards solving a problem.
    a. algorithm   c. insight
    b. heuristic   d. novel construction

4. The solution discussed in the text of using a soft bathtub or shower
    was reached through
    a. insight   c. algorithms
    b. means-end analysis   d. surface structure

5. The textbook example of the two string problem, that was solved with
    the use of the pliers, illustrated the phenomenon of
    a. incubation effect   c. functional fixedness
    b. dyslexia   d. none of the above

6. Your textbook suggests that when you become stuck the most success-
    ful solution may often be to consult an expert.
    a. true   b. false

7. The individual who proposed that language affects people's thoughts
    and perceptions of the world (linguistic relativity) was
    a. Benjamin Whorf   c. Noam Chomsky
    b. Franklin Bass   d. Vicki Washoe

8. If the Whorfian hypothesis is wrong then Eskimos have acquired so many
    snow terms due to the great variety of snow in their environment, and
    not due to their language.
    a. true   b. false

9. By the time human beings are two months old they begin to produce a
    wide range of phonetic sounds.
    a. true   b. false

10. Comedians who imitate various languages and accents rely on

a. actual foreign words   c. phonemes
b. foreign sentences   d. both a and b

11. During the one-word stage
    a. the first true sentences are spoken
    b. telegraphic speech begins
    c. both a and b
    d. none of the above

12. Recent studies have confirmed that children in the one-word stage
    are only learning the names of various objects, actions, or concepts
    and actually do not understand what their word means.
    a. true   b. false

13. Children eventually acquire _____ that adults commonly use to
    express meaning and convey information.
    a. rigid word order   c. function "words"
    b. phonetic expansion   d. none of the above

14. One way we have learned that people begin to form their sentences
    before they say them is by examining
    a. Spoonerisms
    b. mental set
    c. telegraphic speech
    d. primate speech

15. Wernicke's area is located in the _____ side of the
    brain in the _____ lobe(s).
    a. right, parietal
    b. left, frontal
    c. left, temporal and parietal
    d. left, frontal and occipital

SELF TEST II

1. Psychologists study thinking, problem solving, and language because
   these are the very essence of the human experience.
   a. true   b. false

2. Problem solving
   a. can be routine   c. requires you to achieve a goal
   b. can be creative   d. all of the above

3. Heuristics, as opposed to algorithms
   a. are often used by people to solve problems
   b. are sometimes faster at reaching a solution
   c. often require taking steps that seem most likely to approach the goal
   d. all of the above

4. The nine dot problem shown in the text illustrated
    a. routine problem solving   c. mental set
    b. incubation effects   d. all of the above

5. It has been found that no amount of experience can overcome functional fixedness.
    a. true   b. false

6. _____ allows you to use signs or symbols within a grammar to create a _____.
    a. learning, focal color
    b. language, novel construction
    c. semantics, mental set
    d. genetics, semantic code

7. In English some colors are basic and are described by short, simple words. These are known as the
    a. primary colors   c. focal colors
    b. basic 10   d. all of the above

8. The English language makes use of 26 letters and _____ phonemes.
    a. 100   c. 250
    b. 14   d. 46

9. The babbling stage
    a. begins when phonetic expansion occurs
    b. would initially sound the same among infants the world over
    c. comes to an end between 9 and 14 months
    d. all of the above

10. Children seem to acquire _____ and _____ first.
    a. concrete nouns, verbs
    b. abstract adjectives, verbs
    c. abstract nouns, adjectives
    d. concrete nouns, prepositions

11. Grammar is a broader term than _____ because it includes both _____ and _____.
    a. linguistics, syntax, phonology
    b. phonology, phonology, semantics
    c. syntax, syntax, phonology
    d. language, speaking, writing

12. The stage following the two-word stage has been labeled by Roger Brown as the
    a. three-word stage
    b. third-order stage
    c. novel construction stage
    d. none of the above

13.   Children using telegraphic speech <u>need</u> to use rigid word order to convey clearer meaning to their words.
    a. true   b. false

14.   The linguist who proposed the transformational grammar theory was
    a. Roger Brown   c. Beatrice Gardner
    b. Noam Chomsky   d. Francine Patterson

15.   The bundle of nerve fibers that connects Wernicke's area to Broca's area is called the
    a. corpus callosum   c. arcuate fasciculus
    b. language channel   d. geniculate nucleus

ESSAY QUESTIONS

1.   Describe how Watson's "subvocal speech" explanation was refuted.

2.   Construct a solution to a problem not covered in the textbook using means-end analysis.

3.   Explain the difference between mental set and functional fixedness and identify when they are most likely to have an adverse effect.

4.   Describe the experiment with the Dani and focal colors and explain how the results support or refute Whorf's linguistic relativity hypothesis.

5.   Describe the efforts to teach language to the great apes. Describe an interactionist position concerning this issue.

ANSWER SECTION

Guided Review
1.   *Kohler, Sultan, insight*
2.   *insight, two sticks*
3.   *thinking, problem solving, language*
4.   *thinking, symbols, objects, concepts*
5.   *subvocal speech*
6.   *curare, mental*
7.   *concept, properties (or characteristics)*
8.   *concrete, abstract*
9.   *concepts, classify (or categorize)*
10.   *problem solving*
11.   *routine, creative*
12.   *initial state*
13.   *break*
14.   *incubation*

15. *algorithms, heuristics, systematic*
16. *similarity, final goal*
17. *general problem solver*
18. *means-end, goal, intermediate*
19. *Luchin, mental set, obvious*
20. *mental set, boundaries*
21. *functional fixedness*
22. *routine, mental set, functional fixedness, creative problem solving*
23. *stuck*
24. *scientific, hypotheses*
25. *routine, problems*
26. *communication, language*
27. *signs, symbols, grammar, novel*
28. *Benjamin Whorf, linguistic relativity*
29. *Eskimos, words, language*
30. *two*
31. *focal colors, colors, language*
32. *language*
33. *phonemes, 6, 7*
34. *6 months, language*
35. *phonetic expansion*
36. *deaf, babbling, experience*
37. *tonality*
38. *tonal, pitch, inflections*
39. *phonetic contraction*
40. *accent, phonemes*
41. *word, concrete, verbs, abstract, adjectives*
42. *individually (or alone), sentences, one-word*
43. *syntax, grammar, phonology*
44. *syntax, sentences*
45. *vertically, horizontally*
46. *sentences, single (or one)-word*
47. *two hundred*
48. *two-word stage*
49. *sentences, telegraphic*
50. *function, subject, verb*
51. *semantics*
52. *world, function*
53. *wugs*
54. *caretaker speech, baby talk*
55. *language*
56. *language*
57. *syntax, meaning*
58. *spoonerism, Spooner*
59. *sentences*
60. *psycholinguist, transformational grammar*
61. *surface structure, deep structure, deep structures*
62. *twin, rare*
63. *nativist, language, language acquisition device, language*

64.   *Vicki, chimpanzee*
65.   *Washoe, American Sign Language*
66.   *Francine Patterson, gorilla, four hundred*
67.   *syntax (or language), lemon*
68.   *language, interactionist*
69.   *learning, brain (or neural)*
70.   *instrumental*
71.   *Paul Broca, left, frontal, aphasia*
72.   *Broca's, grammatical*
73.   *left, temporal, arcuate fasciculus*
74.   *articulation*
75.   *grammatically, semantic*
76.   *angular gyrus, auditory*
77.   *semantic*
78.   *spoken, written, dyslexia*
79.   *Peter Goldmark, playing record*

Self Test I

1.   b
2.   b
3.   a
4.   b
5.   c
6.   a
7.   a
8.   a
9.   b
10. c
11. d
12. b
13. c
14. a
15. c

Self Test II

1.   a
2.   d
3.   d
4.   c
5.   b
6.   b
7.   c
8.   d
9.   d
10. a
11. c
12. d
13. a
14. b
15. c

CHAPTER 9

Motivation

BEHAVIORAL OBJECTIVES

After completing this chapter, the student should be able to:

1. Compare the concept of homeostasis to a thermostat.
2. Evaluate past and current findings pertaining to the hypothalamocentric hypothesis of hunger motivation.
3. Explain thirst in terms of intracellular and extracellular mechanisms.
4. Contrast Schachter's internally-externally controlled findings on obesity with explanations related more to bodily factors and conditions (i.e., brown fat, temperature, sodium-potassium pumps, etc.).
5. Discuss the sex drive in humans and animals with reference to the chemical and hormonal factors involved.
6. Explain the sociobiological view of motivation.
7. List three stimulus motives and describe the effects of sensory deprivation.
8. Draw a pyramid showing Maslow's hierarchy of motives.
9. Clarify what is meant by the expression, "a grand theory of motivation."
10. Tell someone about learned helplessness studies involving rats, human infants, and fifth grade students.
11. Name two motives studied in detail by researcher David McClelland, and describe his findings.
12. Explain why it is not always a good idea to give a tangible reward to someone who is behaving in a desirable manner.
13. Compare and contrast a person who is future oriented with one who is living in an expanded present.
14. Explain Solomon's theory (which says a terrifying experience can result in great happiness, and an exhilarating experience can lead to unhappiness) using the concept of emotional contrast.

KEY TERMS AND CONCEPTS

biological motives   need

drive
homeostasis
homeostatic mechanism
satiation
hypothalamocentric hypothesis
VMH
dorosolateral portion of the
   hypothalamus
aphagia
adipsia
duodenum, liver, glucose
rate of metabolism
obese
internal and external cues
"internal-external" hypothesis
  for obesity
fat cells
sodium-potassium pumps
brown fat
CCK
intracellular mechanisms
extracellular mechanisms
sex drive
testosterone
pheromone
sociobiology
DNA
stimulus motives

sensory isolation/deprivation
Yerkes-Dodson (law)
learned motivation
social motivation
Maslow's hierarchy of motives
learned helplessness
locus of control
psychological reticence
learned industriousness
power motive
personal enclave pattern
imperial motivation group
conquistador pattern
need for achievement (n-Ach)
achieving society theory
intrinsic motivation
altruism
extrinsic motivation
token economies
social-temporal theory of motivation
future-oriented
expanded present
Zen masters
habituation
opponent process theory of motivation
affective or emotional contrast
critical decay duration

NAMES TO REMEMBER

Harry Harlow
Stanley Schachter
Edward Wilson
Abraham Maslow

David McClelland
David Winter
Philip Zimbardo
Richard L. Solomon

GUIDED REVIEW

1. Psychologists study motivation to discover _____ a
   behavior occurs.

2. As a need increases, the _____ or _____
   to satisfy that need also increases.

3. The only way to see motivations is to _____ the behavior
   that is generated by them.

4. Biological motivations like hunger and thirst exist from _____, that is, they don't have to be _____.

5. The built-in regulatory system that attempts to maintain the status quo is called _____.

6. A need usually produces a _____, which is the motivational force for action.

7. The homeostatic mechanism for food intake in most people is extremely _____.

8. Patients whose stomachs have been removed still feel _____ and _____.

9. Evidence indicates that the homeostatic mechanism for hunger may be located in the _____ of the brain.

10. One study shows that cuts or lesions in a rat's VMH resulted in _____.

11. Lesions in a rat's lateral hypothalamus resulted in an animal which would not eat (called _____) and would not drink (called _____).

12. A satiated monkey who received hypothalamic liquid and tissue from a food deprived monkey (injected into the area of the hypothalamus) became _____ immediately.

13. One researcher argued that the hypothalamus is not related to hunger and thirst, but is merely an "_____ _____."

14. Receptors which act as hunger sensors may be located in the _____ and the _____ (which then transmit information along the _____ nerve to the hypothalamus).

15. Recent research suggests that the hypothalamus really is a _____ and _____ center and not just a center for activation.

16. Stanley Schachter's research indicated that overweight people attend more to _____ cues in the environment, and normal weight people attend to _____ cues to tell them when to eat.

17. Obese subjects ate more when accelerated clocks neared "_____."

18. The internal-external dichotomy is overly _____.

19. The number of fat cells a person has is determined by (a) _____ and by (b) the amount of _____ the person gets during infancy.

20. Many overweight people have fewer chemical _____ - _____ pumps. The more _____ a person has the more _____ per day will be burned.

21. People with _____ body temperatures may be more likely to be obese.

22. "_____" fat keeps body temperature high and burns excess calories.

23. Appetite can be stimulated by _____ the hypothalamus.

24. Evidence exists that many obese people have a _____ _____ not caused by overeating or excess weight.

25. The hormone _____ is secreted by the gastrointestinal tract and apparently signals the brain to stop eating.

26. One fourth of body water is located in the spaces between _____, two thirds is within the _____, and one twelfth is in the _____.

27. Two types of sensor mechanisms relating to thirst regulation are _____ and _____ mechanisms.

28. Loss of blood and diarrhea affect _____ fluid.

29. Rats with frontal area brain damage will drink only if the _____ fluid level is reduced. This suggests _____ control mechanisms for each of the fluid level locations.

30. Injections of _____ directly into the lateral hypothalamus produces _____.

31. The more physiologically advanced a species is, the less its _____ behavior is governed directly by hormones.

32. Sexual activity in males _____ with age. However, _____ levels do not decrease as males age. Sexually active 70-year-olds have _____ testosterone levels.

33. In lower animals the male sex hormone, _____, is directly related to male sexual behaviors for both _____ and _____ animals.

34. Female animals often secrete a _____ which sexually attracts the male of the species. In humans, _____ have not been conclusively identified.

35. Recent research suggests monkeys and humans may prefer certain times for sex based, at least in part, on _____ secreted by the female.

36. Studies have shown that both monkeys and humans become _____ with their sexual partners after long periods of time with them.

37. To maintain sexual interest in a monogamous society it may be necessary to use interesting _____, _____, _____, and particularly _____ during which sex is avoided.

38. Theorists who believe that all human behavior is motivated only by the need to pass on genes to the next generation are called _____.

39. Many people find the idea of sociobiology _____ and _____.

40. The motives to obtain sensory stimulation, to be active, to explore, and to manipulate things are called _____ motives.

41. Subjects placed in a dark, soundproof room with their limbs padded may experience _____ _____.

42. Sensory deprived people often _____ and create their own sensations.

43. Yerkes and Dodson suggested that the most efficient performance occurs at a _____ level of arousal.

44. It is possible to _____ to become hungry by pairing the thought of food with insulin production through classical conditioning.

45. Motives acquired through learning and culture are referred to by the term "_____ _____."

46. One of the most popular "grand theories" of motivation is Maslow's _____ of motives.

47. In Maslow's motivational format, the _____ motives are
     the most basic and most demanding in the hierarchy.

48. The motivation to realize one's full potential is called _____
     _____.

49. Grand theories like Maslow's often _____ to predict
     individual circumstances and situations, and therefore modern motiva-
     tional theory generally focuses on _____ areas rather than
     attempting to develop one grand theory.

50. Rats shocked on both sides of a two-compartment box, human infants
     who can't control their mobiles, and various minority groups with an
     external locus of control may all have developed _____
     _____.

51. Learned helplessness tends to _____ to new situations.

52. People and animals who have little opportunity to control their environ-
     ment and who are always having things done to them or for them,
     quickly learn not to _____.

53. If you feel you are in charge of your environment and have control
     over it, you have an _____ locus of control.

54. Learned helplessness begins to set in only after psychological
     _____ has repeatedly failed.

55. Some researchers have been successful in teaching those who have
     learned to be helpless that they can be _____. This has
     been called learned _____.

56. McClelland found that the more alcohol a person drank, the more
     _____ images he or she imagined.

57. The need to have impact, control, and influence on others is the defini-
     tion of _____ motivation.

58. People who have high power motivation, a low need to be with others,
     and little inhibition in using power were classifed by McClelland as
     exhibiting the "_____ pattern."

59. Some people responding to photographs or drawings demonstrated a
     high need to _____ (abbreviated by McClelland N-Ach).

60. People with a high need to achieve tend to do _____
     in school than those with a low need.

61. An _____ act is one that is not motivated by self interest.

62. In many cases, _____ motivation is superior to _____ motivation in creating and maintaining behavior.

63. Fifth graders who were told they were neat and tidy people littered _____ than those who were given reasons why they should not litter.

64. Rewarding children for drawing actually undermined the _____ motivation behind the drawing; as a result, they drew _____ than children who had never been _____.

65. People in mental institutions who are rewarded with tokens for appropriate behavior are involved in a _____ _____.

66. Using tokens may undermine behavior that is already _____ motivated.

67. Two recent "grand" theories of motivation are Zimbardo's _____-_____ theory and Solomon's _____-_____ theory of motivation.

68. Zimbardo's social-temporal theory is based on people's perception of _____.

69. Organized people with a high need to achieve are very _____-oriented.

70. People from lower class backgrounds and also Zen masters are often _____-oriented.

71. American schools train children to be highly _____-oriented.

72. Among Zen masters, _____ is very difficult to attain (or is nearly nonexistent).

73. Drugs, sex, music, vandalism, and crime are more characteristic of a _____ orientation.

74. Excessive worry is characteristic of a _____ orientation.

75. By using _____ a person's time orientation can be changed.

76. One researcher thinks learned disabled children are living in an expanded _____ and are not motivated because they don't perceive the _____ as most people have been taught.

77. The central theme of Solomon's opponent process theory is that most learned motivations are _____.

78. The fact that pleasure can eventually lead to sadness, and pain can eventually lead to happiness illustrates Solomon's concept of emotional _____.

79. The four stages of emotional contrast are (1) initial resting state, (2) the A process, or first _____ peak, (3) the B process, which is the _____ – _____, and (4) a return to the _____ state.

80. If the A process is extremely stimulating, the B process is likely to be _____ _____ in the _____ direction.

81. Survivors of a suicide leap from the Golden Gate Bridge said they were now _____ and _____ their lives.

82. Solomon noted that in repeating a behavior the initial A state becomes _____ potent and the B state actually _____.

83. "A" will become weaker and "B" stronger only if the behavior is repeated over and over. This won't happen if there is a long enough time interval between the experiences. Solomon called this phenomenon the _____ _____ _____ of the opponent process.

SELF TEST I

1. Monkeys who were given raisins for working puzzles
   a. were unable to learn any of them except the two-piece jigsaw type
   b. acquired human-like puzzle-solving ability
   c. became angry and upset when given puzzles and no raisins
   d. actually learned them faster than monkeys who were given chocolate M & M's.

2. People who have had their stomachs removed
   a. still experience hunger
   b. no longer have hunger sensations
   c. have the experience of satiation, but very little hunger
   d. have not been studied sufficiently to draw any valid conclusions about whether or not they feel hungry.

3. Stanley Schachter reported that overweight subjects were more responsive to _____ than were subjects of normal weight in their eating behaviors.

a. internal cues   c. the sight of food
b. the passage of time   d. both b and c

4. Thirst
   a. increases if salt is injected into the hypothalamus
   b. is a homeostatic mechanism controlled by the brain, hormones, and organs far from the brain
   c. is complex and not fully understood
   d. all of the above

5. Which of the following has been suggested by researchers to maintain sexual interest in a monogamous society?
   a. interesting clothing   c. lulls of no sex
   b. interesting hairstyles   d. all of the above

6. Stimulus motives appear to be
   a. learned
   b. unlearned
   c. both a and b
   d. none of the above; stimulus motives are not discussed with reference to the processes of learning

7. In Maslow's system the highest level needs (wherein you are concerned with developing your full potential) are referred to as _____ needs.
   a. love and belonging
   b. self-esteem and esteem
   c. self-actualization
   d. none of the above

8. Infants who were given control over their mobiles at the beginning of a 14-week study
   a. learned to turn their heads to make the mobile work
   b. failed to learn to operate the mobile
   c. learned to make the mobile move by making gurgling noises through an intercom system
   d. failed to learn to operate the mobile with their heads, but after extensive training did so with their feet

9. A need to have an impact on others and to control and influence them
   a. is the definition of power motivation
   b. reflects Maslow's third level in the need hierarchy
   c. refers to the drive for success
   d. both a and b

10. Which of the following investigators has been very prominent in his studies of the need to achieve?
    a. Yerkes and Dodson   c. Stanley Schachter
    b. David McClelland   d. Philip Zimbardo

11. After drawing for a time, some children were given a good player certificate as a reward for drawing. The children who did not get the reward were _____ likely to draw _____ those who got the reward.
     a. more, than
     b. less, than
     c. equally, as
     d. none of the above; the children who were not rewarded became angry and refused to draw anymore

12. Which of the following kinds of people are very future-oriented?
     a. those with a high need to achieve
     b. those who are very organized
     c. people who are highly influenced by the desires of gambling casino operators
     d. both a and b

13. The sense of exhilaration and jubilance that follows the terrifying experience of a first-time parachute jump is called
     a. emotional contrast   c. extrinsic motivation
     b. habituation   d. affective rebound

14. According to Solomon, when people engage repeatedly in the same kind of emotional contrast, the A state _____ while the B state _____ .
     a. becomes less potent, actually grows
     b. actually grows, becomes less potent
     c. becomes less potent, becomes less potent
     d. actually grows, actually grows

15. The behavior of the young man who was hit by lightning on the golf course illustrated
     a. a future orientation time frame
     b. emotional contrast
     c. compensatory behavior under stress
     d. both b and c

SELF TEST II

1. A built-in regulatory system that attempts to maintain the status quo is known as
    a. biological motivation   c. both a and b
    b. homeostasis   d. none of the above

2. One argument against the hypothalamocentric hypothesis of eating behavior was developed by Valenstein and contended that the hypothalamus is not directly an eating center but is merely a/an _____ center.

a. drinking
b. waking

c. activating
d. orienting

3. Thirst regulation is controlled by _____ mechanisms.
   a. intracellular
   b. extracellular

   c. both a and b
   d. none of the above

4. In lower animal species, a substance called _____,
   which sexually attracts the male, is often secreted by the female.
   a. testosterone
   b. pheromone

   c. CCK
   d. GABA

5. The concepts of sociobiology
   a. are disturbing to many people
   b. maintain that love and kindness are selfish genetic acts
   c. both a and b
   d. none of the above

6. Drinking behavior is
   a. affected by learning
   b. an internal biological drive
   c. both a and b
   d. none of the above; drinking behavior is strictly homeostatic

7. Rats who are shocked on both sides of a two-compartment box
   a. soon give up jumping to the other side
   b. learn to be helpless
   c. give up swimming when placed in water-filled mazes
   d. all of the above

8. If you believe that the locus of control resides in _____
   then you are likely to _____.
   a. the environment, experience learned helplessness
   b. the environment, try harder to reach your goals
   c. you, experience learned helplessness
   d. none of the above

9. People who have a low need to be with others and are very willing to
   use their power were classified by McClelland as the
   a. personal enclave pattern
   b. imperial motivation group
   c. conquistador pattern
   d. alcohol induced superman pattern

10. An act of sharing that is not motivated by self interest is said to be
    a. egocentric
    b. altruistic

    c. hedonistic
    d. heliocentric

11. Which of the following is considered to be a <u>modern</u> "grand" theory
     of human motivation?
     a. McClelland's need to achieve theory
     b. Solomon's opponent-process theory
     c. Seligman's learned helplessness theory
     d. Maslow's hierarchical theory

12. It has been suggested that learning disabled children may be living in
     a. the past
     b. an expanded present
     c. the future
     d. both b and c

13. In Solomon's theory, if the A process is extremely stimulating, then
     the B process is likely to be _____ stimulating.
     a. mildly
     b. moderately
     c. extremely
     d. all of the above depending on the type of extremely stimulating
        A process being experienced

14. To engage in an addicting behavior repeatedly with very little time in
     between will
     a. avoid the critical decay duration
     b. enhance the addiction
     c. produce an emotional contrast in which the A process becomes weaker
        and the B process stronger
     d. all of the above

15. Your pet rat was attacked last month by the family cat. Although you
     heard the squealing and intervened, the rat was pretty badly hurt by
     the time you got there. The rat is recovering nicely now but seems
     to have a ravenous appetite and can't get enough to eat. You suspect
     a. a severed vagus nerve
     b. brain damage in the VMH
     c. lesions in the dorsolateral portion of the hypothalamus
     d. aphagia

ESSAY QUESTIONS

1. What is the role of the hypothalamus in hunger motivation? Include
    past and current findings in your discussion.

2. Compare the effects of chemical and hormonal forces including phero-
    mones on the sex drives of humans and animals.

3. Explain in detail Maslow's hierarchical theory of motivation. Mention
    strengths and criticisms of the theory.

4.   Discuss learned helplessness, give examples, and show how the concept may apply to those in institutions.

5.   Outline and briefly discuss the key features of Zimbardo's social-temporal theory and Solomon's opponent process theory of motivation.

ANSWER SECTION

Guided Review
1.   *why*
2.   *motivation, drive*
3.   *observe (or watch)*
4.   *birth, learned*
5.   *homeostasis*
6.   *drive*
7.   *sensitive*
8.   *hunger, satiation*
9.   *hypothalamus*
10.   *overeating (or obesity)*
11.   *aphagia, adipsia*
12.   *hungry*
13.   *activating center*
14.   *duodenum, liver, vagus*
15.   *hunger, thirst*
16.   *external, internal*
17.   *lunchtime*
18.   *simplistic*
19.   *inheritance (or heredity), feeding (or food)*
20.   *sodium-potassium, pumps, calories*
21.   *cooler*
22.   *brown*
23.   *cooling*
24.   *biochemical defect*
25.   *cholecystokinin (or CCK)*
26.   *cells, cells, blood*
27.   *intracellular, extracellular*
28.   *extracellular*
29.   *extracellular, different*
30.   *salt, drinking*
31.   *sexual*
32.   *decreases, testosterone, higher*
33.   *testosterone, male, female*
34.   *pheromone, pheromones*
35.   *hormones*
36.   *bored*
37.   *perfumes, clothing, hairstyles, lulls*
38.   *sociobiologists*
39.   *shocking, disturbing*

40. *stimulus*
41. *sensory deprivation (or isolation)*
42. *hallucinate*
43. *medium (or middle)*
44. *learn*
45. *social motivation*
46. *hierarchy*
47. *physiological*
48. *self actualization*
49. *fail, separate*
50. *learned helplessness*
51. *generalize*
52. *try*
53. *internal*
54. *reticence*
55. *successful, industriousness*
56. *power*
57. *power*
58. *conquistador*
59. *achieve*
60. *better*
61. *altruistic*
62. *intrinsic, extrinsic*
63. *less*
64. *intrinsic, less, rewarded*
65. *token economy*
66. *intrinsically*
67. *social-temporal, opponent-process*
68. *time*
69. *future*
70. *present*
71. *future*
72. *habituation*
73. *present*
74. *future*
75. *hypnosis*
76. *present, future*
77. *addictions*
78. *contrast*
79. *emotional (or affective), after-reaction, resting*
80. *extremely stimulating, opposite*
81. *happy, enjoyed*
82. *less, grows*
83. *critical decay duration*

Self Test I
  1. c
  2. a
  3. d

Self Test II
  1. b
  2. c
  3. c

4.	d	4.	b
5.	d	5.	c
6.	b	6.	c
7.	c	7.	d
8.	a	8.	a
9.	a	9.	c
10.	b	10.	b
11.	a	11.	b
12.	d	12.	b
13.	a	13.	c
14.	a	14.	d
15.	b	15.	b

CHAPTER 10

Emotion

BEHAVIORAL OBJECTIVES

After completing this chapter, the student should be able to:

1. Summarize Stuart Valins' research with false feedback and emotional assessment.
2. Describe the role of the autonomic nervous system in emotional arousal and list the reactions controlled by the autonomic nervous system.
3. List the physiological measurements typically found on a polygraph.
4. Give the major problems associated with the validity of polygraph tests.
5. List and briefly summarize the four theories of aggression and violence described in the text.
6. Contrast the common-sense theory of emotion with the James-Lange theory of emotion.
7. Describe the Cannon-Bard theory of emotion and state how contemporary research has failed to support it.
8. Summarize Stanley Schachter's cognitive theory of emotion.
9. List the universal facial displays of emotion.
10. Explain S. S. Tomkins' study and state its implications.
11. Outline the research on assessing nonverbal cues.
12. Explain Robert Plutchik's psychoevolutionary synthesis of emotion.
13. Describe Plutchik's wheel of emotion and distinguish primary from secondary emotions.
14. List and give the descriptions of Plutchik's functions associated with the primary emotions.
15. Explain Plutchik's theory as it pertains to his map of emotional intensities.

KEY TERMS AND CONCEPTS

false emotional feedback	polygraph
emotion	lie detector
empathy	GSR

frustration-aggression hypothesis
ethological theory of aggression
physiological theory of aggression
learning theory of aggression
common-sense theory of emotion
James-Lange theory of emotion
Schachter's cognitive theory
    of emotion
Tomkins' facial feedback
    theory of emotion
nonverbal cues
Plutchik's psychoevolutionary
    synthesis of emotion

primary emotions
Plutchik's wheel of emotion
functional aspects of emotion
protection
destruction
incorporation
rejection
reproduction
reintegration
orientation
exploration

NAMES TO REMEMBER

Stuart Valins
William James
Carl Lange
Walter Cannon
Phillip Bard

Stanley Schachter
S. S. Tomkins
Robert Plutchik
Charles Darwin
Gordon Bower

GUIDED REVIEW

1. _Stuart_ _Valins_ used a fake microphone to make subjects believe that they were hearing their own _heartbeats_ . He found that subjects preferred Playboy centerfolds who had been associated with bogus _emotional arousal_ .

2. Everyone has _emotions_ , even young babies. As adults we attend to emotions to discern _attitudes_ and _emotional_ _reactions_ .

3. It is frequently hard to describe your own emotions because emotional states are often a mixture of both _pleasant_ and _unpleasant_ feelings.

4. One psychologist has found over _four_ _hundred_ different English words that are used to describe emotions. Many of these words _overlap_ in meaning.

5. _Language_ is a poor indicator of people's emotionality.

6. Emotional behavior is displayed by both _animals_ and _human_ _beings_ . For example, a pigeon or a human being going through _extinction_ will often display emotional behavior.

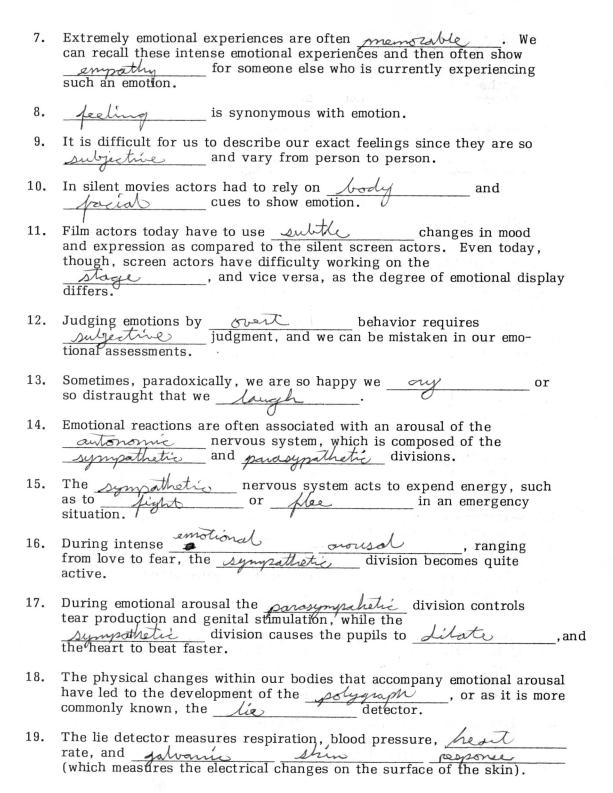

7. Extremely emotional experiences are often _memorable_. We can recall these intense emotional experiences and then often show _empathy_ for someone else who is currently experiencing such an emotion.

8. _feeling_ is synonymous with emotion.

9. It is difficult for us to describe our exact feelings since they are so _subjective_ and vary from person to person.

10. In silent movies actors had to rely on _body_ and _facial_ cues to show emotion.

11. Film actors today have to use _subtle_ changes in mood and expression as compared to the silent screen actors. Even today, though, screen actors have difficulty working on the _stage_, and vice versa, as the degree of emotional display differs.

12. Judging emotions by _overt_ behavior requires _subjective_ judgment, and we can be mistaken in our emotional assessments.

13. Sometimes, paradoxically, we are so happy we _cry_ or so distraught that we _laugh_.

14. Emotional reactions are often associated with an arousal of the _autonomic_ nervous system, which is composed of the _sympathetic_ and _parasympathetic_ divisions.

15. The _sympathetic_ nervous system acts to expend energy, such as to _fight_ or _flee_ in an emergency situation.

16. During intense _emotional_ _arousal_, ranging from love to fear, the _sympathetic_ division becomes quite active.

17. During emotional arousal the _parasympathetic_ division controls tear production and genital stimulation, while the _sympathetic_ division causes the pupils to _dilate_, and the heart to beat faster.

18. The physical changes within our bodies that accompany emotional arousal have led to the development of the _polygraph_, or as it is more commonly known, the _lie_ detector.

19. The lie detector measures respiration, blood pressure, _heart_ rate, and _galvanic_ _skin_ _response_ (which measures the electrical changes on the surface of the skin).

20. The lie detector does not really detect lies, but monitors
nervousness .

21. David Lykken has stated that lie detectors are accurate no more than
two - _thirds_ of the time and that their
most common error occurs when they indicate that a
truthful _person_ has lied.

22. The polygraph test can be faked by elevating the initial
baseline , or by taking _improbamate_ in which case
the chances are only _one_ in _five_ of
being caught telling a lie.

23. Cats and human beings can show emotional behaviors even if they
have never _observed_ them. This suggests that certain
emotional responses are _innate_ .

24. Many human emotional responses are not innate but have been shown
to be the result of _learning_ and culture.

25. The explanation of aggression that contends that aggression occurs
because goals are blocked or because of frustration is known as the
frustration - _aggression_ _hypothesis_ .

26. A theory of aggression and violence taken from ethology contends that
these behaviors occur because of _fixed_ ,
response _patterns_ of _aggression_
found in lower animals. Thus aggression is a natural
response to specific situations.

27. A physiological theory argues that aggression and violence result from
different levels of _hormones_ or _neurotransmitters_ in the
brain .

28. _Learning_ _theory_ argues that aggression and
violence are acquired by observing _aggressive_ models being
reinforced for aggression, and by having _pleasant_ stimuli
associated with aggression.

29. Human reactions to frustration do not seem to be explained by the
frustration _aggression_ _hypothesis_ .

30. Reactions to frustration appear to be more dependent on the
individual and the specific _situation_ .

31. Of all the theories explaining why people are aggressive and violent,
most researchers believe that _learning_ , especially
social _learning_ , are most important.

32. The theory of emotion that contends "we see the bear, are afraid, and then we run," is the *common* - *sense* theory of emotion.

33. The common-sense theory of emotion contends that an emotion must be *felt* before we can *react* *to* *it* .

34. William *James* and Carl *Lange* independently came up with the theory of emotion now known as the *James* - *Lange* theory of emotion.

35. The James-Lange theory suggests that different *visceral* and *muscular* reactions precede each emotion. Thus, the emotion *follows* behavioral responses rather than preceding the response as the *common* - *sense* theory would suggest.

36. "We see the bear, we run, and we feel fearful" would describe the *James* - *Lange* theory of emotion.

37. American physiologist Walter *Cannon* and his student Phillip *Bard* developed the *Cannon* - *Bard* theory of emotion in 1927.

38. The Cannon-Bard theory of emotion argues that visceral and *muscular* responses are not the cause of emotion as the James-Lange theory proposes. This theory argues that arousal and emotion occur *simultaneously* .

39. In 1962 Stanley Schachter developed a theory of emotion in which he proposed that *different* labels may be placed on similar states of arousal depending on how the *situation* is assessed.

40. To test his theory Schachter gave subjects large doses of *adrenaline* , causing subjects to feel a strong state of *psychological* *arousal* . The experiment included two groups of subjects; one group was *informed* , while the second group was *misinformed* about the effects of the supposed vision improving substance.

41. In the Schachter experiment subjects who were *misinformed* became *happy* in the presence of the happy actor and *angry* in the presence of the angry actor. Thus in these subjects emotional arousal was attributed to the *situation* .

42. Schachter's subjects who were correctly informed about the effects of the injection were not *influenced* , since they could account for their *emotional* state.

43. Schachter has demonstrated that general physiological arousal can be subjectively _labeled_, as many different emotions depend upon the immediate situation. His theory is known as the _cognitive_ theory of _emotion_.

44. Five emotional facial expressions have been found to be _universal_. They are _happiness_, _anger_, _disgust_, _sadness_, and _fear_ - _surprise_.

45. Individuals _blind_ since birth, who could never have seen facial expressions, tend to show the universal facial expressions, suggesting that these expressions may be due to a predetermined _genetic_ organization.

46. S. S. Tomkins suggests that _feedback_ from our own facial expressions may be a muscular _precursor_ of emotion.

47. One study supporting Tomkins' view had subjects being given electric _shocks_, and their ratings of perceived pain were less when they tried to avoid any outward signs of _pain_.

48. When we interpret a person's emotional state from nonverbal cues, we rely on _posture_ and _body_ motions as well as facial expressions.

49. _verbal_ cues seem to be more important in determining a person's _moods_ and feelings than any of the nonverbal cues.

50. Investigators have found that _women_ are generally better at reading nonverbal cues.

51. The types of emotions that are seen in our species and in other animals may have evolved because they help species _survive_. That is, emotions may exist because they serve a _function_.

52. Robert Plutchik has developed a theory of emotion he calls a _psychoevolutionary synthesis_ of emotion.

53. Plutchik's theory contends that emotions are _inherited_ _behavior patterns_ that have important functions and that are modifiable by _experience_.

54. Plutchik defines emotion as a _complex sequence_ of events having elements of _cognitive appraisal_, feeling, impulses to action, and overt behavior, all of which involve a _stimulus_ which triggers the chain of events in the beginning.

55. Plutchik has suggested that there are eight ___primary___ emotions: ___sadness___ , ___fear___ , ___surprise___ , ___anger___ , ___disgust___ , ___anticipation___ , ___joy___ , and acceptance, with each being based on a functional purpose.

56. On Plutchik's ___emotion___ ___wheel___ the primary emotions are ___inside___ the wheel, while the secondary emotions, made up of two primaries, are ___outside___ the wheel.

57. Plutchik's theory includes not only behavioral aspects of emotion, but also ___functionale___ aspects which help ensure ___survival___ .

58. The functions of Plutchik's eight primary emotions are: ___protection___ , ___destruction___ , ___incorporation___ , ___rejection___ , ___reproduction___ , ___reintegration___ , ___destruction___ , and exploration.

59. Crying, emitting distress signals, and "babyish" behavior describe behavior with the functional aspect of ___reintegration___ , while biting, striking, cursing, or threatening describe behaviors with the functional aspect of ___destruction___ .

60. According to Plutchik we "run from the bear" because we feel afraid, and also because running leads to ___protection___ .

61. Plutchik's theory is similar to Schachter's theory in that a ___cognitive___ ___assessment___ is made before the feeling is labeled. However, ___innate___ mechanisms that guide our responses are also part of Plutchik's theory.

62. Plutchik views our large cerebral ___cortex___ as something that can help develop and perfect our emotional experiences.

63. Plutchik has also developed a ___model___ that maps ___emotional___ intensities. This ___top___ - shaped figure has similar emotions close to each other, while emotions that are across from each other are ___opposite___ each other. Less intense emotions are more alike and lie at the ___bottom___ of the model.

64. Gordon Bower tested similarities and differences between emotions using ___Plutchick___ model for emotional intensities. He ___hypnotized___ his subjects and manipulated their emotional states while they learned lists of ___objects___ .

65. Bower found that subjects were best able to recall the lists of words when they were in the same ___moods___ they had been in

when they originally learned the lists.

66. _Aaron_ _____ _Copland_ _____ found that the audience's inappropriate reaction to his original work in the movie The Heiress was due to the creation of the wrong _mood_ _____ .

SELF TEST I

1. Stuart Valins studied false physiological feedback and found that
   a. how you assess your "feelings" is part of your emotional makeup
   b. most of the subjects were not influenced by false feedback
   c. cognitive assessments have little to do with emotional assessment
   d. all of the above

2. Mixed emotions or "bittersweet" feelings can be confusing, complex, and difficult to understand.
   a. true   b. false

3. Psychologists rely on subjective reports in order to assess emotions, since these reports are often valid and reliable.
   a. true   b. false

4. Emotional reactions are often associated with an arousal of the _____ nervous system which is made up of the _____ and _____ nervous systems.
   a. autonomic, sympathetic, parasympathetic
   b. central, somatic, peripheral
   c. somatic, peripheral, central
   d. peripheral, central, autonomic

5. Frustrated people may
   a. become aggressive
   b. try harder
   c. give up
   d. any of the above

6. Which of the following statements is _false_?
   a. Stuart Valins demonstrated that a subjective assessment of an emotional state can influence a person's behavior even without any real physiological arousal.
   b. the common-sense theory of emotion argues that an emotion must first be felt before we react with a behavioral response
   c. Valins' false feedback results support the common-sense theory of emotion
   d. the common sense theory of emotion argues that a behavioral response would come last after the stimulus and the emotion

7. Which of the following sequences would best fit the Cannon-Bard theory of emotion?
    a. we see the bear; we run; we are afraid
    b. we see the bear; we are afraid; we run
    c. we see the bear; we run; we label our emotion
    d. none of the above

8. Schachter's test of his theory using adrenaline demonstrated that
    a. correctly informed subjects were highly influenced by the actor, i.e., they, too, became angry or happy
    b. the misinformed subjects were influenced by the action, i.e., they, too, became angry or happy
    c. all subjects exposed to the angry actor became angry
    d. his theory could not account for the results as well as the common-sense theory

9. _____, like _____, argues that different kinds of muscular action must precede the expression of emotions.
    a. W. Cannon, S. Schachter
    b. C. Lange, S. Schachter
    c. S. S. Tomkins, W. James
    d. R. Plutchik, P. Bard

10. Which of the following statements is false?
    a. children are not as efficient as adults in perceiving nonverbal cues
    b. individuals' ability to judge nonverbal cues can differ greatly
    c. men are generally better at interpreting nonverbal cues than women
    d. it is possible that many people can train themselves to be more sensitive to nonverbal cues

11. Robert Plutchik has suggested there are eight _____ emotions.
    a. crossed   c. combined
    b. primary   d. mixed

12. Robert Plutchik has suggested that there are eight fundamental emotions that do not serve a function.
    a. true   b. false

13. According to Plutchik _____ is the function of surprise.
    a. reintegration
    b. orientation
    c. incorporation
    d. protection

14. Robert Plutchik's map of emotional intensities is shaped like a
    a. football field   c. circle
    b. top   d. none of the above

15. Gordon Bower, using Plutchik's wheel of emotion, discovered that
     a. Plutchik's model was contradicted
     b. subjects were best able to recall a list if they were in the same
        mood as when they learned the lists originally
     c. subjects were best able to recall a list if they were in the opposite
        mood as they had originally learned the list
     d. none of the above

SELF TEST II

1.   Which of the following is a reason your author suggests psychologists
     study emotion?
     a. having feelings is an important part of being human
     b. we pay close attention to others to discern their attitudes
     c. emotions constitute the largest research area in psychology
     d. both a and b

2.   Some languages have few words to describe emotions and, therefore,
     people in these cultures are less emotional.
     a. true   b. false

3.   Surprisingly, psychologists have found that correctly judging others'
     emotional state requires little more than objective observation.
     a. true   b. false

4.   The most common error a lie detector is apt to make is to
     a. suggest someone is telling the truth when in fact they are not
     b. show more truthfulness in a person's statements than actually exists
     c. erroneously accuse a truthful person of telling a lie
     d. none of the above

5.   The James-Lange theory of emotion would be best described by the
     sequence
     a. you freeze; you see the bear; you become afraid
     b. you see the bear; you feel afraid; you run
     c. you see the bear; you run; you feel afraid
     d. you see the bear; you freeze; you run

6.   Referring to Schachter's adrenaline study, which of the following
     statements if false?
     a. two groups were used who were misinformed, and two groups were
        used who were correctly informed as to the effects of the injections
     b. misinformed subjects believed they were feeling emotions similar to
        the actors
     c. correctly informed subjects exposed to the angry actor became angrier
        than in any other condition
     d. all subjects in the four conditions were told they were participating
        in a vision experiment

7. The five different facial expressions which have been found to be universal are
    a. fear-surprise, love, surprise, excitement, and hate
    b. happiness, anger, disgust, sadness, and fear-surprise
    c. sorrow, silliness, grief, anger, fear-surprise
    d. none of the above

8. It has been shown that another person's emotional state can be evaluated by noting
    a. body posture and movement
    b. facial expressions
    c. verbal cues
    d. all of the above

9. Robert Plutchik has a theory of emotion known as the
    a. innate evolutionary and learning hypothesis
    b. frustration-aggression hypothesis
    c. psychoevolutionary synthesis of emotion
    d. none of the above

10. Robert Plutchik suggests that
    a. a complex chain or sequence of emotional events is initially triggered by a stimulus
    b. the twelve primary emotions display particular consistency across a wide range of situations involving emotions and personality
    c. behavioral aspects of emotion, as well as functional aspects, are learned, while cognitive aspects are innate
    d. all of the above

11. Robert Plutchik has outlined over 400 basic behavioral patterns of animals and humans.
    a. true   b. false

12. Which of the following statements is true according to Plutchik's theory?
    a. our cognitive capacities have grown and advanced mainly to serve emotion
    b. most emotions serve no function
    c. both a and b would not be true
    d. both a and b would be true

13. Aaron Copland had difficulty with his musical score for the movie The Heiress because
    a. stage actors can't make the transition to the screen very well
    b. his original musical score did not depict the proper mood in one crucial scene
    c. he could not control his temper
    d. he could not relax

14. When trying to assess a friend's emotional state you should attend to
    his or her
    a. facial expressions
    b. overt behavior
    c. verbal cues
    d. all of the above

15. Placing a hot iron on people's tongues was a primitive "lie detector"
    test. If a person had lied the tongue would be dry and it would
    blister because the _____ nervous system had been
    activated.
    a. central   c. parasympathetic
    b. sympathetic   d. digestive

ESSAY QUESTIONS

1. Explain why polygraph results should be viewed cautiously.

2. Compare and contrast the James-Lange and Cannon-Bard theories of
   emotion.

3. Describe Stanley Schachter's classic experiment using adrenaline and
   actors.

4. Summarize Robert Plutchik's psychoevolutionary synthesis.

5. Describe Aaron Copland's problem in the movie The Heiress and explain
   why it occurred and how he solved it.

ANSWER SECTION

Guided Review
1. Stuart Valins, heartbeats, emotional arousal (or accelerated heartbeats)
2. emotions, attitudes, emotional reactions
3. pleasant, unpleasant
4. four hundred, overlap
5. language
6. animals, human beings, extinction
7. memorable, empathy
8. feeling
9. subjective
10. body, facial
11. subtle, stage
12. overt, subjective
13. cry, laugh
14. autonomic, sympathetic, parasympathetic
15. sympathetic, fight, flee

16. *emotional arousal, sympathetic*
17. *parasympathetic, sympathetic, dilate*
18. *polygraph, lie*
19. *heart, galvanic skin response (or GSR)*
20. *nervousness*
21. *two-thirds, truthful person*
22. *baseline, meprobamate, one, five*
23. *observed, innate (or built-in)*
24. *learning*
25. *frustration-aggression hypothesis*
26. *fixed-response patterns, aggression, response*
27. *hormones, neurotransmitters, brain*
28. *learning theory, aggressive, pleasant*
29. *frustration-aggression hypothesis*
30. *individual, situation*
31. *learning, learning*
32. *common-sense*
33. *felt, react to it*
34. *James, Lange, James-Lange*
35. *visceral, muscular, follows, common-sense*
36. *James-Lange*
37. *Cannon, Bard, Cannon-Bard*
38. *muscular, simultaneously*
39. *different (or cognitive), situation*
40. *adrenaline, physiological arousal, informed, misinformed*
41. *misinformed, happy, angry, situation (or context)*
42. *influenced (or aroused), emotional*
43. *labeled, cognitive, emotion*
44. *universal, happiness, anger, disgust, sadness, fear-surprise*
45. *blind, genetic*
46. *feedback, precursor*
47. *shocks, pain*
48. *posture, body*
49. *verbal, moods*
50. *women*
51. *survive, function*
52. *psychoevolutionary synthesis*
53. *inherited behavior patterns, experience*
54. *complex sequence, cognitive appraisal, stimulus*
55. *primary, sadness, fear, surprise, anger, disgust, anticipation, joy*
56. *emotion wheel, inside, outside*
57. *functional, survival*
58. *protection, destruction, incorporation, rejection, reproduction, reintegration, orientation*
59. *reintegration, destruction*
60. *protection*
61. *cognitive assessment, innate*
62. *cortex*
63. *model, emotional, top, opposite, bottom*

64,   Plutchik's, hypnotized, objects (or words)
65.   moods
66.   Aaron Copland, mood

Self Test I		Self Test II	
1.	a	1.	d
2.	a	2.	b
3.	b	3.	b
4.	a	4.	c
5.	d	5.	c
6.	c	6.	c
7.	d	7.	b
8.	b	8.	d
9.	c	9.	c
10.	c	10.	a
11.	b	11.	b
12.	b	12.	a
13.	b	13.	b
14.	b	14.	d
15.	b	15.	b

CHAPTER 11

Human Development

BEHAVIORAL OBJECTIVES

After completing this chapter, the student should be able to:

1. Explain the myth of linear development and tell why it is a myth.
2. Compare Freud's five stages of psychosexual development with Erikson's eight psychosocial stages and give specific examples of behaviors associated with each stage.
3. Describe a newborn infant, and identify at least five typical reflexes in newborns.
4. Summarize research concerning the nature-nurture issue with particular reference to studies of walking, toilet training, and nutrition.
5. Contrast the University of Wisconsin monkey isolation experiments with the foundling home studies of Rene Spitz (in the U.S.) and Dennis (in Beirut).
6. Tell in his or her own words how the effects of adverse early experiences were overcome by Harlow's "patient" monkeys and by Skeels' orphanage children.
7. Identify the key elements and conclusions of Harlow's surrogate mother experiments.
8. Define separation anxiety in his or her own words and explain how it was studied by Mary Ainsworth.
9. List Piaget's four stages of cognitive development and give specific examples of behaviors and activities associated with each stage.
10. Explain why children stop believing in Santa Claus, using Piaget's concepts.
11. Give the findings of recent research on the effects working and non-working mothers have on their children.
12. Describe, and consider the reasons for, the effects of divorce on male and female children and upon their intelligence and achievement.
13. Tell what puberty is and explain the major developmental characteristics and challenges of adolescence.
14. Outline the characteristics of, and the major choices and predicaments facing, young adults in our society including a description of current

trends.
15. Evaluate the reality and extent of the empty nest syndrome as it pertains to middle age.
16. Clarify and set straight the myths and misconceptions of old age.

KEY TERMS AND CONCEPTS

age-related changes
linear development
psychosexual stages
erogenous zones
fixation
psychosocial stages
basic trust
autonomy
initiative vs. guilt
industry vs. inferiority
identify vs. role confusion
intimacy vs. isolation
generativity vs. stagnation
ego integrity vs. despair
reflexes in newborns
maturation
nature-nurture question
cradle board
"accelerators"
"decelerators"
temperament theories
"slow to warm up" babies
autistic
plasticity
"patient" and "therapist"
  monkeys
Skeels study
surrogate mother
creature comfort
cootie
separation anxiety
"strange situation"
secure attachment
ambivalent attachment

avoidant attachment
primary caregiver
secondary caregiver
genetic epistemologist
cognition
sensorimotor stage
object permanence
preoperational stage
preconcepts
animistic thinking
intuitive vs. logical thinking
egocentrism
failure to decenter
reversibility
stage of concrete operations
conservation
horizontal decalage
operations
stage of formal operations
socialization
longitudinal study
sex-differentiating treatment
gender-role deficiencies
peers
puberty
secondary sexual chracteristics
growth spurt
"midlife crisis"
empty nest syndrome
aging
mutation
longevity in a species
genetic death clock

NAMES TO REMEMBER

Sigmund Freud
Erik Erikson
Rene Spitz
H. M. Skeels

Harry Harlow
Mary Ainsworth
Jean Piaget

GUIDED REVIEW

1. Sometime between the ages of one and two years, children become
    _____aware_____ of themselves.

2. Developmental psychology is the study of _____age_____ -
    _____related_____ changes in human behavior over the
    _____lifespan_____ .

3. Although the greatest emphasis by developmental psychologists has
    been placed on the years of _____infancy_____ and
    _____childhood_____ , recent interest in _____adult_____ develop-
    ment has also been growing.

4. Human development is _____concept_____ , and the popular concept
    of _____linear_____ development does not necessarily represent the
    way in which human beings develop.

5. According to Freud, children progress through a series of
    _____psychosexual_____ stages, including the _____oral_____ ,
    _____anal_____ , _____phallic_____ , _____latency_____ , and
    _____genital_____ stages.

6. Today developmental psychologists focus not only on childhood, but on
    the entire _____lifespan_____ .

7. Erik Erikson traces human development through a series of eight
    _____psychosocial_____ stages.

8. Compared with Freud, Erikson placed greater emphasis on _____social_____
    and _____cultural_____ forces, did not feel that failure at a particu-
    lar stage would result in _____irreversible_____ consequences, and
    emphasized the entire _____lifespan_____ rather than the first
    _____six_____ years.

9. Erikson's eight stages of development included basic _____trust_____
    vs. mistrust, _____autonomy_____ vs. shame or doubt, initiative vs.
    _____guilt_____ , industry vs. _____inferiority_____ ,
    _____identity_____ vs. role confusion, _____identity intimacy_____ vs.
    isolation, generativity vs. _____stagnation_____ , and
    _____ego_____ _____integrity_____ vs. despair.

10. Perhaps the most helpless and dependent offspring to be found in the
    animal kingdom are _____human_____ infants.

11. Most newborns at birth have _____blue_____ eyes, weigh between
    _____six_____ and _____nine_____ pounds and have a dis-
    proportionately large _____head_____ .

12. The newborn comes equipped with a number of _reflexes_ including babinski, blink, moro, and rage.

13. If you stroke a baby's foot from heel to toe, the toes fan out, showing the _babinski_ reflex.

14. Genetically determined biological development which progresses relatively independent of experience is referred to as _Maturation_.

15. Hopi infants who were kept on _cradle_ boards, and those who were not, all walked at about _15_ months of age.

16. McGraw's toilet training study and the Dennis and Dennis Hopi infant study showed that children must be maturationally _ready_ before they can learn a particular skill.

17. Environmental experiences may act as " _accelerators_ " or " _decelerators_ " of maturational development.

18. Perhaps children today walk earlier than children in the 1930s because of better _nutrition_ , or because of parents with today's _smaller_ families being more _encouraging_ , or even because of wall-to-wall _carpeting_ .

19. Researchers in 1970 described infants' personalities or temperaments as being _easy_ or _difficult_ .

20. The temperaments of infants have been found to be _stable_ over time.

21. A flat _EEG_ in an infant does not necessarily mean that anything is _wrong_ .

22. Axons in the central nervous system of newborns are not yet _myelinated_ .

23. Infants begin to _smile_ at about the same age the world over. This may be related to the amount of _myelin_ present.

24. Monkeys isolated for six months suffered severe developmental disturbances and rocked back and forth in an _autistic_ way.

25. Different species of monkeys reacted to _isolation_ differently, thus humans may also have unique reactions to _isolations_ .

26. In 1945, Rene Spitz found that infants in a foundling home were developmentally _retarded_ due to lack of attention.

27. Children in the Lebanese foundling home in Beirut were
    _____ retarded, but those who were _____
    gained back the ground they had lost.

28. Studies of Guatemalan children who were raised in near isolation showed
    that by adolescence they had become developmentally _____
    to American children. This shows considerable _____
    in children. That is, they tend to _____
    _____ after adverse conditions.

29. Mrs. A. believed that her second and third children were
    _____. Because of how she raised them they were
    seriously _____ retarded. Thus Mrs. A. produced a
    _____ - _____ prophecy.

30. In 1972 Suomi and Harlow paired six-month-old isolate _____
    monkeys with three-month-old normal _____ monkeys.
    After six months of therapy the patients and therapists were
    _____ in their behaviors.

31. The _____ study in the 1930s placed children from an
    orphanage in the Glenwood State School for retarded adult women.

32. In the Skeels study, the children who moved to the women's school
    averaged _____ points gain in IQ after eighteen months,
    and those who stayed in the orphanage averaged a _____
    point _____ in IQ.

33. The Skeels study suggests that early _____ can often be
    _____.

34. Harry Harlow's research on monkey love casts doubt on the notion that
    _____ leads to the formation of strong attachments be-
    tween infant and mother.

35. In Harlow's experiments, infant monkeys were raised on
    _____ mothers, one made of _____, the
    other of _____.

36. Regardless of which mother provided nursing, the baby monkeys spent
    more time on the _____ mother. Thus _____
    _____ is more important than nursing in the formation
    of attachments.

37. Harlow frightened baby monkeys with plastic _____ and
    found that the babies would run to the _____ mother
    and then become _____ and _____.

38. Baby rhesus monkeys raised without a surrogate mother will not run

to the _____ mother when they see a _____ , they just curl up and _____ with _____ .

39. Human babies, like monkeys, use their mothers as a _____ of _____ from which to explore the _____ .

40. The phenomenon of a baby wanting to stay near its mother, and crying when she leaves has been called _____ _____ .

41. Mary Ainsworth conducted a twenty-minute laboratory test known as the " _____ situation."

42. Earlier separation studies focused on how infants cried when abandoned. Ainsworth focused on the infant's reaction to the _____ of the _____ .

43. Ainsworth observed three attachment reactions in her strange situation experiment. They were _____ attachment, _____ attachment, and _____ attachment.

44. Most researchers prior to 1972 ignored _____ , but recently they have begun to attract attention.

45. Research indicates that infants form strong attachments to _____ caregivers and slightly weaker attachments to _____ caregivers.

46. The way in which we gain knowledge through perception, memory, and thought processing is referred to as _____ .

47. Next to Sigmund Freud, _____ _____ is the most frequently referenced researcher in the psychological literature.

48. Piaget believed that a child's cognitive understanding of the world will be _____ different from an adult's.

49. Piaget's stages of cognitive development are the _____ period, the _____ period, the period of _____ operations, and the period of _____ operations.

50. The sensorimotor stage is characterized by a lack of fully developed object _____ .

51. In every day expression, lack of object permanence means "out of _____ , out of _____ ."

52. A child in the sensorimotor stage looks for objects where they are

most often _____ , rather than where they have last
_____ _____ .

53. Once apes attain object permanence, their cognitive development appears to _____ .

54. In the preoperational stage, the child demonstrates greater and greater use of _____ functions, and has established object _____ . Also the child becomes aware that he or she has a _____ .

55. In the preoperational stage, _____ development increases and children spend time engaging in _____ -
_____ .

56. As children begin to symbolize their environments and internalize objects, they develop immature concepts which Piaget called
_____ .

57. Three-year-olds often refer to every car as _____ car.

58. The belief that inanimate objects are alive is called _____ thinking and is characteristic of the _____ stage.

59. The fact that preoperational children perceive the world only in terms of their own perspective is referred to as _____ .

60. The inability to comprehend more than one aspect of a problem at a time is a cognitive limitation known as the _____ to
_____ .

61. Preoperational children have a difficult time conceiving of doubling back or reversing what has just been done. This is known as
_____ .

62. In the stage of concrete operations, children from _____ to _____ years of age come to understand and apply
_____ , _____ , and _____ .

63. The ability to _____ marks the end of the _____ stage and the beginning of _____ operations.

64. Piaget used the term _____ _____ to refer to the fact that some conservations are mastered before others.

65. Operations are _____ rules.

66. In the stage of _____ operations, individuals can make complex deductions and systematically solve problems by testing _____ solutions.

67. According to Piaget, once the child has entered the stage of
     _____ operations, there are no longer
     _____ differences between the child's thought proces-
     ses and those of an _____.

68. As a description of the development of thought, Piaget's theory is
     _____.

69. Piaget's observations have been repeatedly observed, but explanations
     for _____ cognitive development progresses as it does
     are not _____.

70. Cognitive development at the _____ stage may be closely
     tied to genetics and biological _____, while cognitive
     development in older children and adults may depend more upon
     _____ and _____.

71. Great emphasis is placed in our society upon the _____
     as the primary agent of _____.

72. Most child rearing studies are _____, and
     _____-_____ relationships are difficult
     to infer.

73. In responding to questionnaires and interviews, parents often recall
     things as they wish they _____ _____,
     rather than as they _____ _____.

74. Researchers do not _____ on which child-rearing prac-
     tice is _____. Parents provide _____
     _____ for their children.

75. A study in which the same subjects are repeatedly measured over time
     is called a _____ study.

76. An eight-year longitudinal study showed that young children of
     working mothers are not ordinarily _____ affected by
     their mother's _____.

77. Working mothers tend to _____ for their absence by
     _____ more with their children.

78. Daughters of working mothers perceive the woman's role as more
     _____, and women as more _____
     than do daughters of nonworking mothers.

79. Unemployed mothers may find their homemaking duties overly stress-
     ful because _____ problems are more likely to occur.

80. Employed mothers tend to encourage their children to be more
_____ and _____ - _____
from an early age.

81. Even today, most fathers do not approve of _____
aspirations for their daughters in terms of _____
and _____ choice.

82. Over _____ percent of marriages among young people
will end in divorce.

83. Many children respond to divorce with _____,
_____, guilt, withdrawal and depression. Most children
can adapt to a divorce within a couple of years.

84. Generally, _____ can cope with divorce better than
_____.

85. In general, mothers tend to view their _____ more
_____ after a divorce than they do their
_____.

86. Children raised in single-parent families often perform poorer on
standardized _____ and _____ tests, and
show cognitive _____.

87. Children who are interacting at about the same behavioral level are
considered to be _____, regardless of age.

88. By the age of seven or eight, _____ become important
models as often as a child's _____.

89. There is generally remarkable _____ between a child's
peers and family members in terms of accepted _____
and _____.

90. Choices of friends, language fads, clothing choices, and sexual attitudes are more likely to be influenced by _____, and
future aspirations, academic choices, and political views are more
likely to be influenced by _____.

91. Generally, _____ to peer group standards increases
with age.

92. Physical changes during _____ can cause body image
problems.

93. The development of sexual maturity occurs during a period called
_____.

94. During puberty secondary sexual characteristics emerge, growth accelerates, and body proportions change. This is known as the _____ _____.

95. Adolescents must cope with a number of _____ tasks including sexual relationships, sex roles, independence, and career decisions.

96. By age 60 there is about a 10 percent loss of muscle _____ relative to its peak potential at age _____.

97. The number of _____ young adults in their thirties has _____ since 1960.

98. While many young adults are _____ marriage and others are _____ _____ out of wedlock, many others are marrying and working at being _____ in order to gain the _____ resulting from a healthy inter-action between parent and child.

99. An important task facing young adults is choosing a _____, and such choices are more _____ and _____ today than in the past.

100. By the time the average person is _____ years old, he or she will have made _____ major career changes.

101. Although our culture may praise youth, it is the _____-_____ (ages 40-65) who have the _____.

102. A feeling of desperation related to the fact that time is running out and that one has less time to live than already lived may precipitate a _____-_____ crisis.

103. Despite the popular notion of a mid-life crisis, most middle-aged adults express attitudes of _____-_____ and _____.

104. The depression of "the _____ _____" was not found to be a problem for 159 middle-aged women studied by Rubin. In fact nearly all of them responded to the departure of their children with a sense of _____.

105. In later adulthood (over 65) bones become _____, lung _____ is lessened, and cardiac output at rest becomes less _____.

106. Findings pertaining to old age include the following: _____ is a relatively rare occurrence, _____

relationships among the elderly are normal and healthy, and
_____ and old age are not synonymous.

107. In a survey of 2,800 young, middle-aged and elderly adults, Flanagan
found the two most important factors relating to happiness and satisfaction were _____ and _____
_____.

108. In Flanagan's survey, the poorest predictors of life quality were having
and raising _____, relationships with _____,
_____ others, and participating in _____.

109. The more an older adult can find _____ within a family
or social group and the more he or she can obtain a sense of
_____ with the past, the more enjoyable life will be.

SELF TEST I

1. The study of age-related changes in human behavior over the lifespan
   is
   a. the definition of developmental psychology
   b. based primarily on Sigmund Freud's five psychosocial stages of
      development
   c. primarily in the domain of maturational psychologists
   d. all of the above

2. Which of the following does not belong with the others?
   a. psychosexual stages   c. psychosocial stages
   b. Erik Erikson   d. major emphasis on entire lifespan

3. An older adult who can look back on his or her life with a sense of
   accomplishment and satisfaction is experiencing Erikson's stage of
   a. identity   c. fulfillment
   b. generativity   d. ego-integrity

4. The 1940 McGraw toilet training study indicated that
   a. the twin who was not trained lagged far behind the twin that was
      trained
   b. children must be maturationally ready before they can learn a parti-
      cular skill
   c. the twin who received early training mastered the task at 14 months
      of age
   d. all of the above

5. The axons in the central nervous system of a newborn are
   a. fully myelinated
   b. not yet myelinated
   c. not yet synapsed with other neurons
   d. both a and c

6. The _____ study involved placing half the children from an overcrowded, understaffed orphanage in the Glenwood State School for retarded adult women.
   a. Dennis
   b. Skeels
   c. Harlow
   d. Spitz

7. Baby rhesus monkeys raised without a surrogate mother will _____ when placed in a room with a plastic cootie and and cloth mother.
   a. run to the mother and cling to her body
   b. curl up and shake with fear
   c. approach the cootie and pull off its antennae
   d. none of the above

8. Next to Sigmund Freud, who is the most frequently referenced researcher in the psychological literature?
   a. Jean Piaget
   b. Harry Harlow
   c. B. F. Skinner
   d. Erik Erikson

9. The lack of fully developed _____ is characteristic of Piaget's sensorimotor stage of cognitive development.
   a. socialization
   b. object permanence
   c. syncretic reasoning
   d. secure attachments

10. The belief that nonliving objects like rocks or the sun are alive is
    a. animistic thinking
    b. intuitive thinking
    c. superstitious thinking
    d. none of the above

11. Most family and child-rearing studies
    a. are correlational
    b. are designed to show cause and effect relationships
    c. involve the use of questionnaires and interviews
    d. both a and c

12. Following a divorce,
    a. girls usually have more behavior disorders than boys
    b. mothers tend to view their sons more negatively than they do their daughters
    c. both a and b
    d. none of the above

13. Society expects adolescents to eventually
    a. be socially mature in dealing with both sexes
    b. adopt a life philosophy
    c. achieve emotional independence from parents
    d. all of the above

14. In a study of middle-aged women, Rubin reported that
    a. all but one of them suffered from the classical symptoms of empty nest syndrome

b. nearly all of them responded to the departure of their children with a sense of relief
c. both a and b
d. none of the above

15. Which of the following may contribute to a longer lifespan for human beings?
a. replacing worn out vital parts
b. genetic engineering
c. exercise and proper diet
d. all of the above

SELF TEST II

1. According to Freud, a child obtains the greatest satisfaction through genital stimulation during the
a. oral stage
b. anal stage
c. phallic stage
d. latency stage

2. When children are taught how to master tasks or do things for themselves they start to develop
a. generativity   c. initiative
b. industry   d. autonomy

3. The term used to describe a genetically determined biological plan of development, one relatively independent of experience, is
a. maturation   c. human growth and development
b. linear development   d. genetic epistemology

4. Some environmental experiences may act as _____ or _____ of maturational development.
a. natures, nurtures
b. avoiders, confronters
c. extenders, enhancers
d. accelerators, decelerators

5. Dennis reported that children in a Lebanese foundling home in Beirut
a. became developmentally retarded
b. who were adopted grew up to be developmentally normal
c. both a and b
d. none of the above

6. In the Skeels study, _____ of the children originally transferred to the home from the orphanage eventually were adopted
a. none   c. one or two
b. most   d. none of these, the Skeels study involved monkeys, not children

7. A two-year-old who experiences distress and cries when his or her
    mother leaves is experiencing
    a. maternal departure syndrome
    b. separation anxiety
    c. the strange situation effect
    d. failure to decenter

8. The way in which we gain knowledge through perception, memory, and
    thought processing is referred to as
    a. human development   c. intuitive thinking
    b. plasticity   d. cognition

9. As children begin to symbolize their environments and develop the ability
    to internalize objects and events, they develop immature concepts which
    Piaget called
    a. preconcepts   c. images
    b. animistic thinking   d. cognition

10. The ability to _____ marks the end of the preoperational
    stage and the beginning of the stage of concrete operations.
    a. think transductively   c. conserve
    b. socialize   d. think animistically

11. Daughters of working mothers perceive the woman's role as
    _____ satisfying and/but women as _____
    competent than do daughters of nonworking mothers.
    a. more, less   c. more, more
    b. less, more   d. less, less

12. Regarding accepted values and behaviors,
    a. a child's parents and peers are usually in remarkable agreement
    b. eight-year-old children tend to look to their peers as often as
       they look to their own families
    c. both a and b
    d. none of the above

13. By the time the average person is thirty-five, he or she will have
    made _____ major career changes.
    a. two   c. twelve
    b. seven   d. seventeen

14. During old age (over 65)
    a. senility is a rare occurrence and does not occur in the normal course
       of aging
    b. sexual relationships among the elderly are normal and healthy
    c. both a and b
    d. none of the above

15. Your sister's two-year-old daughter reacted with separation anxiety when your sister left the room. When she returned, the child gave her a happy greeting and manifested secure attachment behavior. In observing this, you become convinced that
    a. your sister probably responds to the child's cries at some times and ignores them at other times
    b. your sister probably responds rapidly to the child's cries
    c. the child is often disobedient to your sister's verbal commands
    d. both b and c

ESSAY QUESTIONS

1. Compare and contrast Freud's and Erikson's stages of development.

2. What effects do early isolation and deprivation have upon monkey and human development? Cite research to support your answer.

3. Evaluate the following statement in the light of Harlow's research: The development of love and attachments of an infant toward its mother is based upon nursing.

4. Discuss the stages of cognitive development described by Jean Piaget. Give the names and examples of the cognitive processes which occur during each stage.

5. List and compare the major developmental tasks and challenges faced by adolescents, young adults, the middle-aged, and older adults in our society.

ANSWER SECTION

Guided Review
1. *aware*
2. *age-related, lifespan*
3. *infancy, childhood, adult*
4. *complex, linear*
5. *psychosexual, oral, anal, phallic, latency, genital*
6. *lifespan*
7. *psychosocial*
8. *social, cultural, irreversible, lifespan, six*
9. *trust, autonomy, guilt, inferiority, identity, intimacy, stagnation, ego integrity*
10. *human*
11. *blue, six, nine, head*
12. *reflexes*
13. *Babinski*
14. *maturation*

15. cradle, fifteen
16. ready
17. accelerators, decelerators
18. nutrition, smaller, encouraging, carpeting
19. easy, difficult
20. stable
21. EEG, wrong
22. myelinated
23. smile, myelin
24. autistic
25. isolation, isolation
26. retarded
27. developmentally, adopted
28. equal, plasticity, bounce back
29. defective, developmentally, self-fulfilling
30. patient, therapist, indistinguishable
31. Skeels
32. 29, 21, decrease
33. deficits, overcome
34. nursing
35. surrogate, wire, cloth
36. cloth, creature comfort
37. cooties, cloth, relaxed, calm
38. cloth, cootie, shake, fear
39. base, operations, environment
40. separation anxiety
41. strange
42. return, mother
43. secure, ambivalent, avoidant
44. fathers
45. primary, secondary
46. cognition
47. Jean Piaget
48. qualitatively
49. sensorimotor, preoperational, concrete, formal
50. permanence
51. sight, mind
52. found, been seen
53. stop
54. symbolic, permanence, self
55. language, make-believe
56. preconcepts
57. Daddy's
58. animistic, preoperational
59. egocentrism
60. failure, decenter
61. reversibility
62. 7, 11, decentering, reversibility, conservation
63. conserve, preoperational, concrete

64. *horizontal decalage*
65. *logical*
66. *formal, hypothetical*
67. *formal, qualitative, adult*
68. *unequalled*
69. *why, resolved*
70. *sensorimotor, maturation, learning, experience*
71. *family, socialization*
72. *correlational, cause-effect*
73. *had been, actually were*
74. *agree, best, role models*
75. *longitudinal*
76. *adversely, absence*
77. *compensate, interacting*
78. *satisfying, competent*
79. *money*
80. *independent, self-sufficient*
81. *nontraditional, achievement, career*
82. *40*
83. *anger, fear*
84. *girls, boys*
85. *sons, negatively, daughters*
86. *intelligence, achievement, deficits*
87. *peers*
88. *peers, family*
89. *agreement, values, behaviors*
90. *peers, parents*
91. *conformity*
92. *adolescence*
93. *puberty*
94. *growth spurt*
95. *developmental*
96. *strength, 30*
97. *single, increased*
98. *postponing, living together, parents, happiness*
99. *career, complex, difficult*
100. *35, seven*
101. *middle-aged, power*
102. *mid-life*
103. *self-confidence, achievement*
104. *empty nest, relief*
105. *brittle, capacity, efficient*
106. *senility, sexual, illness*
107. *money, health care*
108. *children, relatives, aiding, government*
109. *satisfaction, continuity*

Self Test I		*Self Test II*	
1.	a	1.	c
2.	a	2.	d
3.	d	3.	a
4.	b	4.	d
5.	b	5.	c
6.	b	6.	b
7.	b	7.	b
8.	a	8.	d
9.	b	9.	a
10.	a	10.	c
11.	d	11.	c
12.	b	12.	c
13.	d	13.	b
14.	b	14.	c
15.	d	15.	b

CHAPTER 12

Intelligence and Individual Differences

BEHAVIORAL OBJECTIVES

After completing this chapter, the student should be able to:

1. Define intelligence and explain how positive eugenics influenced its development as an area of study.
2. Describe phrenology and explain how this and other factors fostered an inherited view of intelligence.
3. Give the history and development of the Stanford-Binet intelligence test.
4. Summarize Thurstone's and Guilford's view of intelligence.
5. Define factor load and factor analysis and outline Guilford's model of intelligence.
6. Summarize the differences noted between firstborn and later born children.
7. Contrast Arthur Jensen's view of the intelligence of minorities with Jane Mercer's view.
8. Explain what culture-fair tests are, and state how successful such efforts have been.
9. Summarize the data on the heritability of intellectual capacity.
10. Describe the Milwaukee project and explain why some of the disciplinary problems among the children may have occurred.
11. Give examples of early intervention projects and state their overall effectiveness.
12. Summarize the ongoing Lewis Terman study and explain why Terman's subjects may have been so successful.
13. List and describe the categories of exceptional people.
14. Define creativity and describe attempts to measure and describe it.
15. Summarize the case of Gregory Ochoa and convey an understanding of the effects of labeling individuals.

KEY TERMS AND CONCEPTS

intelligence   phrenology

mental age (MA)
chronological age (CA)
intelligence quotient (IQ)
Binet-Simon Intelligence Scale
Stanford-Binet IQ test
Wechsler Adult Intelligence
    Scale (WAIS-R)
validity
factor load
factor analysis
Guilford's model
operations
contents
products
general intelligence
birth order effect
Zajonc and Markus model
intellectual climate
achievement motivation
cultural bias
"menace of the feebleminded"
mental retardation
culture-fair tests
Raven Progressive Matrices Test
positive correlation
correlation of zero
negative correlation

fraternal twins
identical twins
Milwaukee Project
Head Start Project
Ypsilanti Project
kibbutz
Bayley Mental and Motor Scale
reliable
longitudinal study
Terman's study
exceptionality
physical and sensory exceptionality
social-emotional exceptionality
invulnerables
intellectual exceptionality
Down's Syndrome
educable mentally retarded
mainstreaming
creativity
novelty
appropriateness
transcendence of constraints
coalescence of meaning
convergent productions
divergent productions

NAMES TO REMEMBER

Thomas Edison
L. L. Thurstone
Sir Francis Galton
Alfred Binet
Theodore Simon
L. Wilhelm Stern
Lewis Terman
J. P. Guilford
Arthur Jensen
William Shockley
Sandra Scarr

Jerome Kagan
Jane Mercer
Cyril Burt
Rick Heber
Nancy Bayley
Koko
Lewis Terman
Pauline Sears
Robert Sears
Gregory Ochoa

GUIDED REVIEW

1. Thomas Edison, although a genius, hired L. L. _____
    to do his _____, which he seemed incapable of doing
    himself.

2. Thurstone believed that there are many different kinds of
    _____ .

3. _____ is a general term for a person's abilities for a
    wide range of tasks.

4. The first scientific interest in intelligence, intelligence testing, and
    psychological testing in general can be traced back to the work of
    Sir _____ _____ .

5. An early pseudoscientific attempt to measure "inherited traits" was
    _____ which measured the bumps and indentations
    on people's heads.

6. The first intelligence test was designed by _____
    _____ and _____ _____
    in 1905. The purpose of this test was to determine which school
    children should receive _____ _____ or
    be placed in regular classes.

7. Binet used the term _____ _____ to
    represent the actual age of the child and the term _____
    _____ to represent the child's intellectual age in compari-
    son with others of the same chronological age.

8. L. Wilhelm Stern developed the _____ _____
    which is expressed by the formula IQ = _____ times
    _____ divided by _____ .

9   In 1916 _____ _____ at Stanford University
    developed the _____ - _____ intelligence
    test.

10. A test is _____ if it measures what it claims to measure.

11. _____ is a term that has never been adequately defined.

12. The Revised Wechsler Adult Intelligence Scale (WAIS-R) includes a
    _____ scale and a _____ scale.

13. The WAIS-R and the Stanford-Binet are _____ IQ
    tests, rather than _____ IQ tests.

14. Some IQ tests give more weight or emphasis to certain abilities. This
    is known as a _____ _____ .

15. In 1938 L. L. Thurstone advocated developing tests that would measure
    each ability _____ . In order to accomplish this, he relied
    on a technique known as _____ _____ .

16. J. P. _____ developed a three dimensional model of intelligence based on his factor analysis of intelligence. Each side of the block figure represents a major _____ function.

17. In Guilford's model _____ are the actions taken by a person, while _____ include the information upon which an operation is performed, and the _____ refer to the way in which the information is organized.

18. Thurstone and Guilford have suggested that there are many kinds of _____.

19. The Stanford-Binet IQ test is heavily loaded in favor of _____ skills.

20. Feldman and Bratton (1972), in a Minneapolis school, administered the 18 most common measures of _____. They found 92 percent of all of the _____ were in the top five on at least one measure.

21. Being labeled "gifted" may well depend on which _____ one receives.

22. In 1896 Sir _____ _____ noted that a large number of prominent British scientists were _____ children.

23. Firstborn children appear to have a greater need to _____ and perform better _____.

24. Later born children tend to be impulsive, while firstborns tend to be _____.

25. _____ develop language most rapidly.

26. Zajonc and Markus developed a _____ of _____ _____ designed to predict differences in intelligence scores of children from large and small families.

27. Zajonc and Markus, as well as others, have found that intelligence _____ as birth order position drops. However, this trend seems to _____ for eighth or later children.

28. Birth order differences in IQ scores tend to be only _____ or _____ points.

29. More scientists or astronauts may be firstborns simply because they are more likely to have been given _____ denied later born children.

30. _____ _____, a professor of psychology, has argued that whites have a _____ point IQ advantage over blacks because of _____

31. William Shockley has advocated that _____ have inferior genes.

32. Henry Goddard, supervisor of testing immigrants arriving in New York, concluded that many of the incoming immigrants were _____.

33. It didn't seem to bother Goddard that many of the immigrants tested could not _____ _____.

34. _____ _____ may explain why blacks score lower than whites on intelligence tests.

35. Psychologist Sandra Scarr studied IQ scores of _____ _____ raised by _____ _____.

36. Scarr found that the _____ black children were when adopted, the closer the children came to the average white IQ.

37. Since intelligence tests are often culturally biased, a low IQ score may well represent _____ _____ rather than low intelligence.

38. Jane Mercer found a disproportionate number of _____ and _____ - _____ children had been placed in classes for the _____ _____ based solely on their IQ scores.

39. Mercer devised a scale to measure _____ _____, and based on her work it seems that IQ tests have been occasionally _____.

40. Efforts to remove the biasing effects of language from IQ tests have been attempted with _____ - _____ tests.

41. One of the most widely used culture-fair tests is the _____ _____ _____ test.

42. Psychologists study the _____ of human intelligence by examining people who are related to each other, since relatives share many of the same _____.

43. The more alike pairs of individuals' IQ scores are the closer the correlation coefficient is to a value of _____.

44. A correlation approaching −1.00 indicates an _____ _____.

45. Identical twins reared together or apart have _____ positive correlations, suggesting that _____ may play a large role in intelligence.

46. Cyril Burt did much of the early work on _____ _____ _____ but unfortunately it has been discovered that he _____ his data.

47. Researchers have found that twins reared apart have similar IQs but the samples have been _____ in size and possibly _____.

48. The Milwaukee Project was started to study the effects of _____ _____ on children from _____ _____.

49. Rick _____ selected newborn infants whose mothers all had IQs below _____.

50. In the Heber study mothers of the experimental group received _____, _____ _____, and training in homemaking and child care. The children received personalized _____ at home and then training at special centers until the beginning of first grade.

51. The Milwaukee Project's experimental group was dramatically _____ when compared with the control children by the age of six. The experimental group had an average IQ of _____ as compared with the control's of only _____.

52. Heber found that by the age of ten the _____ group's average IQ had held relatively steady, but the _____ group's average had declined 15 points. It was also noted that the experimental group had more _____ problems.

53. The results of the _____ Project in Michigan indicate that good-quality _____-_____ programs do benefit the disadvantaged.

54. A notable example of institutional enrichment has been demonstrated in Israel where children were raised on a _____.

55. The most successful enrichment programs have been those that have used home _____.

56. Measuring IQ throughout an individual's lifespan has been difficult, since tests for young children and infants generally stress _____ _____, while tests for older children stress _____ and _____ skills.

57. IQ scores do not seem to be consistent or _____ (as psychologists prefer to say) until the child is about the age of _____.

58. Botwinick (1967) found that IQs decline in adults with _____ or lower _____ but do not decline in adults of _____ or above _____ intelligence.

59. On tasks that require _____ older adults do not perform as well as younger adults.

60. In 1921, _____ _____ started a _____ study of gifted children.

61. Terman's 800 male subjects had, by the age of 40, _____ to _____ times the publications, patents, professorships, and professional degrees than a similar random sample would have obtained.

62. All of the women in Terman's study who _____ reported greater job _____ than most women.

63. _____ _____, a well-known psychologist, is now in charge of overseeing the continuing Terman study. He was, ironically, one of the _____ _____ in the Terman study.

64. The Terman "kids" are now in their seventies and compared to similar aged people are _____, _____, and _____. These "kids" also have lower incidences of _____, _____, and _____.

65. People who are extremely intelligent and able, and those who are disadvantaged in processing information or dealing with their environment are both referred to as _____.

66. Exceptionality may be defined by _____-_____, _____-_____, and intellectual dimensions.

67. Besides using available technologies to help people overcome their handi-
caps, it is necessary to _____ the public. For example,
_____ is not a form of mental retardation.

68. _____ _____ is a term usually applied
to people with visual or auditory dysfunctions.

69. Hearing-impaired children often have _____ difficulties
because auditory _____ is necessary for normal language
development.

70. Children who have developed and thrived in situations that would seem
to guarantee an emotional disorder or social instability are referred to
as _____ .

71. People who have biogenetic disorders such as _____
Syndrome are limited in what they can accomplish.

72. The largest group of intellectually retarded people are labeled
_____ _____ _____ and
generally have IQs ranging from _____ to
_____ .

73. Most educable mentally retarded individuals learn at a slower rate and
have _____ _____ _____
than normal.

74. Keeping as many exceptional children in the regular classroom as possible
is a philosophy known as _____ .

75. _____ is the ability to originate something new and
appropriate by transcending common constraints.

76. One method of defining creativity includes judgments based upon four
criteria, _____ , _____ ,
_____ of _____ , and _____
of meaning.

77. Something transcends _____ when it breaks away from
common conceptions.

78. Most creative ideas have meanings that _____ over time,
as _____ motion picture projector idea did.

79. Creative ability is poorly predicted by _____
_____ and Guilford contends that this is so because
most of these tests rely heavily on _____
_____ .

80. Guilford argues that _____ _____ , in which an individual uses his or her knowledge to develop as many solutions as possible, is the key to _____ .

81. Michael Wallach (1970) designed a test of creativity that measures _____ _____ .

82. Like IQ scores, ideational fluency scores among older children appear to be fairly _____ over time.

83. Terman's "kids" did well because they _____ excellent brains and nervous systems and because their _____ stimulated their cognitive and intellectual skills.

84. The case of Gregory Ochoa illustrates the problems of _____ that can result when IQ tests are misused.

SELF TEST I

1. The man who was responsible for the initial efforts to measure intelligence and helped begin the whole psychological testing movement was
   a. Sir Francis Galton
   b. L. L. Thurstone
   c. J. P. Guilford
   d. Jerome Kagan

2. Intelligence tests seem to measure many common skills and abilities, most of which are acquired in school.
   a. true
   b. false

3. Which of the following statements is true?
   a. intelligence tests have not been good measures of creativity
   b. intelligence tests have generally been valid measures of school success
   c. intelligence tests have been helpful in clinical assessments of individuals
   d. all of the above

4. The textbook account of Bruce Jenner's decathlon events (which were dependent on running) illustrated the concept of
   a. motor intelligence
   b. validity
   c. factor loading
   d. adaptive behavior

5. In Guilford's model of intelligence "products" are
   a. one of the three major functions
   b. the way in which the information is organized
   c. the actions taken by the individual
   d. both a and b

6. The fact that highly intelligent children tend to have highly intelligent parents proves that intelligence is inherited.
    a. true   b. false

7. William Shockley would disagree most with the notion that
    a. blacks score 15 points on the average below whites
    b. the difference in IQ between whites and blacks is for the most part due to environmental factors
    c. whites are naturally superior to blacks
    d. he would agree with all of the above

8. The American Association on Mental Deficiency states that mental retardation refers to significantly subaverage general intelligence, usually with an IQ score of less than _____ and with deficits in
    _____.
    a. 50, adaptive behavior
    b. 70, motor skills
    c. 70, adaptive behavior
    d. 50, motor skills

9. Trying to avoid misuses of IQ tests in the past, culture-fair tests that are _____ have been attempted.
    a. individual instead of group tests
    b. language-free
    c. in sign language (ASL)
    d. in Spanish

10. The twins reared apart data have difficulties because
    a. studies have been based only on small samples
    b. "reared apart" means that each twin lived with one parent so that the intellectual environments for both twins remained very similar
    c. a portion of the research has been faked
    d. all of the above

11. The experimental group in the Milwaukee Project had
    a. mothers who received education, vocational rehabilitation, and training in home care
    b. a personalized enrichment in their own home for their first three months
    c. special training at a center until they reached the first grade
    d. all of the above

12. The eventual loss of IQ points among the experimental group in Heber's Milwaukee Project could have been caused by
    a. the fact that the schools were geared to the slow student
    b. the fact that some children began going to school hungry
    c. the talkative tendency of these students who had been trained in language skills
    d. all of the above

13. The most successful enrichment programs have incorporated early home-based intervention.
   a. true   b. false

14. All exceptionally disadvantaged individuals could benefit from
   a. available technologies or new technological breakthroughs
   b. public education informing people of their needs
   c. both a and b
   d. none of the above

15. The ability to originate something new and appropriate by transcending constraints defines
   a. genius   c. ideational fluency
   b. exceptionality   d. creativity

SELF TEST II

1. Phrenology
   a. is the measurement of personality by the contours of the head
   b. included the assertion that learning and experience influence personality
   c. was a scientifically sound investigation of inherited traits.
   d. all of the above

2. MA/CA X 100 defines the
   a. chronological age   c. intelligence correlation
   b. intelligence quotient   d. factor load

3. Intelligence tests are good indicators of creativity as well as intelligence.
   a. true   b. false

4. L. L. Thurstone advocated the existence of many different types of intelligence or abilities rather than a single general intelligence factor.
   a. true   b. false

5. Feldman and Bratton studied _____ in a suburban school
   a. mental retardation
   b. giftedness   c. creativity
                              d. factor load

6. According to Zajonc and Markus's model of intellectual climate, a single mother and her newborn baby would have a climate value of
   a. 0   c. 30
   b. 15   d. $16\frac{1}{2}$

7. Sandra Scarr's study of black children adopted by white parents demonstrated that
   a. a child's background, experience, and culture may influence the child's knowledge and thought processes

b. the younger that black children were adopted, the closer their IQs were to white averages

c. both a and b

d. none of the above

8. As a result of Jane Mercer's Riverside study of children labeled mentally retarded, California has passed a law making it illegal to determine that a child is retarded solely on the basis of IQ scores.

a. true   b. false

9. The psychologist _____ was found to have faked his research data which supported the hereditary view of intelligence.

a. L. L. Thorndike   c. Arthur Jensen

b. Cyril Burt   d. David Ochoa

10. Which of the following results represent Heber's Milwaukee Project findings?

a. by age six all of the children in the experimental group were intellectually superior to those in the control group

b. language skills and problem solving abilities were the same for both the experimental and control groups

c. no difference in IQs was noted between experimental and control groups

d. none of the above

11. The Ypsilanti Project demonstrated that children in enrichment programs

a. scored higher on reading and math

b. scored higher on language achievement

c. had fewer antisocial and delinquent tendencies

d. all of the above

12. Most successful early intervention projects have used

a. home-based intervention

b. hot meals

c. project centers

d. none of the above

13. A _____ study is a research approach that studies individuals over time and usually involves measurements at periodic intervals.

a. case   c. horizontal

b. longitudinal   d. correlational

14. _____ is a term usually applied only to those with visual or auditory dysfunctions.

a. common-sense dysfunction

b. sensory exceptionality

c. see-hear syndrome

d. none of the above

15. The type of thinking that generates many different solutions to a problem is known as
    a. convergent production
    b. divergent production
    c. mainstreaming
    d. operations

ESSAY QUESTIONS

1. Explain why Thomas Edison needed the help of L. L. Thurstone.

2. List the verbal and performance subtests on the Wechsler Adult Intelligence Scale.

3. Explain the Zajonc and Markus model of intellectual climate.

4. Identify some of the problems that contaminate the twin studies used to support the inheritability of intelligence.

5. Describe the difficulties in measuring intellectual change over time.

ANSWER SECTION

Guided Review
 1.   Thurstone, mathematics
 2.   intelligence
 3.   intelligence
 4.   Francis Galton
 5.   phrenology
 6.   Alfred Binet, Theodore Simon, special education
 7.   chronological age (or CA), mental age (or MA)
 8.   intelligence quotient, MA, CA, 100
 9.   Lewis Terman, Stanford-Binet
10.   valid
11.   intelligence
12.   verbal, performance
13.   individual, group
14.   factor load
15.   once, factor analysis
16.   Guilford, intellectual
17.   operations, contents, products
18.   intelligence
19.   verbal
20.   giftedness, students
21.   test
22.   Francis Galton, firstborn
23.   achieve, academically

24. *reflective*
25. *firstborns*
26. *model, intellectual, climate*
27. *declines, reverse*
28. *three, four*
29. *opportunities*
30. *Arthur Jensen, fifteen, inheritance*
31. *blacks*
32. *feebleminded*
33. *speak (or comprehend) English*
34. *cultural bias*
35. *black children, white families*
36. *younger*
37. *cultural bias*
38. *black, Mexican-American, mentally retarded*
39. *adaptive behavior, misused*
40. *culture-fair*
41. *Raven Progressive Matrices*
42. *inheritance, genes*
43. *+1.00*
44. *inverse relationship*
45. *high, inheritance (or genetics)*
46. *twins reared apart, faked*
47. *small, contaminated (or biased)*
48. *intellectual stimulation, deprived environments*
49. *Heber, 80*
50. *education, vocational rehabilitation, instruction*
51. *superior, 120.7, 87.2*
52. *control, experimental, disciplinary*
53. *Ypsilanti, early-intervention*
54. *kibbutz*
55. *intervention*
56. *motor skills, verbal, cognitive*
57. *reliable, ten*
58. *average, intelligence, superior, average*
59. *speed*
60. *Lewis Terman, longitudinal*
61. *10, 30*
62. *worked, satisfaction*
63. *Robert Sears, original children*
64. *healthier, happier, richer, suicide, alcoholism, divorce*
65. *exceptional*
66. *physical-sensory, social-emotional*
67. *educate, epilepsy*
68. *sensory exceptionality*
69. *language, feedback*
70. *invulnerables*
71. *Down's*
72. *educable mentally retarded, 50, 69*

73. *shorter attention spans*
74. *mainstreaming*
75. *creativity*
76. *novelty, appropriateness, transcendence, constraints, coalescence*
77. *constraints*
78. *coalesce, Edison's*
79. *IQ (or intelligence) tests, convergent productions*
80. *divergent production, creativity*
81. *ideational fluency*
82. *stable*
83. *inherited, environments*
84. *mislabeling*

Self Test I
1. a
2. a
3. d
4. c
5. d
6. b
7. b
8. c
9. b
10. d
11. d
12. d
13. a
14. c
15. d

Self Test II
1. a
2. b
3. b
4. a
5. b
6. b
7. c
8. a
9. b
10. a
11. d
12. a
13. b
14. b
15. b

CHAPTER 13

Personality

BEHAVIORAL OBJECTIVES

After completing this chapter, the student should be able to:

1. Compare the type theory of Hippocrates with that of William Sheldon.
2. Distinguish a central trait from a secondary trait in Allport's theory.
3. Distinguish surface from source traits in Cattell's theory.
4. Explain how personality traits may be situationally dependent.
5. List and explain the three parts of personality in Freud's psychoanalytic theory.
6. Contrast the underlying dynamics and features of the Oedipus complex with those of the Electra Complex.
7. List and describe the six psychosexual stages of development.
8. Give an example of an oral and anal fixation.
9. Give one or two key features of the psychoanalytic personality theories of Carl Jung, Alfred Adler, and Otto Rank.
10. Mention contributions (strengths) and criticisms (weaknesses) of Freud's psychoanalytic theory.
11. Compare Dollard and Miller's theory with that of Freud's.
12. Outline the major principles and theorists connected with behavioral theories of personality and social learning theory.
13. Compare and contrast the theories of Gordon Allport, Kurt Lewin, and Carl Rogers.
14. State the central underlying themes of humanistic theory.
15. Tell what the MMPI is and what it measures.
16. Explain the meaning of the terms reliability, validity, and standardization as they apply to psychological tests.
17. Compare and contrast the Rorschach and the TAT.

KEY TERMS AND CONCEPTS

personality	melancholic
personality type theories	phlegmatic

sanguine
choleric
humors
endomorph
mesomorph
ectomorph
introverts
extroverts
traits
trait theory
cardinal traits
central traits
secondary traits
surface traits
source traits
16PF
psychoanalytic theory
slips of the tongue
unconscious processes
id, ego, superego
pleasure principle
reality principle
libido
Oedipus complex
pleasure bond
penis envy
Electra complex
narcissistic
hysteria
psychosexual stages
erogenous zones
negative fixation
positive fixation
collective unconscious
inferiority complex
birth trauma
drives, cues, responses,
    reinforcement
experimental neurosis
altruism

generalized expectancy
situationally-dependent
predispositional forces
humanistic theories
self
phenomenological
functional autonomy
Field Theory
life space
principle of contemporaneity
self theory
self actualization
MMPI
standardized instrument
MMPI validity scales
MMPI clinical scales
Terman-Miles Masculinity-Feminity Test
androgynous
California F Scale
authoritarianism
predictive validity
criterion validity
reliability
Rorschach ink blot test
TAT
projective tests
ambiguous stimuli
personality and verbal style
behavioral assessment
humanistic personality assessment
Q sort
self image
ideal self
interviews
empathy
client-centered therapy
nonverbal cues
body language

NAMES TO REMEMBER

Hippocrates
William Sheldon
Carl Jung
Gordon Allport
Raymond B. Cattell
Sigmund Freud

Alfred Adler
Otto Rank
John Dollard
Neal Miller
John B. Watson
B. F. Skinner

Albert Bandura   Kurt Lewin
J. B. Rotter   Carl Rogers

GUIDED REVIEW

1. The essence of any science of psychology is _behavior_ *predictability* .

2. A consistency in behavior that remains stable under varying conditions refers to a person's _personality_ .

3. Psychologists wonder if personalities are _internally_ governed or _externally_ governed.

4. According to psychologists, the word personality refers to the _whole_ person, not just to part of him or her.

5. Early personality researchers were interested in classifying people according to certain personality _types_ .

6. There are many _types_ *theories* of personality, each with a different emphasis.

7. The Greek physician, _Hippocrates_ , classified personality according to body humors.

8. According to Hippocrates, a listless and tired personality type was called _phlegmatic_ and occurred because of too much _phlegm_ .

9. According to Hippocrates a sad personality type was called _melancholic_ and occurred because of too much _black bile_ .

10. In 1940 William _Sheldon_ presented a correlation between _physique_ and personality.

11. In Sheldon's system a thin person will be labeled an _ectomorph_ , a fat person an _endomorph_ , and a muscular person a _mesomorph_ .

12. A person with a _cerebrotonic_ temperament, according to Sheldon, has an ectomorphic physique.

13. Sheldon's findings relating physique and temperament may have been due to _biases_ among observers and raters.

14. Carl Jung's theory of personality classified individuals as being _introverts_ or _extroverts_ .

15. Approximately ___20___ million Americans currently consider themselves to be shy.

16. Personality type theories are both appealing and at the same time limited because of their ___simplicity___ .

17. Because type theories of personality are oversimplifications, personality theorists more often use a ___trait___ approach.

18. Important underlying and enduring qualities of a person are called ___traits___ .

19. Although traits may be good descriptions of behavior, they ___explain___ nothing.

20. The psychologist ___Allport___ talked about cardinal traits, central traits, and secondary traits.

21. Allport's ___cardinal___ traits are the most general and enduring, while ___central___ traits are far more common, and ___secondary___ traits are often called attitudes.

22. Raymond Cattell used the statistical technique of ___factor analysis___ to condense and combine many overlapping traits.

23. Raymond Cattell developed the 16 personality factor questionnaire, commonly abbreviated as the ___16 PF___ .

24. A criticism of trait theory is that many personality "traits" may be ___situationally___ dependent.

25. Because environmental circumstances as well as traits influence behavior, there are probably no strict ___trait___ theorists.

26. Freud is the founder of ___psychoanalytic___ theory.

27. Two techniques Freud used to probe the unconscious mind were the interpretation of ___dreams___ and the analysis of ___slips___ of the tongue.

28. A person who has accepted all or most of Freud's theory is called a ___psychoanalyst___ .

29. Freud's theory is considered to be a ___grand___ explanatory theory because it tries to explain ___most___ of human behavior.

30. The three parts of personality according to Freud are the ___id___ , the ___ego___ , and the ___superego___ .

31. The id operates according to the _pleasure_ principle.

32. The ego functions according to the _reality_ principle.

33. The _superego_ represents social and traditional values in Freud's theory.

34. Freud believed that the id, ego, and superego were constantly in _conflict_.

35. Psychological energy or _libido_ is drained by conflicts between the three parts of the personality.

36. According to Freud, an infant's id receives gratification from the mother during nursing, thus creating a ~~Oedipus~~ _pleasure_ ~~complex~~ _bond_ between infant and mother.

37. A young boy who unconsciously wishes his father to be dead so the boy's id can have the mother all to itself is experiencing the _Oedipus_ complex.

38. To resolve the Oedipus complex, the young boy comes to _identify_ with the father by _acting_ exactly like him. In so doing the boy develops a _heterosexual_ identity as a male.

39. Freud believed that the first few years of a child's life were very powerful determinants of his later adult _personality_.

40. The counterpart of the Oedipus complex in boys is the _Electra_ complex in girls.

41. Freud said girls come to desire their fathers because of _penis_ envy.

42. Freud felt that women could never be as psychologically _whole_ as men and were likely to become _narcissistic_.

43. Freud's ideas about women are expressed in his phrase, "anatomy is _destiny_."

44. The instinctive drives that Freud talked about were _sexual_ behavior and aggression.

45. Sexual desires and aggressive tendencies clash with social inhibition and produce _anxiety_ which is controlled by the ego's use of _defenses_.

46. A person who cannot see but has nothing wrong physically with her eyes is said to be __hysterically__ blind.

47. Freud believed all hysterias were __functional__.

48. The first three psychosexual stages of development are centered about the __erogenous__ zones.

49. Whereas the __oral__ stage produces pleasure through sucking and chewing, the __anal__ stage is related to elimination, retention, and toilet training.

50. A child's greatest pleasure during the __phallic__ stage comes from stimulating the genitals.

51. A person who has problems progressing through the psychosexual stages of development may become __fixated__ at any given stage.

52. Not enough satisfaction in a given stage may produce a __negative__ fixation, and too much satisfaction may produce a __positive__ fixation.

53. Stinginess and selfishness in later life may be, according to Freud, due to unsatisfactory toilet training experiences resulting in an __anal__ __retentive__ personality.

54. Freud said sexual feelings become dormant during the __latency__ stage (ages 6 to 12).

55. From puberty to adulthood, heterosexual desire awakens during the __genital__ stage.

56. Carl Jung believed people have a personal unconscious and a __collective__ unconscious.

57. The term "inferiority complex" was coined by __Alfred__ __Adler__.

58. Psychological birth trauma is an important concept in the writings of __Otto__ __Rank__.

59. Freud's idea of __unconscious__ motivation is a major contribution which has been supported by research.

60. Many of Freud's ideas have been difficult to test with the __scientific__ method.

61. No one has ever demonstrated conclusively that __dreams__ mean anything.

62. The first six years of a person's life are not as _important_ to the formation of later adult personality as Freud thought.

63. John Dollard and Neal Miller attempted to translate the ideas of Freudian psychoanalysis into the language of _behavior_ theory.

64. For Dollard and Miller, the major factors of personality dynamics are _drives_, cues, _responses_ and reinforcement.

65. Dollard and Miller translated Freud's idea of instinctive drives conflicting with social taboos into _approach_ tendencies conflicting with _avoidance_ tendencies.

66. B. F. Skinner and the other behaviorists believe that forces in the _environment_, rather than internal factors, determine behavior.

67. Behaviorists argue that _conditioning_ is responsible for the development of personality.

68. Evidence indicates that there are individual differences in _personality_ just after birth; this argues against the notion that personality is solely due to _environmental_ experience.

69. Albert Bandura is considered to be a _social_ _learning_ theorist.

70. Including _cognitive_ viewpoints within a behavioral framework is a relatively recent trend.

71. J. B. Rotter believes an important variable in determining a person's personality is the person's _expectations_ about future outcomes.

72. Instead of the term "trait," Rotter uses the term "_generalized expectancy_."

73. Whereas trait and psychoanalytic theories view personality as _stable_ across many situations, behavioral and social learning theories view an individual's personality as being _situationally - dependant_.

74. Humanistic theories of personality are interested in the concept of _self_, stress that people tend to grow as human beings and to _realize_ their potential, and believe that people have _free_ will.

75. Humanists often believe that for each person there is no objective world. This is a _phenomenological_ view.

76. Gordon Allport was one of the earliest researchers to emphasize that each individual is *unique* .

77. Allport's concept of *functional* *autonomy* means that any activity may become a goal in itself, although it was originally started for other reasons.

78. Kurt Lewin is associated with *field* theory.

79. According to Lewin, an individual's own personal world is his or her psychological *life* space.

80. Carl Rogers' theory of personality is often called *self* theory.

81. Rogers thinks the major cause of *maladjustment* occurs when one's sense of self is perceived as being opposed to one's goals.

82. Humanistic theory has been criticized because focusing on one's self does not explain the *causes* of behavior.

83. Humanists have also been criticized for ignoring *environmental* forces, and for their lack of rigorous *experimentation*.

84. The best known instrument for measuring personality traits is the (abbreviation only) *MMPI* .

85. Because the MMPI has been administered to thousands of people for purposes of future comparison with other subjects, it is said to be a *standardized* instrument.

86. In addition to ten basic personality scales, the MMPI contains three *validity* scales which detect faking, defensiveness, and a tendency to exaggerate one's problems.

87. The MMPI is useful in making *general* assessments of one's personality but usually cannot predict specific or unique individual responses.

88. A person scoring about equal on the masculine and feminine scales of the Terman–Miles test is said to be *androgynous* .

89. The California F Scale measures the trait of *authoritarianism*

90. In one study, 76% of those who scored high on the California F Scale were members of the *I R* party.

91. If scores on a personality test accurately reflect behavior then the test is said to have predictive *validity* .

92. A test that actually measures what it says it measures is a ___valid___ test.

93. A test that gives consistent results and is stable over time is said to be ___reliable___ .

94. The ___Rorschach___ ink blot test and the (abbreviation only) ___TAT___ attempt to reflect unconscious aspects of personality.

95. Personality measuring instruments which contain ambiguous stimuli (such as the Rorschach and TAT) are known as ___projective___ tests.

96. Whereas the Rorschach contains inkblots, the TAT contains a series of ambiguous ~~TAT~~ ___pictures___ .

97. A person taking the TAT is asked to make up a ___story___ about each picture.

98. ___Projective___ tests are viewed by some psychologists as useful and adequate and by others as invalid and unreliable.

99. The style and speed of a person's ___speech___ can give important clues to his or her personality.

100. Behaviorists use the technique of ___behavior modification___ to shape or change an individual's personality.

101. Behaviorists deal only with ___observable___ aspects of behavior and rely extensively on ___experimental___ methods.

102. Humanistic approaches to personality assessment try to find objective ways of assessing a person's ___subjective___ experience.

103. An investigator who asks a subject to sort cards containing self concept statements is using the humanistic personality assessment technique called ___Q___ ___sorting___ .

104. A person going through the Q sort cards a second time is probably sorting them according to his or her ___ideal___ self.

105. Humanistic psychologists often use personal ___interviews___ to explore the other person's self concept and emotions.

106. To assess aspects of someone's personality by examining posture, gestures, and movements is to study ___non-verbal___ cues or ___body___ language.

107. Criticism has been leveled at humanistic assessment methods for their lack of ___rigor___ .

108. Uncovering creative forces, discovering enduring characteristics, and learning more about people is the common ___goal___ of all personality assessment.

SELF TEST I

1. In Cattell's formula, r = f(ps), which of the following is <u>not</u> true
    a. r stands for response
    b. p stands for personality
    c. s stands for subject
    d. f stands for function.

2. In Sheldon's approach to personality, a chubby individual has a/an _____ body build and a _____ temperament.
    a. endomorphic, viscerotonic
    b. mesomorphic, somatotonic
    c. ectomorphic, cerebrotonic
    d. none of the above

3. One criticism of trait theory is that
    a. many personality traits may be situationally dependent
    b. it has not been tested thoroughly with mathematical and statistical precision
    c. it is a gross oversimplification
    d. all of the above

4. Freud referred to an infant boy's derived gratification through nursing as _____ between infant and mother.
    a. a libido mesh   c. penis envy
    b. a pleasure bond   d. an Oedipus link

5. What instinctive drives did Freud believe were conflicting with cultural taboos?
    a. sex and aggression
    b. hunger, thirst, and sexuality
    c. the Oedipus complex, libido, and the pleasure principle
    d. self preservation and the need for immediate gratification

6. Which two stages of psychosexual development were considered by Freud to be less important than the others?
    a. latency and genital   c. anal and latency
    b. phallic and genital   d. latency and phallic

7. Regarding Freud's theory of personality,
    a. much of it has not been supported by scientific data
    b. it is regarded as valuable because it helped generate much research
    c. it has been difficult to test many of Freud's ideas with the scientific method
    d. all of the above

8. Which of the following supports the beliefs of the behaviorists?
    a. there is evidence that there are individual differences in personality just after birth
    b. personality traits will change if the environment is manipulated sufficiently
    c. both a and b
    d. none of the above

9. For each of us there is no objective world; there is only our own subjective or personal experience of the world. This represents a _____ approach.
    a. phenomenological   c. choleric
    b. psychoanalytic   d. androgynous

10. Which of the following is a humanistic psychologist?
    a. Albert Bandura   c. Carl Rogers
    b. Sigmund Freud   d. B. F. Skinner

11. The MMPI is a _____ test because it has been given to thousands of people, and their scores can be used as a basis for comparison.
    a. standardized   c. reliable
    b. projective   d. personality

12. Which test measures the trait of authoritarianism?
    a. MMPI   c. California F Scale
    b. Rorschach ink blot   d. Terman-Miles

13. Tests which contain ambiguous stimuli that can be interpreted in different ways by different subjects are
    a. projective tests
    b. objective tests
    c. found by research to have very high validity
    d. both a and c

14. A subject placing cards in different piles is providing information about his or her self-image and ideal self. The method being used is
    a. behavioral assessment   c. Q sorting
    b. that of criterion validity d. self analysis

15. That weird dream you've been having night after night has really begun to bother you. You feel that psychoanalysis might help you learn more about your personality by uncovering the possible unconscious conflicts responsible for the dream. You are especially interested in the interpretation of your _____ score.
    a. Q sort   c. MMPI
    b. Rorschach   d. behavioral assessment inventory

SELF TEST II

1. Which of the following does not represent a personality type approach:
    a. Hippocrates' theory   c. Allport's theory
    b. Sheldon's theory   d. Jung's introvert-extrovert model

2. According to Allport, the basic units that make up an individual's
    personality, and which are very common and important in all people,
    are
    a. cardinal traits   c. primary traits
    b. central traits   d. secondary traits

3. The ego, according to Freud
    a. has no objective knowledge of reality
    b. is the internal representation of social values
    c. is primarily biological
    d. must deal with reality

4. In order to resolve an Oedipus complex, a six-year-old boy must
    a. realize that the mother is his real rival
    b. break the pleasure bond
    c. identify with (behave and act like) his father
    d. first develop a homosexual preference for males

5. Sucking and chewing are the chief sources of an infant's pleasure during
    the
    a. Electra complex
    b. oral stage of development
    c. phallic stage of development
    d. pre-toddler stage of psychosexual development

6. Alfred Adler coined the term
    a. introvert-extrovert   c. inferiority complex
    b. androgynous   d. Electra complex

7. B. F. Skinner believes that personality is a function of
    a. internal conflicts   c. unconscious processes
    b. forces in the environment   d. cardinal traits

8. Which personality theories view the individual's personality as mainly
    situationally-dependent?
    a. social learning theories   c. psychoanalytic theories
    b. trait theories   d. both a and b

9. Kurt Lewin is the founder of an approach to personality called
    a. field theory
    b. physique and temperament theory
    c. androgyny
    d. functional autonomy

10. Which personality instrument measures personality traits?
    a. TAT   c. APA
    b. MMPI   d. WISC

11. A person who is excitable and who rushes from one thing to another without finishing anything may score quite high on the MMPI _____ scale.
    a. hypochondriasis   c. hysteria
    b. paranoia   d. hypomania

12. A psychological test that is consistent, yielding scores that are stable over time is
    a. reliable   c. standardized
    b. valid   d. projective

13. The behavioral approach to personality assessment focuses on
    a. internal qualities such as traits
    b. experimental methods and direct observation
    c. emotion and thought
    d. both b and c

14. Humanistic assessment methods have been criticized for their
    a. overuse of projective techniques
    b. lack of empathy
    c. overly structured approach using factor analytic tests
    d. lack of rigor

15. The guy next door is always lifting weights, jogging, and eating bran. He is energetic, assertive, and courageous, and could easily double for the incredible hulk. This neighbor of yours has a _____ physique and a _____ temperament.
    a. mesomorphic, somatotonic
    b. ectomorphic, cerebrotonic
    c. endomorphic, viscerotonic
    d. ectomorphic, viscerotonic

ESSAY QUESTIONS

1. Compare and contrast type theories with trait theories of personality. Make specific reference to the theorists and the concepts they developed.

2. Discuss Freud's psychoanalytic theory of personality. Include an analysis of the parts of personality, the unconscious, the Oedipus complex, and the stages of development.

3. How do behavioral and social learning theories differ from psychoanalytic and trait theories?

4. Discuss humanistic personality theory and assessment techniques. Mention key investigators and key concepts.

5. Explain the meaning of reliability and validity in psychological testing.

6. Compare and contrast the MMPI with the Rorschach and TAT.

ANSWER SECTION

Guided Review
1. *predictability*
2. *personality*
3. *internally, externally*
4. *whole*
5. *types*
6. *theories*
7. *Hippocrates*
8. *phlegmatic, phlegm*
9. *melancholic, black bile*
10. *Sheldon, physique*
11. *ectomorph, endomorph, mesomorph*
12. *cerebrotonic*
13. *biases*
14. *introverts, extroverts*
15. *20*
16. *simplicity*
17. *trait*
18. *traits*
19. *explain*
20. *Allport*
21. *cardinal, central, secondary*
22. *factor analysis*
23. *16PF*
24. *situationally*
25. *trait*
26. *psychoanalytic*
27. *dreams, slips*
28. *psychoanalyst*
29. *grand, most*
30. *id, ego, superego*
31. *pleasure*
32. *reality*
33. *superego*
34. *conflict*
35. *libido*
36. *pleasure bond*
37. *Oedipus*
38. *identify, behaving (or acting), heterosexual*

39. *personality*
40. *Electra*
41. *penis*
42. *complete, narcissistic*
43. *destiny*
44. *sexual*
45. *anxiety (or conflict), defenses*
46. *hysterically*
47. *functional*
48. *erogenous*
49. *oral, anal*
50. *phallic*
51. *fixated*
52. *negative, positive*
53. *anal retentive*
54. *latency*
55. *genital*
56. *collective*
57. *Alfred Adler*
58. *Otto Rank*
59. *unconscious*
60. *scientific*
61. *dreams*
62. *crucial*
63. *behavior (or learning)*
64. *drives, responses*
65. *approach, avoidance*
66. *environment*
67. *conditioning*
68. *personality, environmental*
69. *social learning*
70. *cognitive*
71. *expectations*
72. *generalized expectancy*
73. *stable, situationally-dependent*
74. *self, realize (or actualize), free*
75. *phenomenological*
76. *unique*
77. *functional autonomy*
78. *field*
79. *life*
80. *self*
81. *maladjustment*
82. *causes*
83. *environmental, experimentation*
84. *MMPI*
85. *standardized*
86. *validity (control)*
87. *general*

88. androgynous
89. authoritarianism
90. Republican
91. validity
92. valid
93. reliable
94. Rorschach, TAT
95. projective
96. pictures
97. story
98. projective
99. speech
100. behavior modification
101. observable, experimental
102. subjective
103. Q sorting
104. ideal
105. interviews
106. nonverbal, body
107. rigor
108. goal

Self Test I		Self Test II	
1.	c	1.	c
2.	a	2.	b
3.	a	3.	d
4.	b	4.	c
5.	a	5.	b
6.	a	6.	c
7.	d	7.	b
8.	b	8.	a
9.	a	9.	a
10.	c	10.	b
11.	a	11.	d
12.	c	12.	a
13.	a	13.	b
14.	c	14.	d
15.	b	15.	a

CHAPTER 14

Coping with Conflict and Stress

BEHAVIORAL OBJECTIVES

After completing this chapter, the student should be able to:

1. Describe Brady's "executive monkey" experiment and explain the implications of this study.
2. List and give an example of the four types of conflict.
3. Describe the Three-Mile Island accident and the stress reactions that resulted from it.
4. List and explain the three stages of the general adaptation syndrome.
5. List the symptoms common to chronic stress.
6. Describe Steven Locke's stress study which relied on blood samples, and discuss the implications of this study.
7. Discuss the factors that qualify interpretations of the Holmes and Rahe Social-Readjustment Rating Scale.
8. Describe the Alpha, Beta, and Gamma personality types and explain how each type is related to illness.
9. Define "little murders" and explain what happens if these begin to "pile up."
10. Define and contrast fear and anxiety.
11. Explain the implications of Stephen Suomi's monkey study as it relates to stress and inheritance.
12. Describe the research that indicates stress reactions may be due to biological predisposition.
13. Explain the occasion of Jo Roman's death.
14. Define and give an example of denial, rationalization, reaction formation, projection, and intellectualization.
15. Explain the various coping strategies that an individual can use in order to adjust to stress.

KEY TERMS AND CONCEPTS

executive monkey   stomach ulcers

duodenal ulcers
conflict
stress
unique stressors
approach-approach conflict
approach-avoidance conflict
avoidance-avoidance conflict
double approach-avoidance
   conflict
acute stressors
general adaptation syndrome
   GAS
alarm reaction stage
corticoid hormone
resistance stage
exhaustion stage
chronic stress symptoms
immune system
lymphocytes
natural killer cells
social-readjustment scale
prospective research

ability to cope
personality traits
Alpha personality
Beta personality
Gamma personality
"little murders"
anxiety
fear
benzodiazepines
suicide
imitated suicides
self deliverance guide
defense mechanisms
denial
rationalization
sour grapes
sweet lemon
reaction formation
projection
intellectualization
direct coping strategies
systematic relaxation

NAMES TO REMEMBER

George Serban
Hans Selye
George E. Vaillant
Caroline B. Thomas

Stephen Suomi
Jo Roman
Sigmund Freud
Norman Cousins

GUIDED REVIEW

1. In the 1958 Brady et al. experiment, one of each pair of monkeys had _control_ over the _environment_ .

2. Brady concluded that the "_executive_ _monkeys_ " developed _stomach_ and _duodenal_ ulcers because they were in control of the shocks being delivered.

3. _Conflict_ is a state in which ambivalent feelings about something or someone causes stress.

4. Everyone faces _conflict_ in his or her daily life.

5. _Stress_ is a psychological state associated with _psychological_ and _hormonal_ changes caused by conflict, trauma, or other influences.

6. George Serban surveyed over 1,000 people and found new
___socail___ and ___political___ values are inducing
stress in most people.

7. Whenever you have a choice to make you are in a state
of ___conflict___.

8. The most stressful conflicts occur when it is difficult to ___resolve___
the conflict and when the conflict is extremely ___important___.

9. ___Vaccilating___ is likely to make a conflict last longer, and stress
over a long period of time can be ___debilitating___.

10. Generally the easiest type of conflict to resolve is an
___approach___ - ___approach___ conflict. However, this
conflict can be quite stressful when both goal objects are highly desirable but ___mutually___ ___exclusive___.

11. When we are faced with a single goal that contains both positive and
negative elements, we experience ___approach___ -
___avoidance___ conflict. In this type of conflict the
___positive___ aspects of the goal are generally most prominent
when we are at a distance from the goal; but when we are closer to the
goal, the ___negative___ aspects are more salient.

12. The worst kind of conflict to be in is the ___avoidance___ -
___avoidance___ conflict in which there are two goals and they
are both ___negative___.

13. The most complex and common conflict is ___double___
___approach___ - ___avoidance___ conflict. In this type of
conflict there are two goals and each goal represents an
___approach___ - ___avoidance___ conflict.

14. Not all ___stressors___ are the result of conflict. For example,
people living near Three-Mile Island had acute stress reactions due
to a near nuclear ___meltdown___.

15. Researchers studying people living within 55 miles of the Three-Mile
Island reactor found that the amount of stress people suffered was
directly related to how ___close___ they were to the reactor.

16. The people who suffered the most stress near the nuclear reactor tended
to be: ___young___, well educated, ___female___,
married, homeowners, and those with chronic ___emotional___ or
___health___ problems.

17. Psychiatrist Lenore Terr, when interviewing 23 of the kidnapped
Chowchilla school children, found that the effects of stress are often
___long___ ___lasting___.

18. Researchers have found that _Vietnam_ veterans, who were in combat were more likely to abuse alcohol and _drugs_ and to be _arrested_ by police than other veterans.

19. Experienced firemen and police officers may be _overwhelmed_ by a tragedy like the commercial airliner crash in San Diego, California. Direct contact with the _victims_ caused the acute stress. Memories of the accident resulted in _chronic_ stress.

20. Alan Davidson said that the most successful treatment for city workers exposed to the San Diego crash was to provide _empathy_ and _understanding_.

21. Conflict and traumas can cause _stress_, and this can lead to _illness_.

22. Hans _Selye_ refers to the body's physical reaction to stress as the _general_ _adaption_ _syndrom_ or GAS.

23. The general adaptation syndrome consists of three stages: the _alarm_ _reaction_ stage, the _resistance_ stage, and the _exhaustion_ stage.

24. During Selye's alarm reaction stage _corticoid_ _hormone_ levels increase accompanied by _emotional_ arousal and increased _tension_. Also during this stage attempts to cope by using _defense_ _mechanisms_ or by taking direct _action_ can occur.

25. If stress is prolonged, the resistance stage begins and it is characterized by a "_full war effort_" by the individual who is attempting to cope. It is during this stage that individuals may become _fixed_ in their patterns of behavior instead of finding better ways of coping.

26. In the exhaustion stage, Selye contends that a person's defensive measures may become _inappropriate_ and _exaggerated_. Metabolic changes may also occur that inhibit normal _brain_ functioning, resulting in a complete psychological disorganization. As resistance weakens the individual becomes prone to the _illness_ that may accompany stress.

27. The common early symptoms of chronic stress are headaches, gastro-intestinal disturbances, skin rashes and hives, as well as _dizziness_ and _fatigue_.

28. _chronic stress_ can lead to hypertension, aggravated arthritis, inflammation of the large colon (known as

colitis   ), asthma, hypoglycemia, and
diabetes   .

29. Brady's "executive" monkey study has been criticized because subjects were not _divided_ _randomly_ into control and experimental groups.

30. Many forms of illness are possibly related to stress because of the effect stress has on our _immune_ _systems_ .

31. Counting white blood cells (specifically the _lymphocytes_) is one way of assessing the immune system's effectiveness. Schleifer et al. studied men whose wives had terminal _cancer_ and, as the stress continued, the men's white _blood_ count became lower.

32. After the death of a loved one, the bereaved often have increased incidences of _illness_ or _death_ .

33. Researcher Steven _Locke_ exposed subjects' blood samples to human _leukemia_ cells. He found the effectiveness of natural killer cells to be related to how well subjects were _coping_ with _stress_ , not to the actual stress itself.

34. Several clinical observations and animal studies have shown that defects such as cleft palate and hyperactivity may be the result of _stress_ during _pregnancy_ .

35. Pregnant rats subjected to stress have been found to be more likely to produce _abnormal_ _offspring_ . And other animal studies have shown that stress during pregnancy can affect the expression of _genetic_ _traits_ in the offspring.

36. Holmes and Rahe developed the _Social_-_Readjustment_ Rating Scale to indicate the amount of stress we face in life. More than _300_ stress points within a year has been associated with greater incidence of _illness_ and _stress_ related problems.

37. Holmes and Rahe have not shown that stress _causes_ illness since their data are _correlational_ .

38. Locating a healthy population and studying their life stresses or personalities as related to later illness is known as _prospective_ research.

39. George _Vaillant's_ prospective research discovered that the ability to _cope_ with _stress_ generally

results in a _healthy_ person.

40. Caroline Thomas and Barbara Betz have found evidence that links _personality_ traits to specific stress-related disorders.

41. _Alpha_ personalities rely upon themselves, are cautious and nonadventurous. They are also slow to adapt to _new_ _situations_ .

42. _Beta_ personalities are fun-loving and _spontaneous_ . These people tend to be _flexible_ in new situations and clever.

43. _Gamma_ personalities are short-tempered. These people tend to function at _extremes_ , such as being overly cautious or careless.

44. The _Gamma_ personality type has been found to be three times more likely to suffer a major illness than other types.

45. Spilling your drink, getting caught in traffic, etc., are known collectively as " _little_ _murders_ " and can have a cumulative effect leading to a general _adaption_ _syndrom_ .

46. _Anxiety_ is not the same as fear. Fear is _object_ -related.

47. Anxiety levels have generally been found to be higher among those who handle _stress_ poorly.

48. According to Stephen Suomi, stress may be related to an individual's _biological_ predispositions. He found that _heart_ _rate_ change in a one-month-old monkey was a good predictor of how well the monkeys would later respond to stress. He also found that monkeys who were _blood_ _relative_ reacted to stress similarly.

49. Gregory Carey has found that _identical_ twins are much more likely to react similarly to stress than are _fraternal_ _twins_ .

50. Biochemical differences among people have been noted by the presence of specific cells in the brain which are receptive to (chemical name) _benzodiazepines_ . These data suggest that the brain's neurochemistry may regulate how much _anxiety_ we experience when stressed.

51. Suicide has been generally increasing, but is rising quite rapidly among _adolescents_ and the _elderly_ .

52. One investigator found that ____65____ percent of college students had at one time contemplated suicide seriously enough to consider the __means__ .

53. After the suicide of a well known __person__ , single car fatalities increased by 9.12%. Many of these may have been imitative __suicide__ .

54. Generally, __females__ are more likely to attempt suicide than __males__ , while __males__ are three times more likely to commit suicide.

55. Suicide among blacks is predominantly a __youthful__ __phenomenon__ occurring equally between males and females.

56. A Guide to Self Deliverance is a pamphlet that describes the most simple and least painful ways of __committing__ __suicide__ .

57. __Jo__ __Roman__ , a New York artist, planned a party in which she invited her relatives and close friends for the occasion of her __suicide__ .

58. People often handle stress and conflict by using __defense__ __mechanisms__ which distort reality.

59. The term defense mechanism was first used by __Sigmound__ __Freud__ to explain how people protect themselves from unacceptable __unconscious__ thoughts and unwanted realities.

60. Defense mechanisms are __descriptions__ of __behavior__ , not explanations of why behaviors occur.

61. __Denial__ is a defense mechanism through which anxiety and stress are avoided by a refusal to see the situation as it really is.

62. __Rationalization__ does not imply a rational action but rather is a defense mechanism whereby one's view of a conflict or a behavior is altered.

63. A type of rationalization, in which we justify not being able to have something, is often referred to as "__sour__ __grapes__ ," after the Aesop fable.

64. A "__sweet__ __lemon__ " rationalization is used when we try to enhance what we are stuck with, that is, we try to make something seem better than it is.

65. A __reaction__ __formation__ occurs when a person expresses the opposite of his or her true motives or desires.

66. We are using *projection* when we see our own undesirable attributes and thoughts in others.

67. Medical doctors often emotionally distance themselves from those who are suffering by using the defense mechanism of *intellectualization*.

68. Norman Cousins wondered if *stress* could have precipitated his disease. He reasoned that if *negative* *emotions* associated with stress could cause disease, then *positive* *emotions* such as laughter might remedy it.

69. The remission of Cousin's disease may have occurred because he made himself feel happier, which, in turn, raised *endorphin* levels that may have stimulated the body's *immune* *system*.

70. Active rational strategies intended to alleviate stress either by eliminating the stressor or by reducing the psychological effects of stress, are known as *direct* *coping* *strategies*.

71. To avoid rushing to judgment in response to conflict and stress you should first *gather* *information* in order to make the right decision.

72. Having trust in *time* often helps people cope with stress as the passage of *time* reduces our pain and discomfort. Also being with friends can help us cope with stress as this tends to reduce our *self* concerns.

73. Yet another direct coping strategy is to try to think positively and *rationally* while maintaining a sense of *humor*.

74. A final direct coping strategy is to try to become a more *relaxed* person and to use such special techniques as *systematic* *relaxation*.

75. Stress is only likely to be harmful when it is *unresolved*, long-*lasting*, or ineffectively dealt with.

76. In Chinese, the characters for stress mean *danger*, but also *opportunity*. Some stress can be beneficial by *motivating* an individual to take *action*.

77. Hank Siegal contacted released hostage William Quarles to tell him that feeling *guilty* was perfectly *normal*. The *empathy* and understanding helped Quarles.

SELF TEST I

1. In the "executive" monkey study the
   a. two groups of monkeys benefited from the drugs administered
   b. passive helpless monkeys developed the most ulcers
   c. active "executive" monkeys who controlled the shocks developed the most ulcers
   d. groups developed an equal number of ulcers

2. The neighbor of your text's author, who continually climbed up and down the ladder, was in _____ conflict.
   a. approach-approach
   b. avoidance-avoidance
   c. approach-avoidance
   d. double approach-avoidance

3. In _____ conflict you can't help but realize the loss of one goal once you obtain the other.
   a. approach-avoidance
   b. avoidance-avoidance
   c. double approach-avoidance
   d. approach-approach

4. Lenore Terr, a psychiatrist, interviewed most of the kidnapped children from Chowchilla, California. She found that
   a. many of the children still have recurring and disturbing dreams of the experience
   b. reassurances from their parents have done little to reduce the children's fears
   c. both a and b
   d. the children were generally unaffected by their traumatic episode

5. The first veteran police officers who sought counseling after the San Diego airliner crash felt weak and unmanly for seeking help.
   a. true   b. false

6. During the alarm reaction stage of the general adaptation syndrome symptoms such as rash, gastrointestinal upset, hives and sleep loss may occur.
   a. true   b. false

7. Steven Locke measured stress-related symptoms among individuals and then asked subjects how they were coping. Then he
   a. gave subjects stress medication
   b. exposed the subjects' blood to human leukemia cells
   c. measured their suicidal tendencies
   d. all of the above

8. Some "nice things such as marriage, a family get-together, or a vaca-
    tion seem to be stressful.
    a. true   b. false

9. The Harvard stress study which followed individuals for four decades
    demonstrated that
    a. coping skills were unrelated to how well individuals were managing
       their daily lives
    b. physical health was directly related to how well an individual coped
       with stress
    c. physical health was not related to the mental health of individuals
    d. none of the above

10. The type of personality most likely to suffer illness suggested by Betz
    and Thomas is the _____ personality
    a. alpha   c. beta
    b. gamma   d. delta

11. _____ is not object-related, and is different from
    _____, which is object-related.
    a. anxiety, fear   c. stress, anxiety
    b. fear, anxiety   d. conflict, stress

12. Stephen Suomi, who monitored heart beats of stressed one-month-old
    monkeys, found that
    a. primates show little if any stress reactions
    b. reactions to stress may be related to biological predispositions
    c. males may be more susceptible to stress than females
    d. all of the above

13. According to _____, defense mechanisms were necessary
    to protect a person from unacceptable unconscious thoughts and unde-
    sirable realities.
    a. Sigmund Freud   c. Mavis Hetherington
    b. Hans Selye   d. Norman Cousins

14. The defense mechanism of _____ is based on Aesop's
    fable of the fox who couldn't reach the grapes.
    a. denial   c. intellectualization
    b. reaction formation   d. rationalization

15. _____ are designed to eliminate stressors and to harden
    one to the "_____" of daily life.
    a. coping strategies, little murders
    b. defense mechanisms, full war effort
    c. both a and b
    d. none of the above

SELF TEST II

1. A conflict may
    a. cause you to be ambivalent so that you vacillate before making
       a decision
    b. be relatively easy to resolve and require little time to resolve
    c. if prolonged lead to stress reactions
    d. all of the above

2. "Study or Flunk" is a _____ conflict students often face.
    a. approach-approach
    b. approach-avoidance
    c. double approach-avoidance
    d. none of the above

3. Three-Mile Island, the kidnapped Chowchilla, California, children,
    the Vietnam veterans, and the San Diego plane crash were all examples
    of _____.
    a. the general adaptation syndrome
    b. conflict
    c. acute stressors
    d. "little murders"

4. Vietnam veterans who were involved in significant amounts of combat
    became strong and less likely to abuse drugs and alcohol than other
    Vietnam veterans.
    a. true   b. false

5. The physiologist who has proposed the general adaptation syndrome
    is
    a. George Serban   c. George Vaillant
    b. Sigmund Freud   d. Hans Selye

6. Chronic stress has been associated with
    a. the onset of cancer
    b. an increased probability of contracting a contagious disease
    c. the onset of ulcers
    d. all of the above

7. Holmes and Rahe developed the _____.
    a. Stress Unit Profile (SUP)
    b. Social Readjustment Rating Scale
    c. Conflict Indexed Unit Scale
    d. Anxiety Unit Scale (AUS)

8. Most research dealing with stress and illness begins by examining a/an
    _____ suffering from illness
    a. city   c. population
    b. individual   d. animal

9. Caroline Thomas and Barbara Betz have suggested three personality temperaments who react differently to stress, known as _____ personalities.
    a. delta, sigma, and mu
    b. neurotic, psychotic, and normal
    c. alpha, beta, and gamma
    d. none of the above

10. Beta personality types tend to be
    a. confused and short-tempered
    b. fun-loving and spontaneous
    c. self-reliant and steady, but slow to adapt
    d. overcautious and emotional

11. Which of the following statements is true?
    a. there is recent evidence that there may be a biological or genetic explanation of why some people react more to stress than others
    b. anxiety levels have generally been found to be higher among those who handle stress poorly
    c. many psychologists now discount the belief that psychological conflict alone is sufficient to explain anxiety
    d. all of the above

12. Over the last decade there has been an alarming increase in suicide among _____. In fact, it is the third leading cause of death.
    a. adolescents   c. middle-aged blacks
    b. middle-aged whites   d. elderly black females

13. A student who has not started the term paper that is due tomorrow is probably using the defense mechanism of
    a. reaction formation   c. projection
    b. intellectualization   d. denial

14. Doctors and nurses often use _____ as a means of distancing themselves emotionally from patients.
    a. projection   c. sublimation
    b. denial   d. intellectualization

15. _____ is a special technique designed to help an individual _____.
    a. tooling-up, relax   c. systematic relaxation, relax
    b. full war effort, relax   d. none of the above

ESSAY QUESTIONS

1. List and explain the four kinds of conflict discussed in your textbook. Give an example of each, but not those used in the text or study guide.

2. Discuss the findings of the Three-Mile Island nuclear accident and list those who were generally found to suffer the most distress.

3. Identify and explain the three stages of Hans Selye's general adaptation syndrome (GAS).

4. Describe the suicide rates for young and old contrasting the rates for males, females, blacks, and whites.

5. List and describe the coping strategies suggested by your author.

ANSWER SECTION

Guided Review
1. *control, environment*
2. *executive monkeys, stomach, duodenal*
3. *conflict*
4. *conflict*
5. *stress, physiological, hormonal*
6. *social, political*
7. *conflict*
8. *resolve, important*
9. *vacillation, debilitating*
10. *approach-approach, mutually exclusive*
11. *approach-avoidance, positive, negative*
12. *avoidance-avoidance, unacceptable*
13. *double approach-avoidance, approach-avoidance*
14. *stressors, meltdown (or accident)*
15. *close*
16. *younger, female, emotional, health*
17. *long lasting*
18. *Vietnam, drugs, arrested*
19. *overwhelmed, victims, chronic*
20. *empathy, understanding*
21. *stress, illness*
22. *Selye, general adaptation syndrome*
23. *alarm reaction, resistance, exhaustion*
24. *corticoid hormone, emotional, tension, defense mechanisms, action*
25. *full war effort, fixed*
26. *inappropriate, exaggerated, brain, diseases (or illness)*
27. *dizziness, fatigue*
28. *chronic stress, colitis, diabetes*
29. *divided randomly*
30. *immune systems*
31. *lymphocytes, cancer, blood*
32. *illness, death*
33. *Locke, leukemia, coping, stress*
34. *stress, pregnancy*

35. abnormal offspring, genetic traits
36. Social-Readjustment, 300, illness, stress
37. causes, correlational
38. prospective
39. Vaillant's, cope, stress, healthy
40. personality
41. Alpha, new situations
42. Beta, spontaneous, flexible
43. Gamma, extremes
44. Gamma
45. little murders, adaptation syndrome
46. anxiety, object
47. stress
48. biological, heart rate, blood relatives (genetically related)
49. identical, fraternal twins
50. benzodiazepines, anxiety
51. adolescents (or teenagers), elderly (or aged)
52. 65, means
53. personality (or person), suicides
54. females, males, males
55. youthful phenomenon
56. committing suicide
57. Jo Roman, suicide
58. defense mechanisms
59. Sigmund Freud, unconscious
60. descriptions, behavior
61. denial
62. rationalization
63. sour grapes
64. sweet lemon
65. reaction formation
66. projection
67. intellectualization
68. stress, negative emotions, positive emotions
69. endorphin, immune system
70. direct coping strategies
71. gather information
72. time, time, self
73. rationally, humor
74. relaxed, sytematic relaxation
75. unresolved, lasting
76. danger, opportunity, motivating, action
77. guilty, normal, empathy

Self Test I
1. c
2. c
3. c

Self Test II
1. d
2. d
3. c

4.	c
5.	a
6.	a
7.	b
8.	a
9.	b
10.	b
11.	a
12.	b
13.	a
14.	d
15.	a

4.	b
5.	d
6.	d
7.	b
8.	c
9.	c
10.	b
11.	d
12.	a
13.	d
14.	d
15.	c

CHAPTER 15

Abnormal Behavior

BEHAVIORAL OBJECTIVES

After completing this chapter, the student should be able to:

1. Define abnormality showing an awareness of the problems involved in doing so.
2. Name and explain the salient features of four models of psychopathology.
3. State which maladaptive behavior patterns are most prevalent in the United States.
4. Describe DSM-III, and show how it differs from DSM-II in one or two specific ways.
5. List and describe three phobias, and three anxiety states.
6. Distinguish between an obsession and a compulsion.
7. Describe three somatoform disorders giving examples of each.
8. Explain the similarities and differences between psychogenic amnesia and psychogenic fugue.
9. Clarify the difference between multiple personality and schizophrenia.
10. Explain the classifications, symptoms, and possible causes of affective disorders.
11. Discuss schizophrenia, its types, and possible causes, and distinguish between hallucinations and delusions.
12. Mention similarities and differences between three paranoid disorders.
13. Explain the phases and causes of alcoholism mentioning pertinent research findings.
14. Discuss the extent, history, and problems of drug abuse disorders.
15. Name and describe ten psychosexual disorders and ten personality disorders.
16. Describe in detail the Rosenhan study of pseudopatients in mental hospitals.
17. Clarify the position of critics and supporters of DSM-III.
18. Discuss the problem of misdiagnosis of psychopathology, summarizing related research in this area.

KEY TERMS AND CONCEPTS

abnormal behavior
maladaptive
self-defeating
models of psychopathology
the medical model
etiology
the learning model
client vs. patient
the psychoanalytic model
the humanistic-existential model
the legal model
insane
DSM-II
DSM-III
Axis I, II, III, IV, and V
organic disorders
functional disorders
neurosis
neurotic paradox
anxiety disorders
phobia
anxiety states
generalized anxiety disorder
free-floating anxiety
panic disorder/panic attack
obsessive-compulsive disorder
obsessions
compulsions
somatoform disorders
conversion disorder
pseudopregnancy
glove anesthesia
psychogenic pain disorder
hyponchondriasis
malingerers
dissociative disorders
psychogenic amnesia
fugue
multiple personality
affective disorders
psychoses
bipolar disorder
manic-depressive psychosis
unipolar

major depression
endogenous depression
secondary depression
schizophrenia
delusion
hallucinations
cure/remission
disorganized schizophrenia
hebephrenia
catatonic schizophrenic
paranoid schizophrenic
undifferentiated schizophrenia
residual schizophrenia
genetic factors in schizophrenia
biochemical factors in schizophrenia
dopamine hypothesis
pneumoencephalography
CAT findings among chronic schizophrenics
PET scan
paranoid disorders
paranoia
delusions of persecution
delusions of grandeur
shared paranoid disorder
acute paranoid disorder
substance use disorders
alcoholism
initial stage
prodromal phase
crucial phase
chronic phase
biogenetic factors in alcoholism
environmental factors in alcoholism
other substance use disorders
psychosexual disorders
homosexuality
gender identity disorders
paraphilias
psychosexual dysfunctions
personality disorders
drapetomania
pseudopatients
misdiagnosis

NAMES TO REMEMBER

Robert L. Spitzer
William Cullen
Sigmund Freud
Eve White and Eve Black
Sybil
Gordon Bower

Seymour S. Kety
George Winokur
Daniel R. Weinberger
Thomas Szasz
David Rosenhan

GUIDED REVIEW

1. Psychologists study abnormal behavior in order to help those in _need_.

2. Soviet _dissidents_ are often placed in mental institutions.

3. Poor people are more likely to be labeled _psychotic_ than are rich people.

4. For behavior to be considered abnormal, it must be different from the norm and also _maladaptive_ or self-_defeating_.

5. There is a _continuum_ from normal to abnormal.

6. A _model_ is a depiction or a representation that helps one organize his or her knowledge.

7. The _medical_ model assumes that the cause of mental disorder is a biological dysfunction.

8. The medical model depicts abnormal behaviors as symptoms of an underlying _disease_, and those suffering from such disorders are called _patients_.

9. The processes of classical and operant conditioning are important to the _learning_ model of psychopathology.

10. Abnormal behavior resulting from unresolved unconscious conflicts between the id, ego, and superego illustrates the _psychanalitic_ model of psychopathology.

11. Abnormal behavior resulting from failure to fulfill self-potential reflects the point of view of the _humanist_ - _existential_ model.

12. A murderer who didn't understand the difference between right and wrong may be found not guilty in a court of law on the ground of _insanity_.

13. Insanity is a _legal_ term, not a psychological or medical term.

14. In 1968 DSM-II was developed; its revision in 1979 was called _DSM-III_.

15. DSM-III provides an evaluation of a person according to five dimensions or _axes_.

16. The first three axes in DSM-III assess the _immediate_ condition of the person, and the fourth and fifth axes assess the person's _past_ situation and ability to cope with it.

17. Axis II in the DSM-III classification deals with _personality_ disorders.

18. A person whose mental disorder is caused by physical factors such as brain damage is suffering from an _organic_ disorder.

19. A _functional_ disorder is traditionally considered to be caused by psychological (not physical) factors.

20. Very few disorders listed in DSM-III have a known _etiology_.

21. Previously, feelings of inadequacy, anxiety, avoidance, and self-defeating behavior were considered characteristics of _neurotic_ disorders.

22. The fact that people often refuse to give up ineffective self-defeating behavior patterns was known as the neurotic _paradox_.

23. DSM-III has dropped _neurosis_ and no longer includes it as a description of mental disorder.

24. A specific unrealistic fear is a _phobia_.

25. Fear of open spaces or of being in public places is called _agoraphobia_.

26. Generally, phobic disorders are believed to be _learned_.

27. While fear is related to a specific object or situation, _anxiety_ is often not considered to be.

28. A person in a constant state of tension, worry, and dread may be suffering from a generalized _anxiety_ disorder.

29. Because anxiety may not be tied to a specific object, it is often called _free_-_floating_ anxiety.

30. An attack of extreme overwhelming fear, perhaps accompanied by chest pains and breathing difficulty, may be a ___panic___ attack.

31. Repeated unwanted thoughts are ___obsessions___, and ritualistic acts that must be repeatedly performed are called ___compulsion___.

32. Learning theorists argue that phobic disorders and anxiety states are ___learned___; psychoanalysts believe they result from an unre-solved ___clash___ between id, ego, and superego, and the humanistic-existential model considers these disorders to be the result of failure to fulfill one's life ___potential___.

33. ___Somatoform___ disorders involve physical symptoms or symptoms of illness when no illness can be found.

34. Deafness, blindness, shaking, choking, nausea, or glove anesthesia, without a known physical cause, could be symptoms of the somatoform disorder called ___conversion___ disorder.

35. Conversion disorders serve the purpose of helping people ___escape___ from things they would rather not do.

36. The following helps physicians distinguish conversion disorders from real illnesses: Total ___glove___ anesthesia, a patient's attitude of ___indifference___ toward his or her symptoms, symptoms which are ___selective___, and removal of symptoms under ___hypnosis___.

37. Conversion paralysis is much more likely on the ___left___ side of the body.

38. Severe chronic pain, often in the back of vital organs, without medical cause, is called ___psychogenic___ pain disorder.

39. An intense interest in bodily functions and illness and the belief one has a disease in the absence of medical confirmation describes the disorder known as ___hypochondriasis___.

40. The dissociative disorders are psychogenic ___amnesia___, psycho-genic ___fugue___, and ___multiple___ personality.

41. A person who forgets his or her own identity (with no physical cause) is suffering from psychogenic ___amnesia___, and one who also wanders away is suffering from psychogenic ___fugue___.

42. The Three Faces of Eve and Sybil are descriptions of individuals suffer-ing from ___multiple___ ___personality___.

43. Gordon Bower suggests that the effects of multiple personality can be understood as an exaggerated form of ___state___ - ___dependant___ memory.

44. Dissociative disorders are quite ___rare___ , and therefore not much is known about them.

45. The most severe disorders, involving loss of contact with reality and personality distortion, are called ___psychoses___ .

46. The three classifications of psychotic disorders are ___affective___ , ___schizophrenic___ , and ___paranoid___ disorders.

47. Disorders of mood and emotion are ___affective___ disorders.

48. Drastic swings between extreme moods characterizes ___bipolar___ disorder (formerly called ___manic___ - ___depressive___ psychosis).

49. Many researchers believe there may be important genetic or ___biological___ factors involved in bipolar disorder.

50. Cycles of mania and depression may be related to ___biorythms___ that have become abnormal.

51. The neurotransmitter ___norepinephrine___ peaks in January and July and is low in May and October. Drugs such as ___reserpine___ can lower its level and trigger serious ___depression___ .

52. It has been estimated that as many as ___55___ million people in the United States suffer from depression.

53. Studies of adoptees with major depression suggests there may be a ___genetic___ predisposition to depression and suicide.

54. George Winokur found that among depressed persons ___dexamethasone___ suppression of ___cortisol___ doesn't occur very often. Such tests permit researchers to distinguish ___endogenous___ depression from ___secondary___ depression.

55. Depression that occurs regardless of life events is called ___endogenous___ , and that which occurs in response to an environmentally disturbing situation is ___secondary___ depression.

56. Winokur has in effect developed a ___blood___ test for major depression. Dexamethasone induced non-___suppression___ of cortisol indicates endogenous depression.

57. One half of all mental hospital beds are occupied by people diagnosed as _schizophrenic_ .

58. Schizophrenia is most common in _young_ adults. It is not the same thing as _multiple_ personality.

59. A _schizophrenic_ disorder involves a split from reality, flat distorted emotions and bizarre thought processes.

60. A false unrealistic belief maintained in spite of evidence to the contrary is a _delusion_ , and a sense perception in the absence of any appropriate external stimulus (such as seeing things that aren't there) is an _hallucination_ .

61. The _gradual_ onset of schizophrenia is a bad sign because recovery is less likely.

62. It is rarely said that a person's schizophrenia is cured; rather it is said that the schizophrenia is in _remission_ .

63. DSM-III classifies _five_ types of schizophrenia.

64. Inappropriate silliness, obscene behavior, and distorted emotions are characteristic of _disorganized_ schizophrenia (formerly called _hebephrenia_).

65. Odd prolonged positions, waxy flexibility, and alternating between excitement and withdrawal characterize _catatonic_ schizophrenia.

66. The outlook for the _catatonic_ type is generally better than for the _disorganized_ type of schizophrenia.

67. A person who is potentially dangerous and manifests bizarre delusions of persecution and hallucinations may be a _paranoid_ schizophrenic.

68. A mixture of symptoms characterizes the _undifferentiated_ type of schizophrenia, and those who are recovering from a schizophrenic episode may be classified as _residual_ schizophrenics.

69. Numerous causes of schizophrenia have been studied including genetic and environmental factors, _biochemical_ factors, and _structural_ and anatomical factors.

70. Studies of adopted schizophrenics suggest a _genetic_ link. Someone with schizophrenia in his or her family is _more_ likely to become schizophrenic. The likelihood increases in direct proportion to how close the relative is _genetically_ .

71. Kety believes there is a _genetically_____ caused and an _environmentally_____ caused kind of schizophrenia.

72. To date, no internal _hallucination_____ such as LSD has been found to be the cause of schizophrenia.

73. The neurotransmitter _dopamine_____ may be the causal agent in schizophrenia since many antipsychotic drugs block it.

74. The _dopamine_____ hypothesis suggests that schizphrenics may have an excess of dopamine (or too many receptors sensitive to it).

75. Schizophrenia seems to be more of a dysfunction of the _left_____ hemisphere of the brain than of the _right_____.

76. Chronic schizophrenics often have enlarged cerebral _ventricles_____, as suggested by earlier procedures known as pneumoencephalography and confirmed by more recent _CAT_____ (abbreviation only) scan procedures.

77. Structural abnormalities in schizophrenia are found more often among _chronic_____ schizophrenics.

78. Differences between the brains of schizophrenics, bipolar disorder patients, and normal people have been revealed by the _PET_____ scan.

79. The delusions involved in _paranoid_____ _schizophrenia_____ include hallucination and personality disorganization. In _paranoia_____ they do not.

80. Paranoia involves delusions of _persecution_____ or of _grandeur_____.

81. Temporary, variable, illogical, and disorganized delusions triggered by a stressful situation characterize an _acute_____ paranoid disorder.

82. Approximately _10_____ million Americans have abused alcohol and many of them are alcohol dependent.

83. In the initial stage of alcoholism a person may (a) _increase_____ the consumption of alcohol (b) drink first thing in the _morning_____, and (c) do something he or she later _regrets_____.

84. In the _prodromal_____ phase of alcoholism blackouts may occur.

85. The final two stages in the pattern of alcoholism are the _crucial_____ phase and the _chronic_____ phase.

86. There is increasing evidence that alcoholism may be related to _biological_ and _genetic_ factors.

87. Children of alcoholics react more intensely to _alcohol_ than children of nonalcoholics.

88. The percentage of people in the United States who are likely to be alcoholics is _greater_ among those who have alcoholics in their families.

89. Among people born to alcoholic parents but reared by adoptive parents, _alcoholism_ is much greater than would be expected.

90. Heavy use of alcohol can destroy _neurons_ in the brain.

91. Alcoholism in _Russia_ is twice as severe as it is in the United States.

92. Substance abuse disorders usually begin for _social_ or _psychological_ reasons.

93. People who use drugs may develop a _tolerance_ necessitating higher doses to avoid withdrawal or to maintain an effect.

94. The drugs most likely to be used in various combinations are alcohol, _marijuana_, hashish, barbituates, and _heroin_ .

95. Substance abuse disorders can often end in _death_ if not treated.

96. Although it is hoped that _education_ will help reduce substance use disorders, it is often difficult to _educate_ adolescents about the dangers of drug abuse.

97. Drug use by _parents_ has been found to be positively correlated with children's drug use.

98. Psychosexual disorders include categories in which harmful or unusual sexual actions become the _primary_ _mode_ of arousal.

99. The American Psychiatric and American Psychological Associations do not consider _homosexuality_ to be abnormal because it is so prevalent.

100. A persistent desire to be a member of the opposite sex indicates a _gender_ identify disorder.

101. Preferring animals as sexual partners characterizes _zoophilia_ .

102. Becoming sexually aroused by children reflects the sexual disorder called _pedophilia_ .

103. Inflicting pain on another for one's own sexual arousal illustrates the disorder of sexual _sadism_ .

104. Personality disorders tend to disrupt social _relationships_ .

105. Generally, people with personality disorders do poorly in _therapy_ .

106. A person who demands attention, expects special treatment, and has an exaggerated sense of self-importance may be experiencing a _narcissistic_ personality disorder.

107. A person who fights, lies, steals, lacks feelings for others, and who is manipulative and impulsive may be diagnosed as an _antisocial_ personality.

108. A person who is a perfectionist, does not enjoy life, is a workaholic, and who makes similar demands of others may be diagnosed as having a _compulsive_ personality disorder.

109. Some who argue with DSM-III are worried that almost any behavior pattern may be considered _deviant_ depending on who is doing the observation and assessment.

110. The psychiatrist, Thomas Szasz, says mental illness is a _myth_ .

111. Supporters of DSM-III argue that competent clinicians know the _limitations_ of the system.

112. David Rosenhan sent perfectly normal _pseudopatients_ to mental hospitals to determine if they would be recognized as normal.

113. In Rosenhan's study _none_ of the pseudopatients was detected by the hospital staff as being sane.

114. Some researchers have _disagreed_ with Rosenhan's methods and conclusions.

115. Organic disorders and functional disorders are subject to _misdiagnosis_ .

116. One of the most difficult functional disorders to accurately assess is _schizophrenia_ .

SELF TEST I

1. Psychologists study abnormal behavior
   a. to learn more about behavior
   b. to help those in need
   c. to remove the insane to the safety of an asylum
   d. both a and b

2. Which model of psychopathology depicts unconscious desires and conflicts as the basis of abnormality?
   a. medical
   b. learning
   c. psychoanalytic
   d. humanistic-existential

3. Mental disorders are
   a. always qualitatively different from normal behaviors
   b. the same in type, quality and degree as normal behaviors
   c. often extremes of normal behaviors
   d. rarely found to interfere with a person's life except in extreme cases

4. Because it was considered so broad and all-encompassing, the term _____ was dropped from DSM-III and is no longer included.
   a. hallucination
   b. suicide
   c. psychosis
   d. neurosis

5. Conversion disorders
   a. involve conscious malingering and faked symptoms
   b. serve the purpose of helping people escape from something they'd rather not do
   c. usually involve symptoms that are markedly different from those of a real physical disorder
   d. all of the above

6. A disorder in which a person loses memories, flees or leaves home, and winds up in a new place is called
   a. endogenous wanderlust
   b. amnesia
   c. fugue
   d. paraphilia

7. Kety has demonstrated through his research that there may be a _____ predisposition to depression and suicide.
   a. sociological
   b. neurological
   c. genetic
   d. environmental

8. A strong unrealistic belief that is maintained in spite of ample evidence that it is false is a/an
   a. delusion
   b. hallucination
   c. compulsion
   d. both a and c

9. Studies in Norway and the United States indicate that there is a much stronger tendency for _____ to both have schizophrenia than for _____ to have schizophrenia.
   a. identical twins, fraternal twins
   b. fraternal twins, identical twins
   c. two sisters, two brothers
   d. two brothers, two sisters

10. Those suffering from _____ schizophrenia are more likely to have structural abnormalities in the brain.
    a. acute   c. both a and b
    b. chronic   d. none of the above

11. Blackouts often first occur during which phase of alcoholism?
    a. initial   c. crucial
    b. prodromal   d. chronic

12. A strong and persistent desire to be a member of the opposite sex reflects
    a. a paraphilia
    b. a gender identity disorder
    c. transvestism
    d. a psychosexual stage

13. A perfectionist who works a lot, does not enjoy life, and who insists others do his or her bidding may be experiencing a _____ personality disorder.
    a. borderline   c. compulsive
    b. dependent   d. passive-aggressive

14. Which psychologist sent normal "pseudopatients" to mental hospitals to see if the staff could detect them?
    a. Gordon Bower   c. Thomas Szasz
    b. Seymour Kety   d. David Rosenhan

15. Your cousin Jill recently went through a "pregnancy." Her menstrual cycle stopped, she had morning sickness, and an enlarged abdomen. She even experienced labor pains. However, there was no baby. She had never been pregnant. No physical problem was detected. What might the doctor diagnose?
    a. psychosis   c. hypochondriasis
    b. conversion disorder   d. dissociative disorder

SELF TEST II

1. Which model of psychopathology depicts mental disorders as caused by biological dysfunctions?
   a. medical   c. psychoanalytic
   b. learning   d. humanistic-existential

2. Which legal test for determining guilt by reason of insanity is the most stringent (and most difficult to prove), that is, only those who are severely disturbed could be classified as insane under its stringent standard?
   a. M'Naghten Rule
   b. Irresistible Impulse
   c. Durham Rule
   d. American Law Institute (Model Penal Code)

3. A mental disorder caused by psychological factors (with no known physical basis) is traditionally called a/an _____ disorder.
   a. organic
   b. functional
   c. psychotic
   d. somatoform

4. A ritualistic act that a person must repeat over and over again (such as washing one's hands every 15 minutes) is a/an
   a. obsession
   b. compulsion
   c. panic attack
   d. conversion reaction

5. A person who wants to believe he is ill when no physical illness is present is a
   a. malingerer
   b. compulsive patient
   c. narcissistic substance abuser
   d. hypochondriac

6. Disorders of mood and emotion are called _____ disorders.
   a. schizophrenic
   b. paranoid
   c. affective
   d. neurotic

7. Which of the following subjects consistently showed a normal suppression of cortisol in their blood when injected with dexamethasone?
   a. those with no depression
   b. those with secondary depression
   c. those with endogenous depression
   d. both a and b

8. Delusions of persecution would most likely be found in someone diagnosed as a _____ schizophrenic.
   a. paranoid
   b. hebephrenic
   c. catatonic
   d. none of the above

9. Research has shown which among the following not to be true?
   a. schizophrenia may have a genetic basis
   b. schizophrenia may be related to deviant patterns of family speech and communication
   c. an internal hallucinogen similar to LSD has been found to be the cause of schizophrenia
   d. certain kinds of schizophrenics have enlarged brain ventricles.

10. In _____, hallucinations and severe personality disorganization occur, but in _____ they do not.

    a. paranoia, paranoid schizophrenia
    b. acute paranoid disorder, paranoia
    c. paranoia, acute paranoid disorder
    d. paranoid schizophrenia, paranoia

11. Substance abuse disorders generally begin
    a. because of genetic predispositions
    b. for social or psychological reasons
    c. because of other mental disorders
    d. both a and c

12. Individuals with personality disorders
    a. exhibit problems similar to psychosis
    b. suffer much anxiety because they feel responsible for the troubles
       they cause
    c. typically perceive their problems as being related to luck or to the
       faults of others
    d. generally do quite well in therapy

13. Who believes that psychiatry has been used as a political weapon depriving
    people of their liberties, and that mental illness is a myth?
    a. David Rosenhan   c.   Thomas Szasz
    b. Seymour Kety   d.   Wilhelm Wundt

14. _____ disorders are often subject to misdiagnosis.
    a. organic   c.   both a and b
    b. functional   d.   none of the above

15. You are writing an English term paper and want to focus on the maladap-
    tive behavior pattern in the United States that affects more people than
    any other. What will be the topic of your paper?
    a. alcoholism
    b. depression
    c. schizophrenia
    d. bipolar disorder

ESSAY QUESTIONS

1. Discuss the behavior of a paranoid schizophrenic from the point of
   view of the medical model, the learning model, and the legal model.

2. Describe DSM-III, contrast it with DSM-II, and explain how the concept
   of neurosis fits into each system.

3. Compare and contrast conversion disorder with hypochondriasis. How
   could someone with either of these disorders be distinguished from a
   person with a real physical problem?

4. Explain the key features of gender identity disorders, psychosexual dysfunctions, and seven of the paraphilias.

5. Distinguish between endogenous and secondary depression. Discuss the recent research that suggests there may be a blood test for major depression.

ANSWER SECTION

Guided Review
1. need
2. dissidents
3. psychotic
4. maladaptive, defeating
5. continuum
6. model
7. medical
8. disease, patients
9. learning
10. psychoanalytic
11. humanistic-existential
12. insanity
13. legal
14. DSM-III
15. axes
16. immediate (or present), past
17. personality
18. organic
19. functional
20. etiology (or cause)
21. neurotic
22. paradox
23. neurosis
24. phobia
25. agoraphobia
26. learned
27. anxiety
28. anxiety
29. free-floating
30. panic
31. obsessions, compulsions
32. learned, clash (or conflict), potential
33. somatoform
34. conversion
35. escape
36. glove, indifference, selective, hypnosis
37. left
38. psychogenic

39.　hypochondriasis
40.　amnesia, fugue, multiple
41.　amnesia, fugue
42.　multiple personality
43.　state-dependent
44.　rare
45.　psychoses
46.　affective, schizophrenic, paranoid
47.　affective
48.　bipolar, manic-depressive
49.　biological
50.　biorhythms
51.　norepinephrine, reserpine, depression
52.　55
53.　genetic
54.　dexamethasone, cortisol, endogenous, secondary
55.　endogenous, secondary
56.　blood, suppression
57.　schizophrenic
58.　young, multiple
59.　schizophrenic
60.　delusion, hallucination
61.　gradual
62.　remission
63.　five
64.　disorganized, hebephrenia
65.　catatonic
66.　catatonic, disorganized
67.　paranoid
68.　undifferentiated, residual
69.　biochemical, structural
70.　genetic, more, genetically
71.　genetically, environmentally
72.　hallucinogen
73.　dopamine
74.　dopamine
75.　left, right
76.　ventricles, CAT
77.　chronic (or long-term)
78.　PET
79.　paranoid schizophrenia, paranoia
80.　persecution, grandeur
81.　acute
82.　ten
83.　increase, morning, regrets
84.　prodromal
85.　crucial, chronic
86.　biological, genetic
87.　alcohol

88. greater
89. alcoholism
90. neurons
91. Russia
92. social, psychological
93. tolerance
94. marijuana, heroin
95. death
96. education, educate
97. parents
98. primary mode
99. homosexuality
100. gender
101. zoophilia
102. pedophilia
103. sadism
104. relationships
105. therapy
106. narcissistic
107. antisocial
108. compulsive
109. deviant
110. myth
111. limitations
112. pseudopatients
113. none
114. disagreed (or taken issue)
115. misdiagnosis
116. schizophrenia

Self Test I
1. d
2. c
3. c
4. d
5. b
6. c
7. c
8. a
9. a
10. b
11. b
12. b
13. c
14. d
15. b

Self Test II
1. a
2. a
3. b
4. b
5. d
6. c
7. d
8. a
9. c
10. d
11. b
12. c
13. c
14. c
15. b

CHAPTER 16

Therapy

BEHAVIORAL OBJECTIVES

After completing this chapter, the student should be able to:

1. Describe the therapies Johann Christian Reil used on his patients.
2. Outline the history of therapy from the Greek and Roman era up through the modern era of psychology.
3. List the somatic therapies and convey an understanding of each of them.
4. Summarize the major objections to electroconvulsive shock treatment.
5. Define frontal lobotomy and summarize its development.
6. Evaluate the effectiveness of modern psychosurgery.
7. Summarize the positive and negative effects of deinstitutionalization.
8. Distinguish between directive and nondirective psychotherapies and compare and contrast insight and action psychotherapies.
9. Describe psychoanalysis including the processes of free association, dream interpretation, resistance, and transference.
10. Describe client-centered therapy and define unconditional positive regard and reflective listening.
11. Compare and contrast rational emotive therapy and Gestalt therapy.
12. Describe the behavioral therapies: Classical conditioning therapy, systematic desensitization, and operant behavioral therapy.
13. Briefly summarize cognitive restructuring and hypnotherapy procedures.
14. Describe one of the various treatment programs used in treating serious substance use disorders.
15. Evaluate the effectiveness of modern psychotherapy.

KEY TERMS AND CONCEPTS

noninjurious torture
trephining
trephine
rational view of mental disorders

Malleus Maleficarum
general paresis
organic theory
somatic therapies

chlorpromazines
psychopharmacological therapy
antipsychotic drugs
phenothiazines
major tranquilizers
tardive dyskinesia
antidepressants
mood elevators
tricyclics
MAO inhibitors
Elavil
Marplan
endogenous depression
antimanic drugs
lithium carbonate
antianxiety drugs
minor tranquilizers
Valium
electroconvulsive shock therapy
insulin shock therapy
psychosurgery
frontal lobotomy
leucotome
cingulotomy
deinstitutionalization
psychotherapy
insight therapy
action therapy
directive therapy
nondirective therapy
psychoanalysis
free association
dream interpretation
psychic censor
resistance
transference
neoFreudians

client centered therapy
client versus patient label
unconditional positive regard
reflective listening
existential therapy
rational emotive therapy
Gestalt therapy
group therapy
psychodrama
sensitivity training
encounter groups
transactional analysis
behavior therapy
classical conditioning therapy
aversive conditioning
systematic desensitization
fear hierarchy
operant behavioral therapy
operant techniques of behavior
    modification
cognitive behavior modification
cognitive restructuring
hypnotherapy
self-hypnosis
alcohol dependence
detoxification
chlordiazepoxide
Antabuse
A.A.
opiate addiction
methadone
clonidine
lofexidine
antagonistic therapy
naltrexone
nicotine dependence
spontaneous remission

NAMES TO REMEMBER

Johann Christian Reil
Philippe Pinel
Dorothea Dix
Clifford Beers
Manfred Sakel
Ugo Cerletti
Lucio Bini
Sigmund Freud

Carl Rogers
Albert Ellis
Frederick (Fritz) Perls
J. L. Moreno
Eric Berne
Joseph Wolpe
H. J. Eysenck
Mary Smith
Gene Glass

GUIDED REVIEW

1. Dr. Johann Christian Reil used various forms of crude "*Shock* " *therapy* ranging from shooting cannons to having an assistant dress as a *ghost* .

2. Dr. Reil called his techniques *noninjurious* *torture* .

3. A primitive form of "therapy" in which an opening was chipped through the skull was called *trephining* .

4. Before the scientific method was developed people believed that *emotional* disorders resulted from *supernatural* forces.

5. The Greeks and the Romans favored *humane* *treatment* of individuals with mental disorders.

6. The fall of the Roman Empire resulted in the fall of a *rational* view of mental disorders and the rise of *religious* *demonology* .

7. During the middle ages people who suffered from mental disorders were believed to have been invaded by a *spirit* or a *devil* .

8. Malleus Maleficarum, meaning the *witch's* *hammer* , described ways of identifying *witches* .

9. Due to the development of the *printing* press the early writings of the Greeks and Romans became known during the *Renaissance* .

10. In *asylums* built during the middle ages people with emotional disorders were tortured or killed. During the Renaissance these people were still treated like *animals* in that they were often *chained* and *shackled* .

11. *Phillippe* *Pinel* , a Frenchman, tried an experiment in 1792 in which he removed the chains and shackles from inmates and treated them as sick people rather than as witches or animals.

12. *Dorothea* *Dix* , a reformer, tried to improve conditions for the emotionally disturbed, but, unfortunately, she initiated the practice of *isolating* patients, which was not generally to their benefit.

13. During the mid-1800s physicians and anatomists discovered that abnormal behavior could result from damage to the *brain* or

_nervous_____ system.

14. In the late 1800s _Sigmund_____ _Freud_____ led a movement by psychiatrists that suggested abnormal behavior might be the result of unresolved _unconscious_____ _conflicts_____.

15. A Mind That Found Itself written by _Clifford_____ _Beers_____, described the author's _emotional_____ breakdown and subsequent recovery. This book stimulated efforts to develop therapies for mental disorders.

16. When your author returned to Brooklyn State Hospital, he noticed an absence of _screaming_____ due to the development of new _antipsychotic_____ drugs.

17. Therapies that affect the body and its chemistry are known as _somatic_____ therapies.

18. The chlorpromazines have been replaced by the _phenothiazines_, such as thorazine, stelazine, compazine, and Mellaril, which are often referred to as the _major_____ _tranquilizer_.

19. _Antipsychotic_ drug is a more appropriate label for the phenothiazines than "major tranquilizers."

20. The antipsychotic drugs concentrate in the language, _emotion_____, and _sensory_____ areas of the brain which are related to psychotic symptoms.

21. Because antipsychotic drugs make patients calm and easier to manage, they have tended to be _overused_____ and often drug "therapy" is in reality a form of _crowd_____ control.

22. Prolonged use of antipsychotic drugs often leads to uncontrollable body and facial twitching which are characteristic symptoms of _tardive_____ _dyskinesia_____.

23. Tardive dyskinesia has been estimated to occur in _one_____ -_fifth_____ of all patients taking antipsychotic drugs.

24. Antipsychotic agents are declining in use, not only because of their side effects, but also because they are ineffective in treating chronic forms of _schizophrenia_.

25. Mood elevators or _antidepressants_ drugs are of two types: The _tricyclics_____ and the _monoamine_ - _oxidase_ _inhibitors_____.

26. The case of Ruth H. demonstrated the success story of _lithium_____ _carbonate_____ in treating

bipolar disorder.

27. Valium and Librium are referred to as _antianxiety_ drugs or minor _tranquilizers_ .

28. The minor tranquilizers are used to treat people with personality problems in which _tension_ or _anxiety_ are the main symptoms.

29. Benjamin _Rush_ practiced a form of shock therapy that began by creating a _boil_ on his patients' necks. The shock came when he popped the boil to excite an " _atomic discharge_ " from the neighborhood of the brain.

30. Austrian neurologist Julius Wagner von Jauregg unsuccessfully used an extract of tubercule bacillus to induce an explosively "cureative" _fever_ . He did have some success by injecting the _malaria_ organism into patients who had syphilis.

31. Austrian clinician Manfred Sakel began using chemical _shock_ therapy on schizophrenics by injecting them with _insulin_ .

32. Insulin shock therapy has generally been replaced with _electroconvulsive_ shock therapy (abbreviated _E C T_).

33. ECT is used in modern treatment of severe _depression_ and the depressive lows caused by _bipolar_ disorder.

34. Several researchers are concerned about long-term ECT therapy, as it may cause _permanent_ _memory_ impairment.

35. In _psychosurgery_ particular areas of the brain are destroyed in order to alleviate severe psychiatric disturbances.

36. The first reported surgical destruction of a portion of an uninjured brain in order to change _behavior_ was done by Gottlieb _Burkhardt_ in 1891.

37. Antonio de Egas _Moniz_ , a Portuguese neurologist, developed the technique of destroying the _prefrontal_ areas in monkeys and this marked the beginning of modern _psychosurgery_

38. Moniz used an icepick-like device, known as a _leucotome_ to perform psychosurgeries known as _prefrontal lobotomy_ .

39. After increasing in popularity, interest in psychosurgery began to decline by 1970 due to: Effective _drug_ treatments,

disappointing surgical results, and increased concern with
_____patients_____ rights.

40. A modern psychosurgery procedure gaining in popularity is the
_____cingulotomy_____ in which the _____cingulate_____
_____gyrus_____ of the cerebral cortex is destroyed or removed.

41. Cingulotomies are most often done on patients who suffer from severe
_____pain_____ or who have severe _____psychiatric_____ disorders.
The main side effect of the surgery has been a decreased
_____ability_____ to _____draw_____ among some patients.

42. A recent study found that among psychosurgical patients
_____52_____ percent improved markedly with no resulting
_____neurological_____ damage or deficits.

43. Most past cases of severe neurological damage from psychosurgery
occurred because of the extensive _____cutting_____ that was done.
The popular novel and film " _____One_____ _____flew_____
_____over_____ _____the_____ _____cuckoos_____
_____nest_____ " depicts a patient damaged by psychosurgical
techniques.

44. Taking patients out of state and county mental institutions is known as
_____deinstitutionalize_____ . This process has resulted in the development of
community _____mental_____ _____health_____ centers.

45. Deinstitutionalization has resulted in state and county mental hospital
populations dropping by _____two_____ - _____thirds_____
since 1955. Yet hospital admissions are up _____129_____ %,
indicating many patients are being _____readmitted_____ again and
again.

46. Deinstitutionalization has often failed because of a lack of
_____money_____ and a lack of _____local_____ support.

47. _____Psychotherapy_____ is defined as any noninvasive psychological technique designed to bring about a positive change in someone's behavior,
personality, or adjustment.

48. Some psychotherapies emphasize _____insight_____ in which individuals are aided in developing a better understanding of their situation or problem. Other therapies, called _____action_____ therapies,
focus on changing troublesome habits or problems.

49. _____Directive_____ therapies attempt to guide and direct the client or
patient to solutions whereas _____nondirective_____ therapies place most
of the responsibility on the client.

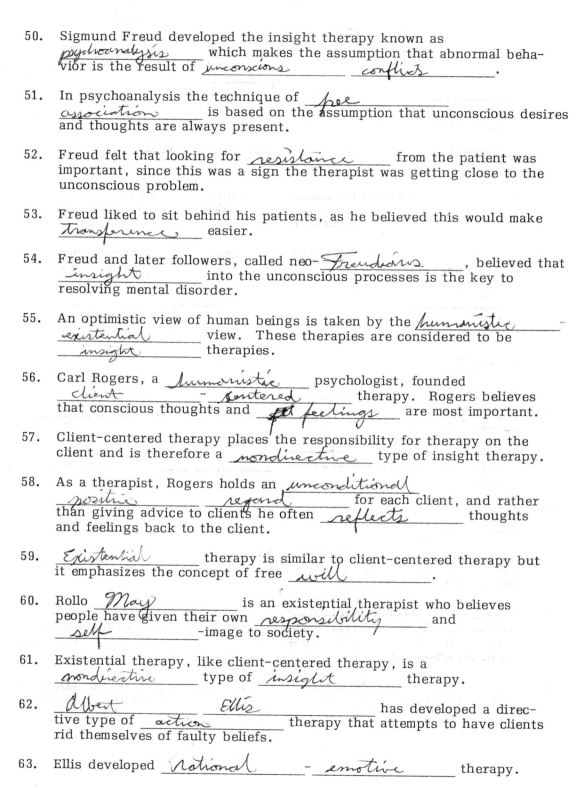

50. Sigmund Freud developed the insight therapy known as
psychoanalysis which makes the assumption that abnormal behavior is the result of _unconscious_ _conflicts_ .

51. In psychoanalysis the technique of _free_
association is based on the assumption that unconscious desires and thoughts are always present.

52. Freud felt that looking for _resistance_ from the patient was important, since this was a sign the therapist was getting close to the unconscious problem.

53. Freud liked to sit behind his patients, as he believed this would make _transference_ easier.

54. Freud and later followers, called neo-_Freudians_ , believed that _insight_ into the unconscious processes is the key to resolving mental disorder.

55. An optimistic view of human beings is taken by the _humanistic_ _existential_ view. These therapies are considered to be _insight_ therapies.

56. Carl Rogers, a _humanistic_ psychologist, founded _client_ - _centered_ therapy. Rogers believes that conscious thoughts and _feelings_ are most important.

57. Client-centered therapy places the responsibility for therapy on the client and is therefore a _nondirective_ type of insight therapy.

58. As a therapist, Rogers holds an _unconditional_ _positive_ _regard_ for each client, and rather than giving advice to clients he often _reflects_ thoughts and feelings back to the client.

59. _Existential_ therapy is similar to client-centered therapy but it emphasizes the concept of free _will_ .

60. Rollo _May_ is an existential therapist who believes people have given their own _responsibility_ and _self_ -image to society.

61. Existential therapy, like client-centered therapy, is a _nondirective_ type of _insight_ therapy.

62. _Albert_ _Ellis_ has developed a directive type of _action_ therapy that attempts to have clients rid themselves of faulty beliefs.

63. Ellis developed _rational_ - _emotive_ therapy.

64. Fritz Perls developed _Gestalt_____ therapy, an action type
of _directive_____ therapy.

65. The goal of Gestalt therapy is to _balance_____ and
_integrate_____ emotions, thoughts, and actions, and this theory
emphasizes the _here_____ _and_____
_now_____ rather than past experiences.

66. One of the earliest group therapies was _psychodrama___, developed
by J. L. _Moreno_____ who first used the term _group_____
psychotherapy.

67. During _sensitivity_____ training, people learn to become more
aware of the needs and _feelings_____ of others.

68. Breaking through false fronts and defenses is the goal of
_encounter_____ groups. These experiences can be psychologically painful, as individuals encounter themselves by having others
_challenge_____ their assertions and _beliefs_____.

69. Another directive insight therapy is _transactional_
_analysis_____, which is described by _Eric_
_Berne_____ in his book, Games People Play.

70. In transactional analysis there are three role types: The
_parent_____, the _adult_____, and the
_child_____.

71. The form of therapy that is based on learning theory and the principles of conditioning is known as _behavior___. therapy. This
kind of therapy focuses on observable _behaviors_____ rather than
feelings, dreams, or thoughts.

72. Behavioral therapists draw their techniques from three behavioral areas:
_classical_____ conditioning, _operant_____ conditioning,
and _social_____ learning.

73. During aversive conditioning, which relies on the principles of
_classical_____ conditioning, a client may receive an _aversive_
_stimulus_____ when undesirable behavior is emitted.

74. John Wolpe has developed a behavioral therapy known as
_systematic_____ _desensitization_____. This therapy begins by
creating a _hierarchy_____ of _fears_____ and proceeds
as the client learns to _relax_____ when progressively more
intense fear is visualized.

75. A behavioral therapeutic approach based on the principles created by
B. F. _Skinner_____ is based on operant principles.

76. __Token__ __economies__ make use of conditioned reinforcers, such as poker chips, to modify behavior.

77. Another behavioral technique is the use of __behavior contracts__ in which those concerned agree on a behavior desired by each other.

78. Cognitive behavior modification, or __cognitive restructuring__, is a therapeutic treatment in which the client and therapist form __hypothesis__ that can be tested. Then __experiments__ are arranged to aid the client in disconfirming his or her erroneous __assumptions__ about the world.

79. Cognitive behavior modification is most helpful with clients who perceive their worlds as harmful or dangerous and who engage in __absolutist__ thinking.

80. Many modern therapists use __hypnosis__ in conjunction with behavior therapy, for instance, in order to help clients to relax more deeply during systematic __desensitization__.

81. One of the oldest applications of hypnosis is in the control of __pain__.

82. Since hypnosis often enhances recall of __memories__, it has been useful at times for treating __dissociative disorders__.

83. Hypnotic induction can be accomplished while alone through the use of __self__ __hypnosis__.

84. The first step in treating an alcoholic is to __detoxify__ him or her and then, possibly, to use chlordiazepoxide to help alleviate __withdrawal__ __symptoms__.

85. Many therapies have been developed to help the alcoholic, but to date, the organization __A__ __A__ has been most effective.

86. Therapeutic treatment for opiate dependence is similar to therapies for alcoholics and may be applied, in situations in which people are addicted to narcotics such as __heroin__ or __morphine__. The therapy must eliminate both the __physical__ and __psychological__ dependence.

87. Recently Dr. Mark Gold has had some success using the drug __clonidine__ and a newer drug __lofexadine__ to eliminate withdrawal symptoms.

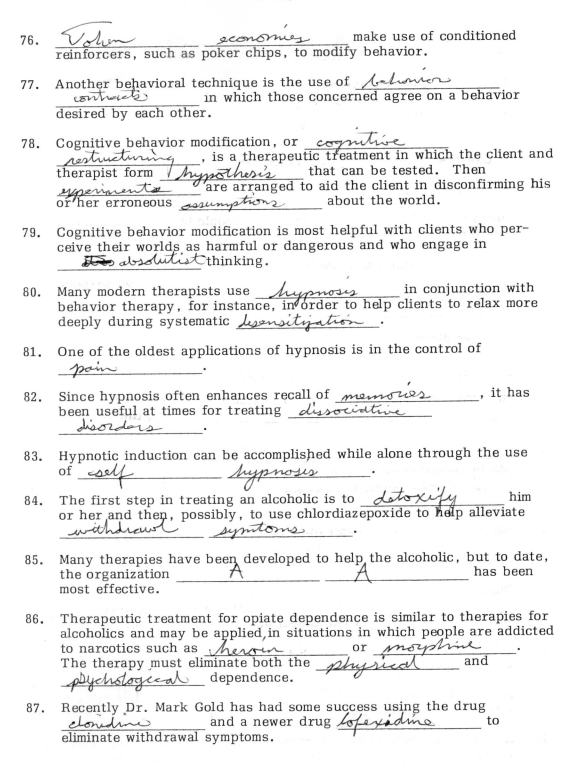

88. Stanley _Schachter_ has found that _blood_ _nicotine_ levels correlate well with urinary pH levels.

89. The use of _bicarbonate_ of _soda_ has been found to reduce cigarette _cravings_ because the nicotine is washed from the blood more _slowly_ .

90. People probably smoke more under stress partly because _blood_ acid and _stomach_ acid levels increase the speed at which nicotine is washed from the blood.

91. In 1952 H. J. _Eysenck_ assessed the effectiveness of _psychotherapy_ . He concluded that _two_ - _thirds_ of any group with behavioral problems will recover or improve significantly within _two_ years, regardless of whether they receive therapy.

92. Clients or patients who are most likely to recover are those who are least _maladjusted_ , have a short history of _symtoms_ , are _motivated_ to change, and are _middle_ or _upper_ class.

93. Mary Smith and Gene Glass conducted the most extensive analysis of the _effectiveness_ of _psychotherapy_ . They found all _psychotherapies_ to be more effective than no _treatment_ .

94. Judy R. had a _bird_ phobia and was treated through the use of _behavior_ therapy. After creating a hierarchy in order to conduct a _systematic_ _desensitization_ , Judy acted out the hierarchy instead of just _imagining_ it.

95. Judy R.'s therapy employed a _model_ for her to imitate and also relied upon _cognitive_ restructuring.

SELF TEST I

1. The doctor who used primitive "shock" therapies like unexpectedly shooting off a cannon or thrwoing sleeping patients into icy water was
   a. Benjamin Rush
   b. Philippe Pinel
   (c.) Johann Christian Reil
   d. Julius Wagner von Jauregg

2. Which of the following statements is true?
   a. the Greeks of Hippocrates' time felt mentally disturbed people should be burned at the stake
   (b.) the Greeks and Romans supported the humane treatment of the mentally disordered

c. all of the descriptive categories of mental disorder used by the
   Greeks and Romans were discarded by modern researchers, since
   all were based on mythical gods
d. all of the above

3. The organic psychosis that results from the disease of syphilis is
   a. general paresis   c. malleus maleficarum
   b. phenothiazine   d. major depression

4. _____ are generally the most widely used antipsychotic
   agents, and have replaced _____.
   a. chlorpromazines, phenothiazines
   b. phenothiazines, chlorpromazines
   c. lithium carbonate, marplan
   d. tricyclics, lithium carbonates

5. The study by Weiss (1978) in which monkeys were injected with antipsychotic drugs, demonstrated that
   a. the monkeys had no side effects from the drugs
   b. only unhealthy monkeys had any side effects like tardive dyskinesia
   c. human side effects to antipsychotic drugs are the result of their
      emotional disorders and not the drugs
   d. healthy monkeys developed tardive dyskinesia when the drugs were
      withdrawn

6. The man who is credited with the idea of "instantaneous therapy" through
   sudden shock or trauma was
   a. Lucio Bini   c. Antonio de Egas Moniz
   b. Mark S. Gold   d. none of the above

7. A destruction of a region of the brain to help alleviate psychiatric
   disorders is known as
   a. psychosurgery   c. neuronal inhibition
   b. neurological therapy   d. neuroanalysis

8. Most psychosurgery is now being conducted in order to
   a. learn more about the brain
   b. relieve schizophrenic symptoms
   c. relieve pain or depression
   d. punish unruly patients

9. Which of the following statements is true?
   a. community mental health centers have not necessarily resulted in a
      more humane treatment of patients
   b. the community mental health center is preferred by large state
      institutions, since patients receive quality professional care in
      the latter
   c. the deinstitutionalization movement ensured that mental patients
      would never end up in flophouses or be abandoned on the streets
   d. both b and c

10. Neo-Freudians
     a. no longer use the concept of the unconscious
     b. have considered cultural, social, and interpersonal factors as important
     c. believe the original methods of Freud work well and have not changed them
     d. are the most successful at treating emotional disorders

11. Humanistic and existential therapies attempt to
     a. improve a person's self-concept
     b. have people develop self-acceptance
     c. have people believe in their own abilities
     d. all of the above

12. J. L. Moreno developed _____, which is a form of _____ therapy.
     a. psychodrama, individual
     b. rational-emotive, group
     c. psychodrama, group
     d. transactional analysis, individual

13. According to transactional analysis "crossed transactions" or "diagonal transactions"
     a. are healthy transactions
     b. indicate a person is psychotic
     c. are not healthy interactions
     d. none of the above

14. Forcing a child who played with matches to light hundreds of matches would be a _____ technique known as _____.
     a. operant, response cost
     b. operant, negative practice
     c. classical conditioning, alternating response effort
     d. none of these--that would never be done

15. The famous social psychologist who has been working on nicotine dependence is
     a. Philip Zimbardo   c. Eric Berne
     b. Stanley Schachter   d. Sydney Schaffer

SELF TEST II

1.   Which of the following statements regarding trephining is true?
     a. it was a primitive procedure in which a hole was chipped in the skull
     b. it was performed to allow healing thoughts and spirits to enter the body
     c. trephined skulls suggest that no patient survived the procedure
     d. all of the above

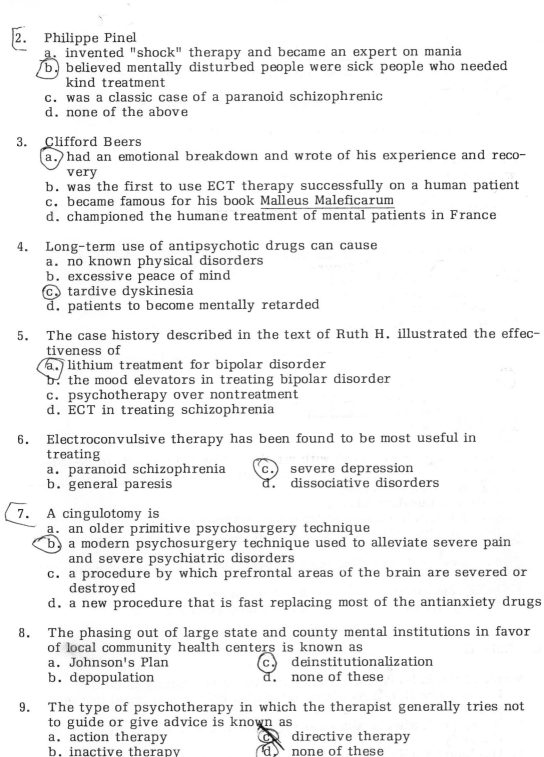

2. Philippe Pinel
    a. invented "shock" therapy and became an expert on mania
    b. believed mentally disturbed people were sick people who needed kind treatment
    c. was a classic case of a paranoid schizophrenic
    d. none of the above

3. Clifford Beers
    a. had an emotional breakdown and wrote of his experience and recovery
    b. was the first to use ECT therapy successfully on a human patient
    c. became famous for his book <u>Malleus Maleficarum</u>
    d. championed the humane treatment of mental patients in France

4. Long-term use of antipsychotic drugs can cause
    a. no known physical disorders
    b. excessive peace of mind
    c. tardive dyskinesia
    d. patients to become mentally retarded

5. The case history described in the text of Ruth H. illustrated the effectiveness of
    a. lithium treatment for bipolar disorder
    b. the mood elevators in treating bipolar disorder
    c. psychotherapy over nontreatment
    d. ECT in treating schizophrenia

6. Electroconvulsive therapy has been found to be most useful in treating
    a. paranoid schizophrenia   c. severe depression
    b. general paresis   d. dissociative disorders

7. A cingulotomy is
    a. an older primitive psychosurgery technique
    b. a modern psychosurgery technique used to alleviate severe pain and severe psychiatric disorders
    c. a procedure by which prefrontal areas of the brain are severed or destroyed
    d. a new procedure that is fast replacing most of the antianxiety drugs

8. The phasing out of large state and county mental institutions in favor of local community health centers is known as
    a. Johnson's Plan   c. deinstitutionalization
    b. depopulation   d. none of these

9. The type of psychotherapy in which the therapist generally tries not to guide or give advice is known as
    a. action therapy   c. directive therapy
    b. inactive therapy   d. none of these

10. Carl Rogers is a _____ psychologist who founded
    _____ therapy.
    a. humanistic, behavioral
    b. behavioral, humanistic
    c. humanistic, client-centered
    d. Gestalt, nondirective

11. _____ is to client-centered therapy as _____
    is to rational-emotive therapy.
    a. Freud, May
    b. Rogers, Perls
    c. Berne, Skinner
    d. Rogers, Ellis

12. Trust walks, in which a blindfolded person is led around by another,
    is most likely to be a part of
    a. encounter groups   c. hypnotherapy
    b. psychodrama   d. sensitivity training

13. Using the principles of classical conditioning in order to create a
    negative association between an electric shock and an undesirable behavior
    is known as
    a. shock therapy   c. pain induction therapy
    b. aversion therapy   d. none of the above

14. The only non-directive action therapy is
    a. psychoanalysis   c. cognitive restructuring
    b. self-hypnosis   d. humanistic therapy

15. Which of the following statements about psychotherapy is <u>false</u>:
    a. individuals in therapy who are most likely to improve are those who
       are least maladjusted
    b. individuals with shorter histories of maladaptive behavior symptoms
       when they begin therapy are most likely to recover
    c. upper class individuals are less likely to recover than middle and
       lower class individuals
    d. experienced therapists are more likely to have successful results
       with clients or patients

ESSAY QUESTIONS

1. Summarize the history of mental institutions beginning in the middle
   ages.

2. Identify the problem from which Ruth H. suffered and explain what
   therapeutic measures were used to help her.

3. Compare and contrast psychoanalysis and client-centered therapy.

4. Describe the case of Jennifer and explain how operant conditioning was used to resolve her problem.

5. Summarize the recent research on smoking conducted by Stanley Schachter.

ANSWER SECTION

Guided Review
1. shock therapy, ghost
2. noninjurious torture
3. trephining
4. emotional (or mental), supernatural
5. humane treatment
6. rational, religious demonology
7. spirit, devil
8. witch's hammer, witches
9. printing, Renaissance
10. asylums, animals, chained, shackled
11. Phillippe Pinel
12. Dorothea Dix, isolating
13. brain, nervous
14. Sigmund Freud, unconscious conflicts
15. Clifford Beers, emotional (or mental)
16. screaming, antipsychotic (or chlorpromazine)
17. somatic
18. phenothiazines, major tranquilizers
19. antipsychotic
20. emotion, sensory
21. overused (or overprescribed), crowd
22. tardive dyskinesia
23. one-fifth
24. schizophrenia
25. antidepressants, tricyclics, monoamine-oxidase inhibitors
26. lithium carbonate, bipolar
27. antianxiety, tranquilizers
28. tension, anxiety
29. Rush, boil, atomic discharge
30. fever, malaria
31. shock, insulin
32. electroconvulsive, ECT
33. depression, bipolar
34. permanent memory
35. psychosurgery
36. behavior, Burkhardt
37. Moniz, prefrontal, psychosurgery
38. leucotome, prefrontal lobotomies
39. drug, patients'

40. *cingulotomy, cingulate gyrus*
41. *pain, psychiatric, ability, draw*
42. *52, neurological*
43. *cutting, One Flew Over the Cuckoo's Nest*
44. *deinstitutionalization, mental health*
45. *two-thirds, 129, readmitted*
46. *money, local*
47. *psychotherapy*
48. *insight, action*
49. *directive, nondirective*
50. *psychoanalysis, unconscious conflicts*
51. *free association*
52. *resistance*
53. *transference*
54. *Freudians, insight*
55. *humanistic-existential, insight*
56. *humanistic, client-centered, feelings*
57. *nondirective*
58. *unconditional positive regard, reflects*
59. *existential, will*
60. *May, responsibility, self*
61. *nondirective, insight*
62. *Albert Ellis, action*
63. *rational-emotive*
64. *Gestalt, directive*
65. *balance, integrate, here and now*
66. *psychodrama, Moreno, group*
67. *sensitivity, feelings (or emotions)*
68. *encounter, challenge, beliefs*
69. *transactional analysis, Eric Berne*
70. *parent, adult, child*
71. *behavior, behaviors*
72. *classical (or associative), operant (or instrumental), social*
73. *classical, aversive stimulus*
74. *systematic desensitization, hierarchy, fears, relax*
75. *Skinner*
76. *token economies*
77. *behavioral contracts*
78. *cognitive restructuring, hypotheses, experiments, assumptions*
79. *absolutist*
80. *hypnosis, desensitization*
81. *pain*
82. *memories (or events), dissociative disorders*
83. *self hypnosis*
84. *detoxify, withdrawal symptoms*
85. *Alcoholics Anonymous (or AA)*
86. *heroin, morphine (or codeine), physical, psychological*
87. *clonidine, lofexidine*
88. *Schachter, blood nicotine*

89. bicarbonate, soda, cravings (or smoking), slowly
90. blood, stomach
91. Eysenck, psychotherapy, two-thirds, two
92. maladjusted, symptoms, motivated, middle, upper
93. effectiveness, psychotherapy, psychotherapies, treatment (or psycho-therapy)
94. bird phobia, behavior, systematic desensitization, imagining
95. model, cognitive

Self Test I		Self Test II	
1.	c	1.	a
2.	b	2.	b
3.	a	3.	a
4.	b	4.	c
5.	d	5.	a
6.	d	6.	c
7.	a	7.	b
8.	c	8.	c
9.	a	9.	d
10.	b	10.	c
11.	d	11.	d
12.	c	12.	d
13.	c	13.	b
14.	b	14.	b
15.	b	15.	c

CHAPTER 17

Social Behavior

BEHAVIORAL OBJECTIVES

After completing this chapter, the student should be able to:

1. Explain why people conform and compare Ron Jones' history class experiment with the social forces operating in Nazi Germany.
2. Discuss the procedures and findings of Milgram's obedience study, and tell what happened in Jonestown, Guyana in 1978, and why.
3. Describe the bystander effect and research that pertains to it.
4. List the various factors that influence a person's likelihood to take action in an emergency situation.
5. Explain the essence of Kohlberg's theory of moral development.
6. Compare Madsen's marble game with the Acme-Bolt trucking game indicating what each tells us about cooperation and competition.
7. List and describe four factors that play a role in bargaining and negotiation.
8. Compare and contrast deindividuation and polarization.
9. Contrast the great-man, great-woman leadership hypothesis with the situational-environmental hypothesis.
10. Describe two experiments pertaining to prejudice and discrimination conducted with third-grade children.
11. Describe an authoritarian personality and tell how it is measured.
12. List five ways for reducing and overcoming prejudice.
13. Tell how attitudes are measured and summarize results of experiments using the bogus pipeline procedure.
14. List several communicator, communication, and listener characteristics that are influential in the changing of attitudes.
15. Name the pioneer investigator of, give the meaning of, and describe research pertaining to, cognitive dissonance.
16. Contrast the impression management hypothesis with cognitive dissonance theory.
17. Distinguish between internal and external attribution explaining the related research and hypotheses.

KEY TERMS AND CONCEPTS

conformity
social norms
social comparison
reference group
Nuremberg trials
obedience
"learner" and "teacher"
bystander effect
diffusion of responsibility
ambiguous situations
task-load
bystander intervention model
morals
Kohlberg's stages of moral
   development
cooperation
competition
Madsen's marble experiment
Acme-Bolt trucking game
unilateral- and bilateral-threat
   conditions
Robbers' Cave experiment
bargaining
negotiation
ingratiation
foot-in-the-door technique
door-in-the-face technique
lowballing
bait and switch
mob mentality
deindividuation
polarization effect
great-man great-woman
   hypothesis

situational-environmental hypothesis
task leaders
social-emotional leaders
great leaders
in-group
out-group
prejudice
discrimination
Jane Elliot's prejudice experiment
authoritarian personality
bogus pipeline
attitudes and self-awareness
persuasive communication
characteristics of the communicator
self-persuasion
characteristics of the communication
two-sided argument
one-sided argument
emotional appeals
mere exposure effect
characteristics of the listener
central route processing
peripheral route processing
intelligence and persuasion
long-term self-esteem
short-term self-esteem
cognitive dissonance
impression-management hypothesis
internal or external attribution
visual perspective hypothesis
information availability hypothesis
self-serving bias
self-directed attention
brainwashed

NAMES TO REMEMBER

Solomon Asch
Stanley Milgram
Ron Jones
Jonestown, Guyana
Jim Jones
Kitty Genovese
Latane and Darley
Lawrence Kohlberg

David Rosenhan
M. C. Madsen
Deutsch and Krauss
C. W. Sherif and M. Sherif
T. W. Adorno
Leon Festinger
Patricia Hearst

GUIDED REVIEW

1. Social psychology is the study of how people affect the
   _____, thoughts, and feelings of _____.

2. People conform for two reasons: (1) they are often _____
   for conforming, and (2) conformity may be the result of social
   _____.

3. Groups of people whom we are like or wish to be like are
   _____ groups.

4. Much research on conformity has grown out of a desire to understand
   the social forces operating in _____ _____.

5. A high school history class taught by Ron Jones in California simulated
   the _____ experience for five days.

6. Social psychologist Stanley Milgram investigated _____
   in a study in which a "teacher" administered what were believed to be
   electric shocks to a "learner."

7. In Milgram's experiment, _____% of the subject-teachers
   went all the way to 450 volts.

8. Three variables accounting for the high level of obedience in Migram's
   study were (1) the presence of a legitimate _____,
   (2) the fact that the victim was in _____
   _____, and (3) that the subject-teacher accepted a
   _____ role.

9. Today, the Milgram experiment would not be considered
   _____ because of the _____ placed on
   the subject-teacher.

10. In a variation of the Milgram study, the percentage of teacher-subjects
    who went all the way to 450 volts was _____ if they
    were in the presence of two other confederate teacher-subjects who
    disobeyed.

11. Nearly 900 people in Jonestown, Guyana committed _____.
    The social psychological influences of _____ and
    _____ were operating that day in Jonestown.

12. More often than not, _____ _____ may
    be stronger than our own personal values, beliefs, and feelings.

13. During the attack and murder of Kitty Genovese, _____
    of the thirty-eight people who watched called the police or helped.

14. When several people witness an emergency, each one thinks someone else will respond or summon help. This is the _____ effect.

15. One reason for the bystander effect is diffusion of _____, and another is the fear of appearing _____.

16. In the experiment in which smoke poured into a room, subjects who were _____ reported it to someone in the outer room. Subjects who were sitting with nonresponding confederates were much _____ likely to do so.

17. People are much <u>less</u> likely to help others in _____ situations.

18. Subjects asked to help search for a lost contact lens were most likely to do so in the _____, _____ - _____ situation.

19. Research with hooded subjects showed that those who maintain their _____ are less likely to help others, and are more likely to _____ someone.

20. According to the bystander-intervention model, a person must complete a five-step process before he or she is likely to give help. The five steps are:
    (a) the event must be _____.
    (b) the event must be interpreted as an _____.
    (c) the person must accept _____ for helping.
    (d) the person has to decide _____ to help.
    (e) _____ must be taken.

21. People can be encouraged to help others by studying _____ _____, by learning appropriate _____ skills (like CPR), by being _____ for helping, and by observing others _____ helping behavior.

22. Lawrence Kohlberg believes that people may progress through six stages of _____ development.

23. The third and fourth stages of moral development in Kohlberg's system are called the _____ level. This is the level reached by most _____.

24. Two or more people working together for their mutual benefit are _____.

25. Vying for a goal that cannot be shared defines _____.

26. In Madsen's marble experiment, _____ was common among four- and five-year-olds; _____ was more common among second through fifth graders.

27. Increased competition among older children occurs because of _____ and _____ .

28. Deutsch and Krauss designed the Acme-Bolt _____ game to study competition and cooperation among adults.

29. The trucking game showed that the chances of cooperation diminish as the ability to _____ one another increases.

30. Sherif and Sherif conducted the _____ Cave experiment.

31. The Sherif study showed that _____ alone was not enough to promote cooperation. It required working together to achieve a common _____ .

32. The bargaining and negotiation technique in which one person makes another feel grateful is called _____ .

33. The two most effective ingratiation techniques are _____ and the giving of small _____ .

34. Getting someone to say "yes" just once to a very small request forms the basis of the _____ -in-the- _____ technique.

35. Asking for a large favor that will certainly be rejected, and then following with a request for a smaller favor is the _____ -in-the- _____ technique.

36. The poorest (but most honest) bargaining technique is to begin by asking for exactly _____ you _____ .

37. Getting someone to agree to a commitment first, and then adding disagreeable specifics later is called _____ .

38. People will do things in _____ that they would never do alone. This is so for at least three reasons: (1) the effects of _____ , (2) a _____ of responsibility, and (3) _____ .

39. Getting so caught up in a group that we lose our self-awareness is referred to as _____ .

40. People with moderate views on an issue often take more radical or extreme views after a group discussion. This is called _____ .

41. One reason for polarization is that we may wish to gain the
    _____ of others by exemplifying their beliefs.

42. Another reason for polarization is that the entire group may shift
    toward the position of the person making the most persuasive and
    convincing _____ .

43. Leadership emerging as a result of the situation and not the individual
    refers to the _____ - _____ hypothesis of
    leadership.

44. The idea that a particular personality makes a leader is referred to as
    the _____ - _____ _____ -
    _____ hypothesis.

45. It has been argued that great leaders combine the best of both
    _____ leaders and _____ -
    _____ leaders.

46. Groups with which a person feels comfortable and a part of are
    _____ - _____ , and groups to which one does
    not belong and which are viewed negatively are _____ -
    _____ .

47. Learned beliefs a person has which lead him or her to be biased toward
    members of particular groups defines _____ .

48. Behavior based upon prejudice is called _____ .

49. Jane Elliott's third grade class learned about _____ by
    discriminating against brown-eyed (and later blue-eyed) classmates.

50. Adorno found that those who are highly prejudiced have
    _____ personalities.

51. Adorno measured authoritarianism with the _____
    _____ Scale.

52. Prejudice can be reduced by bringing antagonistic groups together to
    share a common _____ .

53. Prejudice can also be combatted through _____ , and
    through _____ to increase self-esteem among victims
    of prejudice.

54. A _____ _____ is a system of feelings,
    beliefs, and behaviors with respect to a social object.

55. Our attitudes and views have been shaped systematically by our being

_____ for the "right behavior," and
_____ for anything else.

56. Attitudes are measured by _____ or _____.

57. The _____ pipeline procedure has been used to reduce faking on attitude questionnaires.

58. The bogus pipeline technique tricks subjects into believing that their true opinions will show by the monitoring of _____ responses.

59. Real attitudes are tapped better by the _____ _____ technique than by a _____ used alone.

60. Techniques for changing attitudes often rely on _____ _____.

61. Characteristics of the communicator that affect our attitudes include (1) whether the communicator is an _____, and (2) the communicator's perceived _____ with ourselves.

62. Information people generate themselves is more _____ in determining _____ than is information generated by others.

63. A two-sided argument (presenting both sides of an issue) will lower a recipient's resistance to persuasion best if the recipient initially _____ the idea to be presented.

64. Some communications appeal to the _____.

65. People with _____ self-esteem are _____ likely to be influenced by emotional appeals.

66. It is possible to help people avoid attitude change by _____ them that the speaker intends to change their beliefs.

67. Advertizers use the _____ _____ effect by showing their product as often as possible.

68. Subjects liked their own _____ image photographs best, but liked the direct _____ of their friends' faces best. This illustrates the _____ _____ effect.

69. Two basic routes of persuasion are _____ route processing and _____ route processing.

70. Attitude change through the central route (after careful
    _____) is likely to _____ longer, while
    attitude change through a peripheral route is more likely to be
    _____ .

71. No reliable relationship has been found between _____
    and a person's ability to resist persuasion. However, a _____ -
    _____ argument is more likely to create attitude change
    in those who are more _____ .

72. Subjects who received _____ for telling someone a boring
    task was fun were more likely to really believe it was fun than subjects
    who received _____ for telling the same lie.

73. Those who received only $1.00 experienced _____
    _____ , and changed their opinion of the task to fit
    their behavior.

74. Attempts to reduce cognitive dissonance will generally cause attitudes to
    _____ .

75. People who undergo a severe _____ to experience something
    will rate the experience as _____ valuable than those
    who undergo a mild _____ or none at all.

76. A challenge to cognitive dissonance theory is the _____ -
    _____ theory.

77. We are engaging in _____ whenever we try to find the
    reasons for another's behavior or to understand his or her motivation
    or personality.

78. When we attribute someone's behavior to something we decide whether
    the person's _____ is determining the behavior or if the
    _____ is controlling the behavior.

79. Often people assign blame or give credit on the basis of
    _____ or _____ attribution of behavior.

80. We generally see our own behavior as resulting from _____
    forces, but we generally see the behavior of others to be the function
    of _____ forces. Two explanations of this tendency are
    the _____ _____ hypothesis and the
    _____ _____ hypothesis.

81. The more information we obtain about another person, the more likely
    we are to attribute his or her behavior to _____ factors.

82. The tendency of people to attribute behavior that results in a good

outcome to internal forces, and behavior that results in a bad outcome to environmental factors is called the _____ - _____ _____ .

83. To understand our own feelings by searching inward for feedback is the method of _____ - _____ attention.

84. Subjects who saw their own _____ judged nude slides to be arousing or not arousing based on inner awareness rather than on what they had been _____ beforehand.

SELF TEST I

1. In Asch's classic study of conformity approximately _____ of the subjects agreed at least once with the confederates' lie that the comparison line (which was obviously different) was the same length as the standard line.
   a. 25%   c. 75%
   b. 50%   d. 99%

2. A high school history class taught by Ron Jones simulated the _____ experience for five days.
   a. Nazi   c. Acme-Bolt
   b. Jonestown   d. Hearst

3. The famous study of obedience using a teacher-learner format and increasingly severe electric shocks was conducted by
   a. Solomon Asch   c. Stanley Milgram
   b. Leon Festinger   d. David Rosenhan

4. What social influence was operating to account for the mass suicides in Jonestown, Guyana in 1978?
   a. conformity   c. social comparison
   b. obedience   d. all of the above

5. Two possible reasons for the bystander effect are
   a. social comparison and out-group prejudice
   b. bargaining and ingratiation
   c. emotional instability and fear of retaliation
   d. diffusion of responsibility and fear of appearing foolish

6. Which of the following is not a part of the five step helping process of Latane and Darley's bystander intervention model?
   a. the event must be observed
   b. the event must be interpreted as an emergency
   c. the observer must maintain anonymity
   d. the observer has to decide how to help

7. A bargaining technique where one person makes another feel grateful
    for some reason is called
    a. appreciation   c. cooperation
    b. ingratiation   d. deindividuation

8. Car dealers who wait until you have made a commitment to buy before
    mentioning the cost of sales tax, shipping, and dealer preparation are
    using
    a. the door-in-the-face technique
    b. the foot-in-the-door technique
    c. lowballing
    d. the mere exposure effect

9. Which of the following is a quality shared by many good leaders?
    a. a high degree of verbal skill
    b. maintaining the views of their group
    c. both a and b
    d. none of the above, it depends on which hypothesis of leadership
       is being considered

10. A person with a/an _____ personality rejects out-groups in
    a punitive way, sees others as weak or strong, and shows strict sub-
    mission and obedience to authority.
    a. antisocial   c. Daneriean
    b. authoritarian   d. dissonant

11. A/an _____ is a relatively enduring system of feelings,
    beliefs, and behaviors with respect to a social object.
    a. group impression   c. in-group inclination
    b. collective idea   d. social attitude

12. Which of the following is a communicator characteristic which affects
    people's attitudes?
    a. the communicator being an expert
    b. the communicator's perceived similarity with the audience
    c. the communicator's level of self-esteem
    d. both a and b

13. The greatest and most permanent attitude change occurred in those
    subjects who expected to be interviewed on the issue presented and
    who
    a. found the speaker likeable
    b. found the speaker dislikeable
    c. heard six arguments in favor of the issue
    d. heard two arguments in favor of the issue

14. Whenever we try to find the reasons for someone's behavior or to under-
    stand his or her motivation we are engaging in
    a. attribution   c. social comparison
    b. personality assessment   d. social awareness

15. People tend to take responsibility for good results but attribute bad results to environmental factors. This reflects the
    a. visual perspective hypothesis
    b. information availability hypothesis
    c. self-serving bias
    d. impression management hypothesis

SELF TEST II

1. Social norms are
   a. the ways in which others expect us to conform
   b. spelled out in writing, signs, or notices
   c. unspoken and unwritten
   d. all of the above

2. People conform because
   a. they are often reinforced for conforming
   b. of the influence of social comparison
   c. both a and b
   d. none of the above

3. Before the teacher-learner obedience study was conducted, a group of psychiatrists estimated that _____ of the subject-teachers would go all the way to 450 volts on the shock generator.
   a. 1/10 of 1%   c.   62%
   b. 12%   d   98%

4. What incident has stimulated social psychological investigation into the topic of helping others in emergencies?
   a. the Jonestown, Guyana suicide incident
   b. the Kitty Genovese stabbing incident
   c. the searching for the lost contact lens incident
   d. none of the above

5. Subjects were more likely to help a person search for a contact lens under which conditions?
   a. high-task load, crowded
   b. high-task load, uncrowded
   c. low-task load, crowded
   d. low-task load, uncrowded

6. Which of the following is a reason why Kohlberg's theory of moral development has been criticized?
   a. it correlates poorly with moral behavior
   b. it may be culturally biased in favor of Western ideas of morality
   c. both a and b
   d. none of the above

7. In the Acme–Bolt trucking game, cooperation diminished when the players were given a/an
   a. alternate route   c. gate
   b. inoperable truck   d. bomb

8. People who enter a group discussion with moderate views often become more extreme (more radical or conservative) about the issue after the discussion. This is referred to as
   a. deindividuation   c. ingratiation
   b. polarization   d. extremism

9. People typically have a positive regard toward _____.
   They tend to view _____ in a negative light.
   a. in-groups, other-groups
   b. other-groups, out-groups
   c. in-groups, out-groups
   d. out-groups, in-groups

10. Which of the following (by itself) is not effective in reducing or overcoming prejudice?
    a. bringing antagonistic groups into contact with one another
    b. having antagonistic groups work together toward a common goal
    c. having a group be on the receiving end of prejudice for awhile
    d. putting members of antagonistic groups on the same baseball team

11. Evidence suggests that real attitudes are tapped better by _____ than by _____ used alone.
    a. the contrived biofeedback technique, a questionnaire
    b. the bogus pipeline technique, a questionnaire
    c. a questionnaire, the contrived biofeedback technique
    d. a questionnaire, the bogus pipeline technique

12. Advertizers show their product as often as possible because
    a. of the effectiveness of emotional appeals
    b. self-persuasion is likely to be enhanced
    c. of the mere exposure effect
    d. they believe in the impression-management hypothesis

13. An uncomfortable feeling that occurs when someone acts in a manner inconsistent with his or her real feelings and beliefs is called
    a. cognitive attribution
    b. cognitive dissonance
    c. emotional distress
    d. emotional dissonance

14. Which approach argues that people have a need to appear consistent in the eyes of others, and so will state they have changed an attitude to match their behavior when in fact the attitude has not changed?
    a. the situational-environmental hypothesis
    b. cognitive dissonance theory

c. the impression-management hypothesis
d. the consistency control hypothesis

15. Two of your young friends are playing a "drop the marble in the cup" game which requires cooperation for anyone to win marbles. The likelihood is greatest that both of your friends will win some marbles if
    a. they are both four years old
    b. they are both in the second grade
    c. they are both in the fifth grade
    d. one is a second grader and the other is a fifth grader

ESSAY QUESTIONS

1. Discuss the nightmare in Jonestown, Guyana in light of the social-psychological principles of conformity and obedience. Make specific reference to Milgram's obedience study.

2. Discuss the factors affecting the chances that a bystander will lend aid in an emergency situation. Include an explanation of Latane and Darley's bystander intervention model.

3. Explain how self-respecting, honest, everyday people can take part in mob violence. What social-psychological factors operate?

4. Discuss the meaning of, causes of, and ways to reduce prejudice.

5. We tend to attribute our own behavior to external forces, and the behavior of others to internal (personality) factors. Explain why this is and in so doing mention two hypotheses and consider the concept of self-serving bias.

ANSWER SECTION

Guided Review
1. *behavior, others*
2. *reinforced, comparison*
3. *reference*
4. *Nazi Germany*
5. *Nazi*
6. *obedience*
7. *62*
8. *authority, another room, subordinate*
9. *ethical, stress*
10. *lower (12%)*
11. *suicide, conformity, obedience*
12. *social forces*
13. *none*

14. *bystander*
15. *responsibility, foolish*
16. *alone, less*
17. *ambiguous*
18. *uncrowded, low-task*
19. *anonymity, shock*
20. *observed, emergency, responsibility, how, action*
21. *social psychology, helping, reinforced, model*
22. *moral*
23. *conventional, adults*
24. *cooperating*
25. *competition*
26. *cooperation, competition*
27. *experience, learning*
28. *trucking*
29. *threaten*
30. *Robbers'*
31. *contact, goal*
32. *ingratiation*
33. *flattery, favors*
34. *foot, door*
35. *door, face*
36. *what, want*
37. *lowballing*
38. *groups, modeling, diffusion, deindividuation*
39. *deindividuation*
40. *polarization*
41. *approval*
42. *argument*
43. *situational-environmental*
44. *great-man great-woman*
45. *task, social-emotional*
46. *in-groups, out-groups*
47. *prejudice*
48. *discrimination*
49. *prejudice*
50. *authoritarian*
51. *California F*
52. *goal*
53. *legislation, learning*
54. *social attitude*
55. *rewarded, punished*
56. *questionnaires, scales*
57. *bogus*
58. *physiological*
59. *bogus pipeline, questionnaire*
60. *persuasive communication*
61. *expert, similarity*
62. *powerful, attitudes*

63. *opposes*
64. *emotions*
65. *high, more*
66. *forewarning*
67. *mere exposure*
68. *mirror, photographs, mere exposure*
69. *central, peripheral*
70. *listening, endure (or last), temporary*
71. *intelligence, two-sided, intelligent*
72. *$1.00, $20.00*
73. *cognitive dissonance*
74. *change*
75. *initiation, more, initiation*
76. *impression-management*
77. *attribution*
78. *personality, environment*
79. *internal, external*
80. *environmental, internal, visual perspective, information availability*
81. *environmental*
82. *self-serving bias*
83. *self-directed*
84. *reflection, told*

Self Test I

1. c
2. a
3. c
4. d
5. d
6. c
7. b
8. c
9. c
10. b
11. d
12. d
13. c
14. a
15. c

Self Test II

1. d
2. c
3. a
4. b
5. d
6. c
7. c
8. b
9. c
10. a
11. b
12. c
13. b
14. c
15. a

CHAPTER 18

Sexuality, Attraction, and Intimacy

BEHAVIORAL OBJECTIVES

After completing this chapter, the student should be able to:

1. Compare and contrast the Arapesh, Mundugumor, and Tchambuli tribes' sexual temperaments.
2. List the primary and secondary sex characteristics.
3. Describe the effects of exposing a fetus to high levels of sex hormones.
4. Explain why hormones have been said to have a "double effect."
5. Describe the genetic disorder known in slang terms as "penis-at-twelve" and contrast the transitions made by individuals suffering this disorder in the United States and Santo Domingo.
6. Summarize the research regarding male and female brain differences.
7. Contrast the social learning, cognitive, and psychoanalytic theories of sex-role development.
8. Summarize the study conducted by Richard Green on the effects of parents' sexuality and sexual preference in children's sex role development.
9. Explain how social learning theory and cognitive theory have attempted to explain sexual preference.
10. Define transsexualism and describe transsexual reassignment procedures.
11. Explain how cultures can shape sex-roles.
12. List and describe the factors that influence our attraction to others.
13. Summarize the research on the effects of attractiveness.
14. Explain why we like others according to the reinforcement, exchange theory, and the gain-loss theory.
15. Compare and contrast passionate love with conjugal love.

KEY TERMS AND CONCEPTS

Arapesh tribe
Mundugumor tribe

Tchambuli tribe
love

primary sexual characteristics
secondary sexual characteristics
menarche
gonads
ovaries
testes
adrenal glands
adrenal cortex
estrogens
androgens
thymus gland
pituitary gland
genetic sex
23rd pair of chromosomes
testosterone
freemartins
androgynized
gender identity
dihydrotestosterone
"penis at 12"
monozygotic twins
gender constancy
gender identity
sex-roles
sex-role typing
sexual preference
sex-role modeling
social learning theory of
    gender identity

cognitive theory of gender identity
psychoanalytic theory of gender identity
transsexualism
transsexual reassignment
attraction
liking
closeness-proximity
similarity
complementary needs
competence
attractiveness and liking
reinforcement theory of liking
equity theory
exchange theory
gain-loss theory
passionate love
phenylethlamine
conjugal love
masturbation
nocturnal emissions
wet dreams
spermatorrhea
excitement phase
plateau phase
orgasm
orgasmic phase
resolution phase
refractory period

NAMES TO REMEMBER

Margaret Mead
Harry Harlow
Julienne Imperato-McGinley
Jean Piaget
Richard Green
John Money
Richard von Krafft-Ebing

Claude Francis l'Allemand
Charles Drysdale
Sigmund Freud
Alfred Kinsey
William Masters
Virginia Johnson
Havelock Ellis

GUIDED REVIEW

1. _____ _____, the famous anthropologist,
   noted _____ - _____ among various South
   Pacific tribes.

2. The _____ displayed _____ temperaments
   that would be more typical of 1930 American females.

3. The Mundugumor tribe are a very different tribe in that both men and women are _____ and _____ . Here the women behave in a _____ manner as compared to Westerners.

4. Among the _____ tribe, the _____ and _____ roles are the _____ of Western culture. The _____ are tough leaders, while the _____ are emotional and easily _____ .

5. Margaret Mead suggested that sex-role may be more a function of _____ than of _____ .

6. Psychologists want to know how biological and hormonal aspects of _____ affect _____ .

7. Psychologists also study how our _____ understanding of being male or female shapes our relationships.

8. Additionally, psychologists study how _____ - _____ influences concerning our sexuality can affect us. Psychologists are also interested in intimacy and _____ .

9. Males and females differ in both _____ and _____ sexual characteristics.

10. _____ sexual characteristics appear at _____ . For boys these include the appearance of facial hair and a _____ of the voice.

11. Secondary sexual characteristics of females include development of the _____ and widening of the _____ .

12. The appearance of _____ sexual characteristics indicate that the body is preparing for the capacity to _____ .

13. Males become capable of reproduction when they first _____ _____ and females can once _____ has occurred.

14. _____ are body chemicals carried by the _____ that can affect psychological and physiological development.

15. The sex glands, called _____ , secrete hormones. In the female these are the _____ , and in the male they are the _____ .

16. The male hormones are the _____ and the female hormones are the _____ .

17. It is believed that the secretion of sex hormones is directed by the _____ and _____ glands.

18. If _____ is present during the development of an XY embryo, _____ _____ develop in place of _____ _____ .

19. Girls who were exposed to abnormally large amounts of _____ prior to birth appeared less _____ during their _____ .

20. Boys who had mothers who received large doses of _____ during pregnancy were considered to be less athletic, less _____ , and less _____ than typical boys.

21. German physiologist Arnold _____ found that by castrating roosters he could stop them from fighting with other roosters. Later he concluded that something carried in the _____ affected behavior.

22. Frank Lillie speculated that _____ from the testes of the male _____ _____ masculinized _____ cows, which is why they act like _____ .

23. Young and Goy gave large amounts of _____ to pregnant guinea pigs. The females in the subsequent litters were _____ . Then after removal of their ovaries they acted like _____ .

24. Hormones tend to organize _____ structures in a masculinized or feminized manner before birth.

25. Robert Goy has studied the effects of different levels of _____ and noted various forms of _____ and _____ behavior can be generated by different doses.

26. The effect of hormones at main action sites in the brain have been studied by injecting _____ hormones.

27. _____ and _____ concentrate in similar areas of the brain but different _____ sites in these areas attract one kind or the other. Different _____ cells and _____ pathways develop depending on which hormone affects the area of the brain in question.

28. Julienne Imperato-McGinley studied 38 boys from _____ _____ who had a _____ disorder which made them look like _____ until they reached _____ when they adopted the culturally accepted _____ sex role.

29. Imperato-McGinley also studied children in the United States. These _____ children were raised as _____ and were surgically _____ with five of the eight having serious _____ problems.

30. Adopting male roles may be dependent on the presence of _____ hormones.

31. It is possible that the differences between the Santo Domingo children and the United States sample were due to _____ factors.

32. American "girls" who were surgically forced to become women may have had additional problems, since they could not give _____ and had to have continual _____ injections.

33. Biological variables may not be the only ones responsible for the development of _____ identity. Studies of _____ twins have suggested that environmental factors may also play a role.

34. Differences in the _____ _____ of male and female rats have been established by Diamond and his colleagues.

35. In the female rat the _____ _____ is thicker than the _____ _____ . In the male rat the _____ _____ is thicker than the _____ _____ .

36. If at birth female rats have their ovaries removed or males are castrated the thickness of their hemispheres may be the _____ of what is normal.

37. The structural differences found in rat brains are believed to be the result of _____ action.

38. Male or female hormones administered _____ to rats can affect the _____ of the cortex.

39. Male rats are generally better able to _____ _____ , a task that requires _____ orientation, than are females. Human males are also generally _____ to females on spatial orientation tasks.

40. Female rats exposed to _____ _____ during a _____ period in the womb or immediately after

birth are able to run mazes as well as males.

41. _____ _____ found that female rats learned to avoid an electric shock faster than males, unless they were given _____ _____ .

42. Among men the _____ hemisphere appears to be dominant, while among women the _____ hemisphere is generally dominant.

43. It has been found that _____ are significantly more responsive to _____ and _____ sent to the right hemisphere, while _____ are more responsive when these are sent to the left hemisphere.

44. The fact that the right hemisphere is generally dominant in males may explain why males are superior in geometry and _____ . And the fact that females are left brain dominant may explain why they are generally superior in _____ ability.

45. Many researchers contend that the differences between men and women in mathematical and verbal ability are due to _____ factors.

46. Camilla Benbow and Julian Stanley concluded that males have a _____ and _____ mathematical ability.

47. Genshaft and Hirt (1980) found that girls who were _____ excelled in _____ ability while girls not receiving help showed no _____ .

48. While superior mathematical ability among men and superior verbal ability among women may be the result of _____ , there is still evidence suggesting that _____ can cause changes in the brain.

49. Hormones appear to affect _____ structures and these in turn may influence sexual _____ , but the sexual differences in behavior between men and women are very _____ .

50. In order to investigate our cognitive understanding of _____ and _____ _____ , psychologists have studied children before they were old enough to grasp the meaning of their _____ and then watched as their _____ identity began to form.

51. It appears that children are able to comprehend that they are either _____ or _____ by about the age of _____ .

52. Three-year-olds are better able to judge who is a boy and who is a girl, yet they lack an understanding of _____ constancy.

53. The formation of gender constancy agrees well with _____ _____ description of cognitive development, since gender constancy is fully developed when the ability to _____ appears at appproximately _____ years of age.

54. The _____ process attempts to transmit beliefs and values to children by reinforcing and shaping appropriate _____ _____ behaviors.

55. Children engage in socially _____ – _____ behavior even before they are _____ aware of their gender or its constancy.

56. Fathers tend to emphasize the _____ and _____ of their newborn daughters, and the _____ and _____ of their newborn sons.

57. Mothers are reported to be more _____ with their infant _____ .

58. _____ generally treat boy and girl infants less differently than do _____ .

59. _____ _____ typing refers to the learning of sex roles and may be more influenced by _____ in our culture.

60. A person's _____ identity is believed to be determined to a great degree by _____ as well as by social or biological processes.

61. A parent's _____ preference and sex role _____ are believed to have a very influential effect on a child's developing gender identity.

62. In Freudian or _____ theory the _____ with the father leads to the boy adopting the _____ sex role.

63. According to social leraning theory, a boy becomes attached to his father because the father is the major _____ and _____ in his life.

64. According to _____ theory, the boy first realizes the

_____ of "male" and after understanding he is male
looks to the father as a sex role _____ and becomes
attached to him.

65. Psychoanalytic theory views a girl's sex role development as stemming
     from the _____ complex, while social learning theorists
     are _____ how a girl's sex role development occurs.

66. Richard Green studied children who were being reared by either
     female _____ or by parents who had _____-
     _____ operations. All of these children, except one,
     developed _____ preferences.

67. Among the Sakalavas in Madagascar _____ who are
     considered pretty are raised as _____ and they readily
     adopt the woman's _____-_____ role.

68. John Money studied _____ normal girls who had been
     exposed to excessive amounts of _____ during their
     mother's pregnancies. These girls developed _____
     _____.

69. Money believes that a change of _____ could successfully
     occur before the age of roughly 18 months to three years.

70. _____ is the most extreme form of _____
     _____ in which a person feels that he or she is trapped
     in the wrong sexed body.

71. _____ _____ is a medical procedure that
     anatomically and hormonally enables a person to change sex.
     Approximately three-fourths of these operations have been
     _____ to _____.

72. Both psychoanalytic and _____ learning theories agree
     that transsexualism is related to a weak or reversed _____
     _____. Whatever the reason, it is generally accepted
     that early childhood _____ play an important role.

73. According to Margaret Mead, the _____ process is more
     important than _____ variables in determining a person's
     sex role.

74. Male chimps and male humans are somewhat more likely to engage in
     _____ and _____ play than are females.

75. Trobriand Island _____ have been found to be very
     _____. In addition, Ethel Albert has found cultures in
     which the women do heavy _____ because the men are
     believed to be too _____.

76. There's a greater chance you'll like other people who live
_____ to you. One study found that half of those who
applied for a _____ license lived within
_____ blocks of each other.

77. In a study of college dorms the people most liked tended to be those who
lived _____ door. Also, simply being someone's
_____ will often foster a friendship.

78. Closeness or _____ will not lead to increased liking if
the initial _____ of both people are _____.

79. Whether we like someone often depends on how similar that person's
_____, _____, and _____
are to our own.

80. Byrne and his colleagues found that couples with similar
_____ and _____ were found to be more
likely to express a desire to have another _____.

81. When social psychologists say that opposites attract, they don't mean that
opposite _____ and _____ attract, but
rather, that sharing _____ needs is attractive.

82. We tend to like people who are competent but not too _____.
In one study in which tapes were played the most liked contestant was
the _____ one who had an _____.

83. Researchers have found that physically _____ people
are more often liked in most kinds of social situations.

84. In the Sroufe et al. study money was deliberately left in phone booths
and when a stranger entered the booth he or she most often returned
the money to an _____ _____.

85. Juries, in mock trials, have been found to give _____
_____ sentences to attractive defendants unless the
defendant used his or her _____ _____
to commit the crime.

86. Dion found that fifth and six graders who are physically attractive
are more successful at _____ and _____
the behavior of children of the opposite _____.

87. Physical attractiveness has been positively correlated with
_____ skill, suggesting that being attractive can affect
an individual's _____.

88. Possibly because attractive people value their own opinions, they are
less likely to be affected by _____ pressure.

89. Adams (1977) found that _____ individuals are more
     susceptible to _____ pressure.

90. Attractive people are often perceived as _____ and
     _____ and more likely to have _____
     affairs.

91. The four major theories of liking are _____ theory,
     _____ theory, _____ theory, and
     _____-_____ theory.

92. Senator William Proxmire has criticized psychologists for studying
     _____.

93. Love can be divided into two classifications: _____
     and _____ love.

94. _____ love is an intense emotional reaction and in modern
     Western culture is not only common but _____ to occur.

95. _____ arousal that an individual interprets as love gen-
     erally occurs in passionate love. This was demonstrated in the study
     reported by Adler and Carey of men asking for a date after crossing
     a narrow _____.

96. People who have a history of love affairs and breakups often crave
     _____ following a breakup, which is high in
     _____.

97. John Money argues that the place to look for answers to
     _____ is in the _____.

98. The high divorce rate in the United States may be due in part to newly-
     weds expecting _____ love to remain at a high level.

99. Richard von Krafft-Ebing wrote "_____ _____"
     and his beliefs probably did more to encourage _____
     and _____ concerning sex than any other book.

100. Claude Francois l'Allemand called _____ _____
     _____ and considered it to be a serious disorder.

101. Alfred _____ found that more than half of the married
     women and over two-thirds of the married men in his sample had had
     _____ _____.

102. Kinsey also found that a majority of men and women engaged in
     _____.

103. Masters and Johnson discovered that during sexual arousal both males and females go through the _____ phase, the _____ phase, the _____ phase, and the _____ phase. They also found during the resolution phase men have a _____ _____ in which ejaculation is impossible.

104. Although _____ _____ is not as well known as Sigmund Freud, his investigations of human sexuality were perhaps the beginning of modern _____ _____ .

SELF TEST I

1. Margaret Mead's studies of South Pacific tribes suggested
    a. aggressiveness is innate
    b. sex roles are due to our biology more than to any cultural influence
    c. homosexual behavior is much more prevalent among natives than once believed
    d. none of the above

2. Male hormones are called _____ and female hormones are called _____ .
    a. testes, gonads
    b. androgens, estrogens
    c. estrogens, androgens
    d. none of the above

3. In 1849, when Arnold Berthold castrated roosters, he discovered when the sex glands were reintroduced that
    a. something in the blood controlled behavior
    b. the roosters stopped fighting with one another when the glands were removed
    c. transplanted testicles again yielded fighting behavior
    d. all of the above

4. The researcher who studied samples of children with genetic disorders in Santo Domingo and in America was
    a. Ellis   c. Imperato-McGinley
    b. Mead   d. Money

5. In _____ rats the left hemisphere is thicker than the right hemisphere.
    a. male   c. freemartin
    b. female   d. wild

6. _____ are significantly more responsive to light and sound sent to the _____ , while _____ are more responsive to light and sound sent to the _____ .

a. men, right hemisphere, women, left hemisphere
b. women, right hemisphere, men, left hemisphere
c. men, left temporal lobe, women, right temporal lobe
d. none of the above

7. Three-year-olds, who may be able to judge who is a boy and who is a girl, generally fail to understand _____.
    a. gender identity   c. both a and b
    b. gender constancy   d. none of the above

8. Mothers generally treat boy and girl infants less differently than do fathers.
    a. true   b. false

9. Conclusive hormonal differences between heterosexual and homosexual adults have recently been established.
    a. true   b. false

10. Both psychoanalytic and social learning theories agree that transsexualism is directly related to a weak or reversed gender identity.
    a. true   b. false

11. A variable that can determine whether or not we will like someone is
    a. closeness   c. competency
    b. similarity   d. all of the above

12. Which of the following old adages has psychological research partially supported?
    a. "birds of a feather flock together"
    b. "opposites attract"
    c. both a and b
    d. none of the above

13. At least one study has shown social skill to be _____ with physical attractiveness.
    a. negative correlated
    b. positively correlated
    c. uncorrelated
    d. none of the above

14. Senator _____ riduculed psychology for studying love.
    a. Barry Goldwater   c. William Proxmire
    b. S. I. Hayakawa   d. Edward Kennedy

15. Krafft-Ebing argued that _____ was often the precursor to lust murder and was a loathesome disease.
    a. heterosexuality   c. matriculation
    b. masturbation   d. spermatorrhea

SELF TEST II

1. The penis, scrotum, and testes of the male, and the vagina, ovaries, and uterus of the female are the
    a. primary sexual characteristics
    b. secondary sexual characteristics
    c. freemartins
    d. none of the above

2. A male embryo during development is exposed to _____ under the direction of the _____ chromosome.
    a. estrogens, Y
    b. androgens, X
    c. testosterone, Y
    d. none of the above

3. Hormones
    a. may organize brain structures in a masculinized way prior to birth
    b. may organize brain structures in a feminized way prior to birth
    c. activate brain structures long after birth
    d. all of the above

4. Male children with a genetic disorder that makes them appear female until puberty seem to adjust to the change in sex roles much easier in the Dominican Republic than in America.
    a. true   b. false

5. Human males are not generally as good as females at spatial orientation.
    a. true   b. false

6. Camilla Benbow and Julian Stanley studied male and female differences in mathematical ability and concluded
    a. males are naturally superior to females in mathematical ability
    b. females are naturally superior to males in mathematical ability
    c. that socialization clearly accounts for any differences between males and females
    d. that no real difference exists

7. Socialization has been shown to be unrelated to the development of sex role behaviors.
    a. true   b. false

8. According to psychoanalytic theory
    a. identity with the father results from a drive to avoid retaliation for initially desiring the mother
    b. girls' sex role development stems from the Electra complex
    c. boys adopt the father's ways as their own once identification occurs.
    d. all of the above

9. The most extreme form of gender reversal in which an individual feels
    that he or she is really a member of the opposite sex is known as
    a. homosexuality   c. transsexualism
    b. bisexuality   d. transvestism

10. _____ chimps and _____ humans are
    more likely to engage in rough and tumble play.
    a. male, female   c. female, male
    b. female, female   d. male, male

11. The Priest and Sawyer study conducted in a college dormitory found
    a. people especially liked the person next door more than those farther
       away
    b. people especially disliked the person next door
    c. dormitory residents often like all residents equally regardless of
       proximity or closeness
    d. none of the above

12. So far, mock juries have always given less severe sentences to attrac-
    tive defendants.
    a. true   b. false

13. Which of the following is not a major theory of liking?
    a. reinforcement theory
    b. psychoanalytic theory
    c. equity theory
    d. exchange theory

14. One possible chemical in the brain that may be associated with being
    in love is
    a. phenylethylamine   c. PCP
    b. GABA   d. vasopressin

15. The four phases that Masters and Johnson describe in males and females
    sexual responses are, in order:
    a. excitement, plateau, orgasmic, refractory
    b. excitement, plateau, orgasmic, resolution
    c. excitement, orgasmic, plateau, resolution
    d. none of the above

ESSAY QUESTIONS

1. Describe the cultural differences in sex roles noted by Margaret Mead
    and explain why this type of information is significant.

2. Summarize the findings of modern research using radioactive hormones
    in animal brains.

3. Tell in your own words how we develop our gender identity and support this with studies described in the text.

4. Explain why people have criticized psychology for studying "love" and explain why such research is appropriate.

5. Describe the background and contributions of Havelock Ellis.

ANSWER SECTION

Guided Review
1.   *Margaret Mead, sex roles*
2.   *Arapesh, nonaggressive*
3.   *dangerous, aggressive, masculine*
4.   *Tchambuli, sex, temperament, opposite, women, men, embarrassed*
5.   *culture, biology*
6.   *sexuality, behavior*
7.   *cognitive*
8.   *socio-cultural, love*
9.   *primary, secondary*
10. *secondary, puberty, deepending*
11. *breasts, hips*
12. *secondary, reproduce*
13. *ejaculate sperm, menarche*
14. *hormones, blood*
15. *gonads, ovaries, testes*
16. *androgens, estrogens*
17. *thymus, pituitary*
18. *testosterone (or dihydrotestosterone), male genitals, female genitals*
19. *androgens, feminine, preadolescence*
20. *estrogens, assertive, aggressive*
21. *Berthold, castrating, blood*
22. *hormones, fraternal twin, freemartin, bulls*
23. *testosterone, androgynized, males*
24. *brain*
25. *testosterone, masculine, feminine*
26. *radioactive*
27. *androgens, estrogens, receptor, nerve, nerve*
28. *Santo Domingo, genetic, girls, puberty, male*
29. *male, girls, castrated, psychological*
30. *male*
31. *environmental*
32. *birth, hormone*
33. *gender, monozygotic (or identical)*
34. *cerebral cortex*
35. *left hemisphere, right hemisphere, right hemisphere, left hemisphere*
36. *opposite*
37. *hormone*

38. *prenatally, width*
39. *run mazes, spatial, superior*
40. *male hormones, critical*
41. *William Beatty, male hormones*
42. *right, left*
43. *men, light, sound, women*
44. *mathematics, verbal*
45. *environmental*
46. *superior, natural*
47. *counseled, mathematical, improvement*
48. *culture (or experience, training), hormones*
49. *brain, behavior, subtle*
50. *sexuality, sex roles, sex, gender*
51. *boys, girls, 3*
52. *gender*
53. *Jean Piaget's, conserve, 6 or 7*
54. *socialization, sex role*
55. *sex-appropriate, cognitively*
56. *beauty, delicacy, strength, coordination*
57. *verbal, daughters*
58. *mothers, fathers*
59. *sex role, fathers*
60. *gender, cognitive*
61. *sexual, modeling*
62. *psychoanalytic, identification, male*
63. *rewarder, controller*
64. *cognitive, concept, model*
65. *Electra, unsure*
66. *homosexuals, sex-change, heterosexual*
67. *boys, girls, sex-appropriate*
68. *chromosomally, androgen, undifferentiated genitals*
69. *gender*
70. *transsexualism, gender reversal*
71. *transsexual reassignment, male, female*
72. *social, gender identity, experiences*
73. *socialization, biological*
74. *rough, tumble*
75. *women, aggressive, work, weak*
76. *close, marriage, 14*
77. *next, roommate*
78. *proximity, attitudes, dissimilar*
79. *values, attitudes, beliefs*
80. *attitudes, beliefs, date*
81. *attitudes, beliefs, complementary*
82. *competent, competent, accident*
83. *attractive*
84. *attractive individual*
85. *less severe, good looks*
86. *influencing, changing, sex*

87. *social, personality*
88. *peer*
89. *unattractive, peer*
90. *vain, egotistical, extramarital*
91. *reinforcement, exchange, equity, gain-loss*
92. *love*
93. *passionate, conjugal*
94. *passionate, expected*
95. *emotional (or physiological), footbridge*
96. *chocolate, phenylethylamine*
97. *love, brain*
98. *passionate*
99. *Psychopathia Sexualis, disgust, revulsion*
100. *nocturnal emissions (or wet dreams), spermatorrhea*
101. *Kinsey, premarital intercourse*
102. *masturbation*
103. *excitement, plateau, orgasmic, resolution, refractory period*
104. *Havelock Ellis, sexual research*

Self Test I
1. *d*
2. *b*
3. *d*
4. *c*
5. *b*
6. *a*
7. *b*
8. *a*
9. *b*
10. *a*
11. *d*
12. *c*
13. *b*
14. *c*
15. *b*

Self Test II
1. *a*
2. *c*
3. *d*
4. *a*
5. *b*
6. *a*
7. *b*
8. *d*
9. *c*
10. *d*
11. *a*
12. *b*
13. *b*
14. *a*
15. *b*

STATISTICS APPENDIX

BEHAVIORAL OBJECTIVES

After completing this appendix, the student should be able to:

1. State the purpose of using statistics in research and name the two major categories of statistics.
2. Construct a regular and grouped frequency distribution, a histogram, and a frequency polygon.
3. Identify and explain the meaning of a normal, positively skewed, negatively skewed, and bimodal curve.
4. Compare and contrast the mean, median, and mode, explain when it is appropriate to use each, and pin-point each in a distribution of scores.
5. Explain the concept of variability and convey an understanding of the standard deviation.
6. List three kinds of standard scores and give the mean and standard deviation associated with each.
7. Distinguish between a percent and a percentile.
8. Tell in his or her own words the relationship of Z-scores and the standard deviation to the normal bell-shaped curve.
9. Give the approximate percentages under the normal curve between + and -1 SD, + and -2 SDs, and + and -3 SDs.
10. Define inferential statistics and distinguish between a population and a sample.
11. Compare a null hypothesis with an original research hypothesis and explain the implications of rejecting or retaining the null hypothesis.
12. Contrast an experimental study with a correlational study.
13. Explain the meaning of a positive, negative, perfect, and zero correlation coefficient.
14. Draw a scatter diagram for a set of correlational data and explain the meaning of a straight line dot pattern.
15. Summarize the issue of correlation and causation and state the assumptions that may and may not be made about causation.

16. Analyze a journal research article and intelligently comment on some of the statistical procedures employed.

KEY TERMS AND CONCEPTS

statistics
descriptive statistics
frequency distribution
regular frequency distribution
score value
grouped frequency distribution
histogram
bar graph
frequency polygon
normal bell-shaped curve
positively skewed curve
negatively skewed curve
bimodal curve
central tendency
mean
median
mode
variability
range
standard deviation
squared differences
square root
transformed scores
percentile
standard scores
Z scores
T scores
SAT scores
Scholastic Aptitude Test
Graduate Record Exam
percentages under the
    normal curve
Wechsler Intelligence Test
inferential statistics
predictions
sample

population
probability
chance
null hypothesis
reject
retain
significant difference
original research hypothesis
testing for differences between means
correlation
relationship
variables
experimental study
correlation coefficient
positive correlation
negative correlation
perfect correlation
zero correlation
$r = +1.00$
predict
scatter diagram
correlation coefficient interpretation
cause and effect relationship
causation
correlation and causation
babies and storks
variable X
variable Y
N
r
(Sum of X^2)
(Sum of X)^2
(Sum of XY)
(Sum of X) (Sum of Y)
(Sum of Y^2)
(Sum of Y)^2

GUIDED REVIEW

1. Strategies and techniques designed to help an investigator interpret, understand, and make predictions from research data are collectively called _____.

2. To summarize and boil down large amounts of data you should use
    _____ statistics.

3. In a set of test scores if you list every possible score value once
    from highest to lowest, and then enter beside each score value the
    number of times it occurs, you are making a _____
    _____ distribution.

4. A grouped frequency distribution should be used if the spread of
    score values is _____.

5. A grouped frequency distribution condenses score values into class
    _____ and shows, in the _____ column,
    the number of people falling within each class _____.

6. The visual pattern of a frequency distribution may be shown by con-
    structing a _____.

7. One way to graph a frequency distribution is to use a bar graph (or
    _____), and another way is to construct a frequency
    _____.

8. The vertical edges of each bar in a histogram are plotted mid-way
    _____ the scores so that each score value falls in the
    _____ of the bar.

9. Frequency polygons plot the score frequencies as _____
    which are connected with a _____ _____.

10. Frequency polygons and histograms convey more _____
    than a mass of random scores.

11. Frequency polygons, particularly when large numbers of scores are
    involved, often take on an identifiable _____.

12. In a normal bell-shaped frequency polygon (or curve), most of the
    people score toward the _____ of the distribution.

13. In a _____ _____ curve, most of the scores
    are piling up at the low end, and in a _____ curve,
    most of the scores are piling up at the high end of the distribution.

14. If most of the students in a large class either aced the test or bombed
    it, the shape of the frequency polygon (curve) would be
    _____.

15. If you want to know about the middleness or centralness of a distribu-
    tion of scores, you are interested in a measure of central
    _____.

16. The three measures of central tendency are the _____,
    the _____, and the _____.

17. The arithmetic average obtained by the well known procedure of summing
    the scores and dividing by the number of scores is called the
    _____.

18. The most commonly used measure of central tendency in statistical analy-
    sis is the _____. However, if you have a highly skewed
    distribution with extreme scores it is not appropriate to use the
    _____. In situations in which the mean should not be
    used, the best measure of central tendency is the _____.

19. The point in a distribution where exactly _____ the
    scores fall above it and _____ below it is called the
    median.

20. Given the following scores: 4,5,5,5,5,6,6,7,7,7,8,9. The mode is
    _____.

21. The measure of central tendency which is seldom used because it is
    crude, is the _____.

22. To be concerned with how spread out, dispersed, or scattered a set
    of scores is, is to be concerned with _____.

23. Scores that are tightly clustered together have _____
    variability.

24. Two popular measures of variability are the _____ and
    the _____ _____.

25. To get the _____, subtract the lowest from the highest
    score. Like the mode, the _____ is a _____
    statistical measure, since it takes into account only _____
    scores in the distribution.

26. The most useful measure of variability, which takes into account all
    scores in the distribution, and which represents the average distance
    of the scores from the mean, is the _____
    _____.

27. To calculate the standard deviation, take the _____
    _____ of the average (using N-1) of the squared
    differences.

28. Transformed scores generally fall into two categories, namely
    _____ and _____ scores.

29. If you figure the percent of people who scored at or below the score you got on a test, you are calculating your _____.

30. Z scores have a mean of _____ and a standard deviation of _____, T scores have a mean of _____ and a SD of _____, and the SAT score's mean equals _____ with a SD of _____. Z, T, and SAT scores are classified as _____ scores.

31. The only type of standard score that may yield scores with negative numbers is a _____ score.

32. The results of the _____ _____ Exam are reported in SAT scores.

33. Z scores and the standard deviation are related to the _____ _____ - _____ curve in a fixed and predictable manner.

34. The _____ under the normal curve never change. Thus, about _____ percent of all people taking any test (assuming the scores are normally distributed) fall between +1 and −1 standard deviation on the curve. Over _____ percent fall between +3 and −3 standard deviations, and only _____ percent score above +3 standard deviations.

35. To make predictions and draw conclusions about populations based on data from a sample, you must use _____ statistics.

36. A _____ is all of whatever it is you are interested in: All rats, all Americans, all statistics students, or all fourth graders who are heavy TV watchers.

37. A subpart of a population is a _____, and, if it is chosen at _____, it will likely be a good representation of the _____.

38. Inferential statistics are based on the laws of _____ or _____.

39. If the means of two populations are the same, then the probability is _____ that the two sample means will be considerably different from each other just by chance alone.

40. When you assume that there is no difference between two population means, you are stating the _____ hypothesis.

41. If the probability is extremely low that two sample means differed from each other by chance alone, then you should _____ the _____ hypothesis.

42. Typically, if the probability that the difference between sample means occurred by chance is less than _____ percent, then _____ the null hypothesis.

43. If you reject the null hypothesis, then you have found a _____ _____ between the means.

44. In rejecting the null hypothesis, you are _____ the original research hypothesis that you formulated at the beginning of your study.

45. In _____ studies the researcher tests for significant differences between means, but in _____ studies the degree of relationship between variables is investigated.

46. The correlation or _____ between two variables is expressed as a number known as the _____ _____.

47. If there is a trend or tendency for two variables to change together in the same direction, then the resulting correlation coefficient will be _____.

48. If there is a trend or tendency for one variable to increase as the other variable is decreasing (like absences and grades), then the correlation coefficient will be _____.

49. The strongest possible correlation coefficient is plus or minus _____ and is called a _____ correlation.

50. If you correlate length of big toe and college grade point average for a group of 100 students, the correlation coefficient would likely come out to be about _____.

51. A _____ correlation coefficient indicates no relationship between the variables.

52. With a correlation of plus or minus 1.00 you can _____ perfectly a person's score on one variable if you know their score on the other variable.

53. The visual representation of the direction and strength of a correlation is called a _____ _____.

54. On a scatter diagram, the closer the _____ approach a straight line the _____ the correlation (or relationship); and an exact straight line dot pattern means there is a _____ correlation of + or – _____.

55. The size of the correlation coefficient shows how _____ the relationship is, and the sign (plus or minus) indicates the _____ of the relationship.

56. A correlation coefficient of −.77 is _____ than one of +.69.

57. A correlation coefficient of +.87 would be interpreted as a _____ _____ relationship, −.65 as a _____ relationship, +.24 as a _____ relationship, −.09 as a _____ relationship, and .00 as _____ relationship.

58. The abbreviation for correlation coefficient is _____.

59. Whereas _____ studies help draw conclusions about _____ and effect relationships, _____ studies do not establish causation.

60. Just because two variables are highly correlated does not necessarily mean that one _____ the other. The correlation coefficient gives us no information about _____.

61. It has been found that there is a _____ _____ correlation between the number of babies born in European cities many years ago and the number of _____ nesting in the _____.

SELF TEST I

1. _____ statistics are used to summarize, organize, describe, boil down and make sense out of large amounts of data.
   a. psychological   c. inferential
   b. descriptive   d. behavioral

2. A test distribution wherein nearly everyone received very low scores with fewer and fewer getting higher and higher scores would be
   a. positively skewed   c. normal
   b. negatively skewed   d. bimodal

3. If you subtract the lowest score from the highest score you are figuring the _____ of a set of scores.
   a. correlation   c. range
   b. T score   d. standard deviation

4. _____ have a mean of 50 and a standard deviation of 10.
   a. Z scores   c. SAT scores
   b. T scores   d. spelling scores

5. In using the normal bell-shaped curve, what percent of the population will score between a Z score of +3 and −3?
    a. 13/100 percent   c. about 95%
    b. 68%   d. over 99%

6. If two populations each have a mean of 75, then the probability that the sample mean from population 1 equals 74, and the sample mean from population 2 equals 75 is
    a. high
    b. low
    c. moderate
    d. either a or b depending on the null hypothesis

7. Which of the following terms does not belong with the others?
    a. correlation
    b. standard deviation
    c. relationship
    d. a trend or tendency

8. Which of the following correlation coefficients indicate no relationship between the variables?
    a. −1   c. + or −.5
    b. 0   d. +1

9. Which statistical symbol stands for correlation coefficient?
    a. c   c. n
    b. r   d. XY

10. Your friend Betty received only 64% on her English mid-term, but later learned that she had outscored 90 percent of her class. To know this, she must have calculated a
    a. standard deviation   c. percentile
    b. null hypothesis   d. median

SELF TEST II

1. Which type of frequency distribution condenses score values into class intervals?
    a. psychological   c. regular
    b. behavioral   d. grouped

2. Which of the following is the most commonly used measure of central tendency in statistical analysis?
    a. mean   c. mode
    b. median   d. none of the above

3. The most useful measure of variability is
    a. the Z score   c. range
    b. mean   d. standard deviation

4. If your Z score on a test is -1, then you T score would be
    a. 40   c. 90%
    b. 49   d. 400

5. Usually it is impossible to measure _____ , so researchers
    instead measure _____ .
    a. adult TV viewers, child TV viewers
    b. intelligence precisely, academic performance
    c. populations, samples
    d. entire populations, smaller more manageable populations

6. You can say that you have found a significant difference between the
    means when
    a. they are at least 25 points apart
    b. you retain the null hypothesis
    c. you reject the null hypothesis
    d. the inferential statistics yield a significant correlation

7. Perfect correlations _____ occur with psychological data.
    a. always   c. often
    b. nearly always   d. rarely

8. Which of the following correlation coefficients indicates the strongest
    degree of relationship?
    a. .00   c. +.73
    b. -.76   d. -.10

9. There are only ten people left in your underwater basket weaving class.
    The scores on the final exam are 60, 65, 70, 70, 81, 81, 83, 83, 83, 84.
    What is the mode?
    a. 76   c. 83
    b. 81   d. none of the above

10. The correlation between midterm and final exam scores in Study Skills
    1A is +.83. Ambitious Andy Angus scored above average on the
    midterm. What is your best guess about his performance on the final?
    a. he scored below average
    b. he scored above average
    c. he scored about average
    d. none of these; it is impossible to tell based on the data available

ESSAY QUESTIONS

1. Explain the difference between descriptive statistics and inferential
    statistics and give examples of each.

2. You have developed a new test designed to measure sense of humor
    (humor quotient, H.Q.). You gave it to 9 subjects. Their scores

are listed below. Make a regular frequency distribution, a histogram, and a frequency polygon for the data, and identify the shape of the frequency polygon.
H.Q. scores: 3, 2, 1, 3, 5, 4, 2, 3, 4

3.   Distinguish between the concepts of central tendency and variability and list at least two examples of each.

4.   What does the normal bell-shaped curve have to do with Z scores and the standard deviation? Why is the curve so important in statistical analysis?

5.   What is a null hypothesis? How is it used in inferential statistics? What does it mean when you reject a null hypothesis?

6.   Discuss the issue of correlation and causation.

ANSWER SECTION

Guided Review
1.   *statistics*
2.   *descriptive*
3.   *regular frequency*
4.   *large*
5.   *intervals, frequency, interval*
6.   *graph*
7.   *histogram, polygon*
8.   *between, center*
9.   *points, straight line*
10. *information*
11. *shape*
12. *middle*
13. *positively skewed, negatively skewed*
14. *bimodal*
15. *tendency*
16. *mean, median, mode*
17. *mean*
18. *mean, mean, median*
19. *half, half*
20. *5*
21. *mode*
22. *variability*
23. *low*
24. *range, standard deviation*
25. *range, range, crude, two*
26. *standard deviation*
27. *square root*
28. *percentiles, standard*

29. percentile
30. zero, one, 50, 10, 500, 100, standard
31. Z
32. Graduate Record
33. normal bell-shaped
34. percentages, 68, 99, 13/100 (or .13)
35. inferential
36. population
37. sample, random, population
38. probability, chance
39. low
40. null
41. reject, null
42. 5, reject
43. significant difference
44. supporting
45. experimental, correlational
46. relationship, correlation coefficient
47. positive
48. negative
49. 1.00, perfect
50. zero
51. zero
52. predict
53. scatter diagram
54. dots, higher (or stronger), perfect, 1.00
55. strong (or high), direction
56. stronger (or higher)
57. very strong, strong, weak, very weak, no
58. r
59. experimental, cause, correlational
60. causes, causation
61. high positive, storks, chimneys

Self Test I
1. b
2. a
3. c
4. b
5. d
6. a
7. b
8. b
9. b
10. c

Self Test II
1. d
2. a
3. d
4. a
5. c
6. c
7. d
8. b
9. c
10. b

†